EX-ETIQUETTE
FOR PARENTS

EX-ETIQUETTE FOR PARENTS

Good Behavior After a Divorce or Separation

Jann Blackstone-Ford, M.A., and
Sharyl Jupe

CHICAGO
REVIEW
PRESS

Library of Congress Cataloging-in-Publication Data
Blackstone-Ford, Jann.
Ex-etiquette for parents : good behavior after a divorce or
  separation / Jann
Blackstone-Ford and Sharyl Jupe. — 1st ed.
p. cm.
ISBN 1-55652-551-6
1. Divorced parents. 2. Joint custody of children. 3.
  Parenting. 4. Children of divorced parents. 5. Stepfamilies.
  6. Interpersonal conflict.   I. Jupe, Sharyl. II. Title.
HQ759.915.B54 2004
649'.1—dc22   2004006568

Cover design: Emily Brackett, Visible Logic
Cover photo: Kevin Dodge/Masterfile
Author photo: Courtesy of Melanie Ford
Interior design: Scott Rattray, Rattray Design
© 2004 by Jann Blackstone-Ford, M.A.
All rights reserved
First edition
Published by Chicago Review Press, Incorporated
814 North Franklin Street
Chicago, Illinois 60610
ISBN 1-555652-551-6
Printed in the United States of America
5 4 3 2

CONTENTS

ACKNOWLEDGMENTS

Sharyl and I would like to thank our collective family for their understanding while we were writing this book. It has been a long process and we thank you, Larry, Mel, Anee, Steven, and Harleigh, from the bottom of our hearts for your patience and unwavering support.

We would also like to thank Dr. Susan Bartell for always "just being an e-mail away," for her constant support of the Bonus Families movement, and the shots in the arm when we had writer's block. To Wendy Vainauskas for holding down the fort and taking on the Bonus Families Support Group project when we were in the midst of editing. To Dr. Mike Riera for his kindness, enthusiasm, and true understanding of the Bonus Families movement. To Cynthia Sherry, Lisa Reardon, and the staff at Chicago Review Press for their enthusiasm and support while preparing the manuscript. To our agent, Djana Pearson Morris, for always keeping us focused. And, finally, to the parents and children who contributed their stories and offered their insight, we thank you for your candor and your sincere desire to help others. Without you this book could not have been written.

INTRODUCTION

The first time Sharyl and I met, the meeting was quite cordial. My soon-to-be-husband, Larry, suggested that since he and his ex shared equal custody of the kids, it was time for me to meet the mother of his children. We met. That was it. I didn't talk to her again until after Larry and I were married six months later. She had called him up, they were disagreeing very loudly (as usual), and he just handed me the phone and walked out of the room.

"Here," he snapped before he left. "You talk to her. I can't anymore."

"Huh?" I remember thinking. "I don't want to talk to your ex-wife!"

There I stood, phone in hand, waiting for him to return. He didn't, and as the seconds clicked by I envisioned Sharyl sitting on the other end getting angrier and angrier. When we spoke, I was prepared for the rant of a crazy woman. But much to my surprise, that's not what I heard at all. Instead, after I said hello, she asked in a frustrated voice, "Jann, why does he hate me so much?"

I have to admit, that question threw me. By this time Sharyl and I had settled into our roles of ex and new wife, and neither of us saw the other as anything but a pain in the neck. We rarely talked, and when we did, we were just going through the motions. Her children lived with me 50 percent of the time. Sharyl worked full-time away from home, and since I had a home office, the kids came back to our house after school, even on the weeks they were supposed to be with her. Every day I was more deeply ingrained in their lives, and every day Sharyl got a little angrier.

I decided honesty was the best policy. She wanted to know why her ex hated her, so I told her the truth. Not as directly as my husband had voiced so often, but calmly and with as much reason as could be applied to this particular situation. She thanked me for my frankness and hung up the phone. The next time she called, rather than deal with my husband, she asked for me, and slowly over the years, we have forged quite a friendship.

Sharyl and I would be lying if we said we knew ahead of time what was in store for us when I married her ex-husband. We both had preconceived notions of what life would be like. Growing up with divorced parents, Sharyl saw divorce as the end of interaction with the ex. She lived with her mother, and although she stayed in contact with her father, her parents rarely spoke to each other.

While my parents were not divorced, my father was divorced from his first wife. I had a half-brother twenty-five years older than I. In fact, I regarded him more as an uncle until we got older—and I never met his mother. The thought of my mother interacting with my father's ex was laughable. With this as our background, both Sharyl and I walked into this new life believing divorce made us solitary creatures whose paths would rarely cross.

That is *not* what happened. In 1989 Larry and Sharyl tried something quite innovative for the time. They divorced and agreed to joint physical custody of their kids, Melanie, age seven, and Steven, age four. Joint physical custody means truly equal custody—50 percent of the time with mom and 50 percent of the time with dad. In 1989 that was a rarity, and there were very few resources to look to for help. Both parents were very close to their children—so much so that for more than a year after their initial separation, neither of them could be away from their children longer than a couple of days. I had my own child, Anee, age six, from a previous marriage. She lived with me and visited her father every other weekend, so interacting with my ex on an almost daily basis was not the norm to me. To further complicate matters, Larry and Sharyl could barely talk to each other, and that anger eventually evolved into a Larry-and-Jann-against-Sharyl kind of existence.

Although the adults thought they were keeping their animosity toward each other away from the children, Sharyl and Larry's daughter developed chronic stomachaches and my daughter began to have nightmares. That's when we realized we had to come to our senses. Good behavior after divorce, something we now call good ex-etiquette, is more than just positive interaction between divorced or separated parents—it's also gracefully integrating new partners into the mix. We do not say this because we are advocating a new-age liberal attitude for raising kids in today's hectic, troubled world. We say it because it is inevitable. The majority of parents who are no longer together *will* get involved with someone else, and they will do this while attempting to raise children from a previous relationship.

Times have changed since Emily Post published her first book on good social behavior, in 1922. Back then the rules were more clearly defined, and the words we used to describe each other were obvious. *Husband* or *wife*. People rarely divorced, let alone lived together "out of wedlock." No one called anyone else "my significant other" or "my lover." "My partner" was reserved for business associates. Without a doubt, a new etiquette, even a new language, is needed to match today's more open-ended lifestyle.

What is really needed is a new cooperative attitude between divorced or separated parents. Old-school divorce often resulted in hating one's ex, hating his or her new partner, and certainly never speaking to one's ex-in-laws after the divorce was final. That attitude won't work anymore. Because divorce and remarriage are so prevalent, we all face unpredictable social situations.

CUSTODY TERMS

Legal custody of a child determines who has the right and obligation to make decisions about the child. The parent or parents with legal custody make decisions about such issues as schooling, religious training, and medical or dental care. The different types of legal custody and associated terms are explained below.

Physical custody refers to the parent with whom the child legally resides.

Placement refers to the percentage of time the child resides with each parent.

Sole custody is when one parent has the final word regarding where the child lives and all other decisions that will be made for the child. The noncustodial parent has visitation rights and pays child support. A parent with sole custody is the only parent who may sign legal documents for the child.

Joint custody is when both parents agree to share the legal responsibility of raising their children. Both parents may sign legal documents. Joint custody does not guarantee equal placement, however. The percentage of time a child is required to stay with a parent is determined at the time of divorce. For example, 80/20 placement in favor of the mother means that the child lives with the mother 80 percent of the time and with the father 20 percent of the time, but these parents still have joint custody. Child support is often paid to the parent who houses the child for the greatest amount of time. In this 80/20 example, the father would still pay child support even though the mother and father have joint custody. Unless neglect, drug use, or abuse can be proven, most parents currently receive joint custody of their children after divorce or separation. Marriage to the parent of your child is not a prerequisite for gaining joint custody.

Joint physical custody is when both parents share equally in the child's upbringing. This includes decision making, the signing of legal documents, and placement. The child lives 50 percent of the time with the mother and 50 percent of the time with the father. If one parent makes substantially more money than the other, he or she may be required to pay child support to the lower-income parent.

Shared custody is a blanket term used to describe any custody agreement other than sole custody. Joint custody and joint physical custody are both regarded as shared custody.

That's why in 2000, Sharyl and I started a nonprofit organization called Bonus Families, which is dedicated to the peaceful coexistence between separated or divorced parents and their new families. Unhappy with the negative connotations implied by the term *step-*, we began by searching for another more positive word to describe the step relationship. We happened on the word *bonus* quite by accident. Sharyl and I were watching Sharyl's daughter, then about twelve, play basketball after school. Sharyl explained in passing that Melanie felt uncomfortable introducing me as her stepparent. She had confided to her mother that when she said, "This is my stepmom, Jann," her friends automatically thought she disliked me, which wasn't true. I hated being referred to as a stepparent, but there wasn't really another word to describe me. Sharyl and I tried on words to see if they fit, and when we heard the word *bonus*, we knew it was the right word. A bonus is a reward for a job well done. And with all the hard work it takes to interact with an ex, an ex's new partner, children from both sides, and extended family members, it would be nice to get a bonus. Therefore, when you refer to someone as a bonus—bonusmom, bonusdad, bonusson or bonusdaughter, and even bonusfamily—you are giving a compliment.

Sharyl and I started Bonus Families as a safe haven for stepfamilies on the Internet, but it quickly became much more than that. As a divorce and stepfamily mediator I worked with families in conflict resolution, Sharyl and I taught workshops to help divorced parents cope, and I pooled many of the professionals I had worked with in the past to help write articles and volunteer their time. Our Web site is now one of the most read coparenting and stepfamily sites on the Web, and there are Bonus Families support groups springing up all over the world.

Ex-Etiquette for Parents: Good Behavior After a Divorce or Separation is the culmination of more than ten years of working with divorced or separated parents and their new families. We borrowed the title from the column Sharyl and I write on the Bonus Families Web site, "Ex-Etiquette." It is by far our most visited department. Every month we receive hundreds of requests for help from parents looking for answers to common questions ranging from "Should I go to my stepson's wedding?" to "Should the dog go back and forth with the kids?" to "Help me get along with my ex!" We believe this positive response is because divorced or separated couples are tired of fighting and are looking for more positive ways to interact with each other. Truthfully, nothing we are saying is really new. We are suggesting many of the same strategies relationship experts suggest for maintaining a relationship with a spouse. The way we see it, relationships are relationships, it doesn't really matter if you are divorced or married. If you have children, you still have to communicate, and if the tools are there for one application, they can certainly be used in another. It is our sincere wish that you will find the answers you are looking for in this book.

As you read *Ex-Etiquette for Parents,* you may notice the use of the pronoun *I* and think Jann wrote the book by herself. Nothing could be further from the truth. The singular pronoun was simply our way of making the text easier to read, coping with the problem of constantly having to identify who was speaking, or always using *we.* This book is the result of combined input from Jann and Sharyl. Good ex-etiquette is *always* a combined effort.

Finally, we have tried to make this book free of gender bias. To avoid the continual use of *he or she,* we made it a practice to alternate pronouns as much as possible. For example, we address or refer to a man with an ex-wife as an example in one chapter, and a woman with an ex-husband in the next. Similarly, references to husbands and wives and other traditional family arrangements are not meant to exclude mothers and fathers who are single, who have same-sex partners, or who have chosen not to marry their live-in partners; we simply felt that phrases such as *your husband or significant other* would be too cumbersome for the reader. Please know that this book is designed for *anyone* attempting to coparent after a breakup.

If you would like to contact Sharyl or Jann directly, please feel free to e-mail us through the Bonus Families Web site at jann@bonusfamilies.com or sharyl@bonusfamilies.com. It will even get to us if you send it to jannandsharyl@bonusfamilies.com.

Part I

BASIC EX-ETIQUETTE

Defining and Practicing Good Behavior After Divorce or Separation

1

LAYING THE GROUNDWORK

"Problems cannot be solved by the same level
of thinking that created them."

—ALBERT EINSTEIN

Webster's Dictionary defines *etiquette* as "conventional require-
ments as to proper social behavior." However, "proper social
behavior" and divorce are rarely mentioned in the same breath.
Some think it is ridiculous to believe that parents who could not
get along in a marriage should be able to get along after divorce.
Yet research continues to tell us that our children's emotional
health depends on their parents' relationship. For that reason
alone divorced parents must look for positive ways to talk to each
other and resolve conflicts.

What Is Ex-Etiquette?

As explained by Emily Post, proper etiquette is "a code of behavior based on consideration, kindness, and unselfishness." We currently have no ground rules for a code of behavior when it comes to an ex-spouse. When an ex behaves badly, it's understood that the reason is that he is the ex. Poor behavior seems acceptable and is perpetuated by each generation. When it comes to dealing with—or being dealt with by—an ex, rudeness is the norm. According to the National Institutes of Health, about 1.5 million children experience the divorce of their parents each year—ultimately 40 percent of all children. Perhaps it would be less acceptable if we replaced the word *ex* with *parent*. Then the impact of the bad behavior might be more easily understood.

The essence of ex-etiquette is simply good behavior after a bad divorce. This chapter introduces the necessary mind-set that will allow divorced parents to interact successfully based on what is really important—the children—and discusses how to take the necessary steps to make well-balanced decisions even in the most stressful situations.

In the Beginning

Newly married Lisa and Mike Johnson had an unanticipated problem when they attempted to raise their kids from previous marriages in their new blended family.

"It's embarrassing for me to admit," said Lisa, "but this is my third marriage. I have one child from my first marriage and two children from my second. I also have a child from this marriage to Mike, and he has two children from his previous marriage. We both

share physical custody of the kids, the fifty-fifty split,
which means there are a lot of different parents
involved in the decision making."

With five marriages between them, Lisa and Mike's organizational problems may seem extreme. However, now that 50 percent of all first marriages end in divorce in the United States, and an even more staggering 60 percent of all second marriages end the same way, more and more parents like Lisa and Mike are looking for creative solutions to raising their kids after divorce. These solutions include reaching out past their normal comfort zone to coordinate efforts with their ex—or their current spouse's ex.

I first met Lisa during a mediation session with her second ex-husband, Jason. She was married to Mike, but she and Jason were finding it impossible to coordinate their parenting efforts, and their youngest child had stopped sleeping through the night. They decided to try mediation instead of going to court to adjust their custody agreement. Lisa confided that her marriage to Mike was also in jeopardy because of the chaos created by the ex-spouses. It put so much pressure on the kids that they, too, were showing signs of stress.

Like so many other divorced parents, Lisa had decided that coordinating parenting with Jason was impossible and she'd begun to plan her life around her "new" family with Mike, no longer considering Jason when making decisions for the kids. Rather than help, this caused additional resentment. The adults quickly realized that something else had to be done, but they were at a loss. They needed tools to help them resolve the conflicts. I suggested Lisa start by waving the white flag.

"Wave the white flag?" asked Lisa. "I'm not sure what you mean."

"Wave the white flag," I repeated. "Ask for help. When you are at a loss and you can't figure out what to do, that's when it's time to ask the other person for his or her suggestions. Stop talking and listen."

Both Lisa and Jason seemed surprised by my suggestion, and Lisa made a face in disgust.

"I'm not asking him for anything. He makes me sick, and so does his new wife."

"Then your children will just have to suffer," I replied, and I began to walk toward my office door to let them out. Lisa didn't budge. She sat there, dumbfounded, realizing for the first time that cooperating wasn't just Jason's problem—it was hers too. That's when we finally got down to work.

Wave the White Flag

In most instances waving the white flag means surrendering to the opposing party, but that is not what I'm suggesting at all. In the world of ex-etiquette, waving the white flag can also mean stop forcing your own agenda and ask for help finding the answers. As a divorce and stepfamily mediator, I am trained to help warring parents manage their own conflicts—to look within themselves for the solutions to end the war. I have found that when divorced couples come up against a brick wall, it is because they are usually behaving in the same manner—holding on for the sake of being right and trying not to lose ground. Waving the white flag says to the other person, "I can't figure this out on my own."

Am I saying to give up your cause? Roll over and play dead? Let that $%#^& win? Not at all. I am saying that the responsibility for finding a solution to any problem is shared equally between the opposing parties. The key lies in something Albert Einstein said: "Problems cannot be solved by the same level of thinking that created them." Answers to problems often lie in the most unconventional places; therefore, if you can't solve the problem by yourself, don't be afraid to look to the opposition for a solution. Granted, this is an unconventional approach. Most people throw up their hands and let the courts decide. When this happens, one person wins, the other loses, and both continue to resent each other for years. I try to remind divorced parents—those who ask for help often get it.

Do I Have to Get Along with My Ex?

If you don't have children, you don't have to interact with your ex after your relationship ends. However, if you do have children, it's time to put your own issues aside and look at the bigger picture. In order to successfully co-parent after divorce or separation, you will interact with your ex on a weekly, perhaps even daily, basis. Know this going in and make the necessary adjustments. Don't torture your children by putting them in the position of watching you and your ex continue to argue even after the divorce is final.

The Ten Rules of Good Ex-Etiquette

The "rules of ex-etiquette" are very similar to the unwritten rules of common decency and fair play. However, divorced parents often ask me for a formal list—something they can use to help them keep their wits about them when times get tough. As a result I have devised "The Ten Rules of Good Ex-Etiquette."

1. Put the children first.
2. Ask for help when you need it.
3. No badmouthing.
4. Biological parents make the rules; bonusparents uphold them.
5. Don't be spiteful.
6. Don't hold grudges.
7. Use empathy when problem solving.
8. Be honest and straightforward.
9. Respect each other's turf.
10. Compromise whenever possible.

Putting the Children First

We have all heard this for years, but what does "put your kids first" really mean in the world of ex-etiquette? It means that you must have enough respect for your children to put their needs before yours. Forget about "the principle of the thing" when disagreeing with their other parent. Make your love for the children the principle thing. From this day forward, make all your decisions based on their welfare, no matter if you have to be uncomfortable, swallow your pride, move, do without, or go slower in a new relationship than you would like. Your children did not ask for the separation or divorce. Most children would sacrifice just about anything to keep their parents together, so if you have made the decision to go forward without their parent or to commit to someone who has children from a previous relationship, accept that this child is rightfully your first priority.

Good Behavior After a Bad Divorce: Ex-Etiquette in Action

The Time Consideration

"My ex-husband expects me to give up my time with the kids so he can take them to the World Series! I'm not giving up my time to anyone. What kind of mother would I be?"

By law, if parents accept shared custody of the children after divorce, they are obligated to share the children's time with the other parent. Some parents find it hard to accept that the other parent has equal rights after divorce concerning the children. For this reason, each parent's time with the children becomes the issue. The possibility that their children will have *more* treasured memories with the enemy becomes more important than the children's welfare and happiness.

Sam and Kathy have been divorced for three years. Now that their son, Marcus, is twelve he likes to watch *Monday Night Football* with his dad. Sam and Kathy's fifty-fifty custody agreement allows Marcus to spend every other Monday night with his dad. Therefore, Sam asked Kathy if they could alter the visitation schedule during football season so that he and Marcus could enjoy the game together. Kathy refused to consider giving up one minute of *her* time with *her* son—until Sam offered her an extra night a week.

"I had always vowed that I would not be one of those parents who used their children to get back at the other parent after divorce, but here I was, doing exactly that. All my son wanted to do was watch Monday Night Football *with his dad. In order for him to do that I had to force his dad to trade for an extra Sunday night dinner? Who was this really about? I swallowed my pride and admitted to Sam that I was embarrassed by my behavior. From that day forward Sam's attitude toward me completely changed, and now he is far more open to compromise."*

Ex-etiquette dictates that parents must follow their custody agreement; however, the essence of good etiquette is consideration and politeness. Parents who are more concerned with preventing the other parent from spending additional time with the kids rather than weighing the positive outcome of the act are being selfish and maybe even abusive. The essence of "put the children first" means parents must put their children's needs ahead of their own.

Decide to Cooperate

Some divorced parents do not want to cooperate with an ex. They block communication and schedule things around their "own" family, which consists of "the kids" and their new spouse. A parent who takes this approach to parenting after divorce is actually in denial. He is trying to remake his new life to fit into the conventional family mold. But he's forgetting one thing—they aren't a conventional family.

If your ex is being uncooperative, you can do one of two things—you can buy into his behavior and compete on the same level, or you can look for a new solution. Many exes realize that change is necessary but don't know how to break out of the old patterns of communication. They continue to do the same old things and then state loudly, "I've done all I can do! She is an idiot!"

> *"The thought of cooperating with my ex, after what he put the kids and me through, seems unfathomable to me."*

It's hard work to get along with someone you despise. Find consolation in the fact that you are not doing it for yourself. You are doing it for the people you love the most—your kids. I'm not suggesting that you block a bullet, which many parents say they would do to save their children. I'm suggesting that you cooperate with your child's other parent after divorce. There are three behaviors that lead you to this end.

1. Break the old patterns of communication.
2. Let go of negative emotions.
3. Acknowledge your mutual interests.

Break the Old Patterns of Communication

Breaking an old pattern of communication is not easy. So much of it is mental preparation. What you think about your ex—and the thoughts you run over and over in your mind before you meet—has an effect on your actions when you finally interact. Your behavior can become a negative thought/negative behavior chain reaction. In the psychological community this is referred to as a conditioned response based on past experiences. Examining where and why the term *conditioned response* originated may be helpful.

Ivan Pavlov was a Russian scientist of the early twentieth century. He made a number of important discoveries in the realm of physiology, particularly related to digestion; however, he is best remembered for an experiment in which he "conditioned" dogs to initiate a salivary response to the sound of a bell. Dr. Pavlov began his experiment by measuring the amount of salivation the dogs produced when responding to food. As the experiments continued, he rang a bell at the same time he presented the food. Again, he noted a salivary response. Over time, Pavlov observed the same salivation response when he rang the bell, whether he presented the dogs with food or not. The dogs equated the sound of the bell with getting ready to eat. Pavlov defined this as conditioned response.

In some ways anger against an ex is a conditioned response. If your thoughts conjure up feelings of anger and resentment, you are not likely to want to cooperate. If you can change your thinking process, you can change your behavior and break old patterns of communication. You will have broken the negative thought/negative behavior chain.

Here's a perfect example of how thought processes affect a person's behavior—and what that person must do to break the cycle. It's a personal story, one I have used many times while teaching stepfamily seminars.

My husband and I were married for six months, and during that time Sharyl and I were not the best of friends. Every morning I would sit in front of my makeup mirror, and as I put on my makeup I'd rehearse exactly what I was going to tell her the next time she did something that made me angry. As I put on my foundation, I was a little miffed. As I progressed to the blusher, I was angrier still. By the time I was adding the finishing touches with my mascara, I was livid—and I hadn't said a thing to anyone! This went on day after day. I thought I was keeping it all inside. I didn't think anyone knew how angry I was until one day my husband timidly tiptoed around the corner of the bathroom.

"What are you doing?" I snapped.

"Well," he said. "I was checking to see how much makeup you're wearing. It seems the more makeup you have on, the angrier you are with me."

I had no idea my husband was so perceptive, and I was very impressed. His comment made me realize that *I* was the one making me angry, not Sharyl. As soon as I sat down in front of my mirror each morning I started the same vengeful angry thought process. My anger was simply learned behavior. I had taught myself to be angry!

Since I had learned to be angry in my plight, I decided I could learn *not* to be angry. Rather than rehearse all the bad things in my head each morning, I made myself think about the good things—how happy I was to be married to my husband. How happy I was that the kids had accepted me and seem to be adjusting so well. Everyone was healthy. Every time a bad thought came to my mind about Sharyl I pushed it out and replaced it with a more positive thought about my life.

Lo and behold, the next time my husband crept around the bathroom corner, I said, "Hi honey!" rather than growling at him. But, equally as important, the next time I spoke to Sharyl I didn't have one bad thing to say to her. And oddly enough, she didn't have one bad thing to say to me, either.

This story is a perfect example of how changing your thought process changes your behavior. I was thoroughly convinced that it was Sharyl's fault that we were at odds. If I had not made the necessary changes to break the negative thought chain, to change those negative expectations into positive affirmations, I would still be furious, sitting in front of my mirror and snapping at everyone who crossed my path.

"But I can't make communication with my ex work by myself."

Like most people, you have probably been taught that communication is a two-way street. If one party does not wish to communicate, then it is unlikely things will change, right? Wrong. Things *can* change when only one person is committed to change. Rather than try to change your ex's mind, what you really have to do is change your own. Adopt a new mind-set when dealing with your ex—one that allows you to change your negative expectations into positive affirmations. That way, you don't have to convince your ex to believe something different. All you have to do is change your own belief about your ex. Whatever you believe, you manifest in your life. As proof, take note of my makeup mirror story. I was the only one who changed my thinking. One person, not two. Neither Sharyl nor my husband had any idea I wanted to change the status quo—yet changing my mind brought about that larger change.

If you read through the makeup mirror story again, you will see that the positive affirmations do not necessarily have to be about the problem at hand. Any positive thought works to break the negative thought/negative behavior chain of events. It's the dwelling on the negative that makes you react negatively. Dwell on the positive and you will react positively.

"But ex-etiquette suggestions are for ex-partners who are reasonable human beings. Mine isn't. She doesn't want to cooperate. How do I co-parent and communicate with someone who has no desire to work through problems?"

This book attempts to change the way society in general, and exes in particular, think about interacting with an ex or an ex's new partner. This is built on a two-part premise. First, I believe anyone can be a reasonable human being. It's a choice. If you disagree with your ex and you behave badly, you cannot blame your bad behavior on anyone but yourself. The devil *did not* make you do it. Your ex may drive you nuts, but you choose to react in the manner in which you do. If divorced parents want their children to be free of emotional problems after divorce, they have to learn to ask themselves one question before they respond to the other's behavior: "Is this response for me, or for the well-being of my children?" If the answer is, "for the children," you are on the right track. If the answer is, "for me, because he just makes me so mad," it's time to rethink your approach. Put the children and their needs first and you will be reasonable. Put yourself and your needs first, and you will be unreasonable.

Second—I have to say it—it's time for divorced parents to grow up and take responsibility for their actions. The divorce statistics are astronomical, and there are millions of children affected by their parents' poor behavior. Once you have children it is no longer about you, no matter how much you have been wronged by the other person. I urge divorced parents to stop whining about *rights*, *sides*, *fault*, and *blame*, and to take responsibility for their own actions once and for all.

Let Go of Negative Emotions

The emotions that are most troublesome when dealing with an ex are anger, resentment, jealousy, and envy. All are natural responses to fear on some level. Reason goes right out the window, and what becomes most important is defending one's position. "Forget about the kid's welfare, you don't respect *me*!" Conquering these emotions is a prerequisite to good ex-etiquette. Conquering or controlling negative emotions doesn't mean you don't feel them. The mind-set behind ex-etiquette offers tools to deal with interacting with an ex when you *do* feel angry, jealous, or resentful.

> *"That sounds like you are consciously in denial. That can't be right."*

You are in denial when you don't see or accept something. It's a *subconscious* coping mechanism to avoid something painful. I am suggesting that you deal with something by *consciously* changing your thinking. That's not denial. That's "the wisdom to know the difference."

Divorce is one of the most painful experiences a person can have in life. When polled, people rank it on the same level as death. One of the reasons people cling to their anger, resentment, or even jealousy after divorce is because they inwardly sense that once the emotion is gone, they will have to deal with the pain behind the emotion.

If you let go of the anger you feel for your ex, you will then have to address the pain associated with your divorce—your pain, your ex's pain, and the pain of your children. You will have to look at how you contributed to that pain. Keeping things stirred up camouflages the real issues and blaming the other diminishes your responsibility. Anger protects you. If your ex perceives you as angry and adjusts her behavior, you have control. If you have been wronged, truly wronged, then that makes you *right*. And to be right in the face of divorce—that is bliss. You are the good guy. She is the bad guy. Hold on to that anger, and you will remain the wronged one and the good guy forever.

A school counselor with whom I often work confessed, "My parents have been divorced for thirty years, and my mother can still not be in the same room as my father. She refers to him as "that man" to this day. She's a very unhappy woman."

"Has she remarried?" I asked.

"No," she answered.

Of course she hadn't remarried. I knew the answer before I was told. Staying angry prevented her from moving on.

Staying in a state of anger diminishes your personal power. It eats away at *your* self-esteem and has no effect on the other person. Sure, you may make his or her life miserable, but to do that you have to stay in a miserable state, as well—and therefore, so do your children. My friend, the school counselor, was well into her forties but was still affected, more than thirty years later, by her parent's bad behavior after divorce.

"But my divorce was terrible. Don't I deserve to be happy now?"

Of course you do. We *all* deserve to be happy, including your children, and that is why it is doubly important for you to put your children first after your divorce. Like you, from this day forward, they are also dependent upon every decision that you make. You are a parent, and the moment you decided to become a parent was when this decision to put the children first should have been made, not now.

"But I hate my ex. You don't understand what he has done to me."

It doesn't matter. Someone at some point in our lives has wronged us all. Some of us have been wronged to a greater extent than others, but that does not diminish our responsibility to our children. If divorced parents truly hate each other, they should not attempt shared custody. Studies show that children adjust quicker to life after divorce when both parents are present; however, when angry, vindictive parents attempt shared custody, it actually extends the child's adjustment period and makes matters worse.

Shared custody is only successful when arguments are kept at a minimum and parents can actively solve problems. If you cannot successfully interact with your child's other parent, call the attorneys, put together a parenting plan that establishes one custodial parent and a noncustodial parent with visitation, and work within those perimeters when planning time with your children.

If you want to see your children more often, you *must* look for ways to get along with your ex. You'll notice that I didn't say "like your ex." I said, "get along." It's as simple as that.

"Once you realize you must let your anger go in order to go on . . . how do you do it?

Conquering negative emotions is not easy, especially if you feel justified in your anger. Justified anger is exhilarating! Anger initially gets that adrenaline pumping; it's related to a natural fight-or-flight response that protects animals from predators. If you hang on to your anger for too long, however, as my friend's mother did, it will eventually make you sick and prevent you from moving on with your life.

Acknowledge Your Mutual Interests

Mutual interests are the building blocks for agreement. However, most divorced parents spend their time examining their differences. They don't realize that there still may be mutual interests on which they can base a new working relationship to raise their kids after their divorce or separation. Unless they identify their common interests, exes will not feel it is necessary to come to agreement about anything.

Divorced parents do have at least two mutual interests. First, they both love the same children, and if they put aside their differences they will acknowledge their mutual importance in their children's lives.

Second, both parents see the importance of establishing a separate happy life after divorce. When they are no longer fighting, they can then move on to successful happy lives—and so can their children.

Forgiveness

It sounds good in theory, getting along with an ex-spouse (or her new partner). But what if you are faced with someone leaving you and the kids for someone else? What if drugs and alcohol appear to be more important than building a life together? What if mental illness robs you of the person you once thought was the love of your life? All of these things are out of your control—how do you forgive that? How do you get past it and build a new life?

We go through certain stages of coping when we face any tragedy. The world-famous expert on death, dying, and the after-life, Elisabeth Kübler-Ross, has outlined five common stages of grief in her book *On Death and Dying*. They are adjusted below to conform to the needs of those dealing with the grief associated with a divorce or separation.

1. **Denial:** The "It can't be" stage. This stage is filled with disbelief. Your partner wants to break up, and you think that he will change his mind.

2. **Anger/Resentment:** The "Why me?" stage. You are angry about the situation, about the pain you feel, about the pain the kids feel. It's difficult to control your reactions to anything—especially anything your ex says because you are so furious.

3. **Bargaining:** The "If I do this, you'll do that" stage. You try to negotiate to change the situation. For example, "I'll change if you don't leave."

4. **Depression:** The "It's really happened" stage. You realize the situation isn't going to change. The breakup is for good and there is nothing that will bring the other person back. Acknowledging this situation often brings on depression.

5. **Acceptance:** The "Co-parenting" stage. Though you haven't forgotten what happened, you are able to forgive and move forward. You have let go of the negative emotions you associate with your ex. You are now ready to co-parent.

The problem is that many people get stuck in the first or second stage and can't progress to stage five. These are the parents who fight over time with the children, fight in front of their children, and simply forget to put their kids first because they feel so angry, so wronged, and so justified in their behavior. Forgiveness comes by letting go of the past and correcting their thinking processes. It has nothing to do with who was right and who was wrong.

When you forgive, you don't do it for the person you are forgiving. You do it for you. Most often the person you are forgiving doesn't feel the power of your wrath, but you do. It's your anger that makes your heart beat faster. Only you can break the negative thought/negative behavior chain reaction.

Break the Chain

"Just hearing my ex's voice makes the hair stand up on the back of my neck."

Each time an angry or vengeful thought comes to mind, break the chain. Picture *yourself* happy. See yourself free of the hold those thoughts have on you. Actually picture yourself in your new relationship or in your job in which you are successful—*anything positive that takes your mind away from the angry, vengeful thoughts.* Yes, you are justified in your anger, but owning that only perpetuates the anger. Dwell on what makes you happy. Look for your higher self. If you make that your priority, the anger will seem less important. Don't let yourself dwell on what she has done and how justified you are in your anger ever again. When you hear your ex's voice, instead of thinking what you would *really* like to say to her, picture positive interaction. *Control what you think about your ex and your life will be in control.*

Revenge

"But he has made me so miserable! I have to get him back!"

Chances are you have been angry with your ex for so long that you don't remember how *not* to be angry with him or her. If you feel you have been wronged in some way, the desire for revenge is a natural response. Conquering the need for revenge is a must for proper ex-etiquette. It is very much like conquering anger. It takes a change in mind-set.

Although men and women cope differently, they experience equally agonizing feelings when faced with a breakup. If revenge is what you want more than anything else, you can spend the rest of your life trying to get even. You can throw nails onto your nemesis's driveway, let air out of her tires, or prevent her from seeing the children—anything to make her life miserable. You can try to get even by holding a grudge. You might have the crazy notion that the hate you harbor for the person who has wronged you will somehow make *her* unhappy. The truth of the matter is your nemesis probably couldn't care less what you think or feel. And seeking revenge on your ex does not teach your children to deal with future conflict in their lives. On the contrary, if your children observe you desiring revenge for being wronged, they will likely grow up accepting revenge as the natural order of things. Teaching your children revenge as a way of life will eventually teach them to feel bad about themselves.

Preconceived Notions

Let's say you had a friend who had a dog. The dog recently was lost and when it returned home it was a little disoriented. You think you know the dog pretty well, but when you come over to see your friend, the dog bites you.

Let's analyze what your response might be. You might yell at the dog, and it would perceive you as being angry. If the dog was small enough, you might lash out and smack it on the nose. At that point the dog would know that you are angry, and it might lash out to protect itself. The next time you see the dog, you are on the defensive—you don't want to be bitten again. When the dog sees you, it remembers that you smacked it in the nose; it starts growling out of fear as soon as it sees you. You are afraid that you will once again be bitten and you get in your fighting stance. "No little dog is going to get the best of me!"

Ironically, your relationship with your ex is no different. Both parties are afraid and it's not uncommon for the opposition to mistake your fear for anger and respond accordingly. Good communication doesn't just happen. *You* have to set the stage, which means each time you meet you must do so with a clean slate. Don't carry around preconceived notions based on what has happened in the past. Mentally wash that slate clean and walk into each meeting with an open mind. Just keep repeating to yourself that it's all for the sake of the kids until you have conditioned yourself to both expect and participate in good postdivorce behavior.

Keep the Issues Separate

As in the analogy of the biting dog, the second time you happened upon the dog you anticipated that it would bite you. Because of that preconceived notion, you started your next meeting in a fighting stance. You know the old saying, "The best defense is a good offense." You were ready for anything!

If you respond the same way to your ex, each meeting from the day you split up will begin as a fight. Both of you will be constantly jockeying for position, anticipating the worst, and fighting a battle with no end. To end the constant back and forth you must learn to keep the true issues separate from any negative emotions you might feel.

Let's put this into an everyday application between divorced parents. Here is an example:

"My ex constantly bugs me about the child support being late. I know the money is supplementing her rent and it really pisses me off, so I drag my feet every month. Last month I picked up my son for our

weekend together and his shoes were in really bad shape. I pay child support! Couldn't she at least buy him new shoes?"

There are two very separate issues in question here: the father's late child support and his anger over what he believes is the mother's bad judgment. The issues do not relate to each other, but because he is angry, the father is running the two issues together in his mind and therefore justifies his behavior. The important issue, paying child support on time, is hidden behind the anger. The key? Diffuse the anger and the real issue, child support, will become more obvious.

To diffuse the anger I simply asked the father who he was picturing in his mind as he wrote the child support check. Was he picturing his son, who is in need of shoes, or his ex-wife, whom he believes to be using the child support check to supplement her income? Of course, he said he was picturing his ex-wife and this mental preparation was making him angry and resentful.

"If the child support is for your son," I asked, "why are you picturing his mother in your mind as you write the check?"

"Well," he snarled. "She's the one who controls the transaction."

The operative word was "controls." The father subconsciously felt the mother was in control, which made him angry. By being late on the child support, he was again in control of the situation. His anger was clouding his reason.

"When you go to a department store to buy a present and pay for it by check," I asked, "who do you picture in your mind as you write the check? The salesperson who controls the transaction or the person for whom you are buying the present?"

"The person for whom I am buying the present, of course."

"And that makes you happy. You anticipate how excited the person will be to receive your present and you graciously write the check?"

"Exactly," replied this father.

"Child support is no different."

Child support is not a gift, of course. However, to separate the anger from the act, the mind-set is still the same. To diffuse his anger this father must stop picturing his ex-wife as he writes the support check. If he continues to picture her, each month he will revisit the negative feelings associated with his inability to control her. In other words, he's setting himself up for failure. If he pictures his son smiling, and pushes the angry resentful thoughts associated with his ex from his mind, he will not resent writing the check. Miraculously, the father admitted, once he changed what he thought about as he wrote the check, he had no trouble sending the payment on time.

Building a Working Relationship After Divorce

Once you have learned to deal with the negative thoughts that produce poor behavior and you acknowledge your mutual interests, you are ready to move on to building a new working relationship with your child's other parent. Here are the steps to building a working relationship with an ex:

Approach this as a business relationship. If you disagreed with your boss or a coworker, would you react the same way you do when you disagree with your ex? Probably not. Flying off the handle is not tolerated in business meetings. When you disagree with a coworker it is important to keep your head and find a solution quickly so you can continue to work together. Use the same principle when looking for solutions with an ex.

Have a goal. In this case, your goal would be positive co-parenting after divorce. Once this becomes a mutual goal, you and your ex will be willing to make the necessary concessions to get along. If it is not a mutual goal, both of you will continue to put your needs ahead of those of your children, and blame each other for why life does not run smoothly.

Develop empathy. One of the things that separates humans from the rest of the food chain is the ability to feel empathy. Using your natural empathetic ability will allow you not only to focus on your own feelings, but also to try to identify with what the other parent may be feeling and use that when looking for solutions. I have found that this simple act has led to more creative problem solving than any other tool. For example, this mom realized, "It's very difficult for me not to see the kids for a week at a time. I can only imagine what it is like for my ex when the kids are with me and I realize he must feel equally as bad." Her empathy led to positive results: "With this in mind, if my ex asks for a little extra time here and there, I try to accommodate him. He often returns the favor, and it makes the transition much easier for the kids."

Cultivate respect. When people do not feel respected they are unlikely to cooperate. An easy way to make your ex feel respected is simply to ask her opinion. Ironically, asking the opinion of an ex is the last thing many co-parents will think of. Many co-parents fear that asking for an opinion indicates loss of power. First, power comes from within you, it is not dependent upon your ex. Second, asking for an opinion demonstrates your respect for her. It is a gesture as much as a tool—after all, you don't have to take her advice!

Pick your fights. If it's not a crisis, don't make it into one. If your daughter comes back from her father's house with magenta hair, and it's washable, tell her to wash her hair. If it's permanent dye, call her father and discuss coordinating the rules.

Be honest and straightforward. Honesty is the building block of any relationship. If you cannot trust your ex and your ex cannot trust you, there is no foundation for co-parenting.

Look for the compromise. Many divorced parents frown at the thought of compromise. They automatically assume that they will have to give something up and will therefore not be completely satisfied. Ex-etiquette teaches you to look for the compromise. One of the quickest ways to do that is to *listen* to the opposition. The simple act of listening validates both parties, and it's much easier to find common ground and compromise if both sides feel validated. If you listen, and read between the lines, your ex will tell you what she wants. You can calmly assess her desire and see if a compromise is in order.

Here's an example. A parent says to her ex, "I'll be at your house at 6:00 on Saturday night to pick up Mark for the weekend. Did I tell you my mother is coming into town on Friday? It's too bad she has to leave first thing Saturday morning." What is this parent really trying to say? She is trying to say, "My mother is coming into town on Friday night, and I know she would love to see Mark. I would like to pick up Mark on Friday night instead of Saturday night so he can spend some time with my mother."

Why doesn't she just come out and say that? There may be many reasons, but the most important one is likely past history. If there have been disagreements about visitation in the past, a parent may be gun-shy when suggesting an occasional change. She may simply avoid saying what she means. She may anticipate an argument and just not want to take it on.

To ease tensions and to make Mark's life easier, the listening parent could easily suggest a workable compromise, such as, "Why don't you pick up Mark on Friday after school so he can visit with your mother, and then bring him back on Saturday night?"

This compromise seems obvious to the outside observer, but not to a couple right in the middle of poor ex-etiquette. It's unlikely a warring parent will ever suggest picking a child up *early*. However, that isn't *exactly* what this parent has done. The compromise lies in the fact that he suggested an earlier pick-up, but also an earlier drop-off time. A schedule change was suggested; he did not offer his ex more time with the child. As time moves on and they get used to better communication and compromise, that may be an option. In the beginning, take baby steps. This was an excellent start.

It's your job to compromise if you want healthy kids after divorce. Don't make your child suffer because you are angry with your ex.

Active Listening

Active listening is an excellent tool to help you read between the lines of what your ex is really saying. It involves both verbal and nonverbal behaviors to show you hear and understand. The nonverbal behaviors that are useful are tone of voice, eye contact, and body language. It could include the simple act of leaning forward to let the opposition know you are truly trying to listen. Looking at the ground or picking at your fingernails will not give the other parent the impression that you are listening. No matter how angry you are, make eye contact when you interact with your ex.

Active listening also involves verbal skills. Listen to your ex, then summarize her concern and repeat it back to her. If you are correct in your assumptions, you validate her feelings with your understanding. If your assumptions are wrong, it gives your ex an opportunity to clarify her feelings.

I often use active listening in mediation to help disgruntled divorced parents understand each other's point of view. After listening to both parties explain their concerns, I might begin the session by saying, "So what you are telling me is that you feel your ex-wife is undermining your visits with the children by not helping them to prepare for the visit." The angry parent might then clarify by saying, "Yes, the kids are never ready when I arrive, and they resent having to hurry. This colors our entire visit." Or he might say, "No, it's not that she doesn't help them prepare. They are always ready to go when I arrive to pick them up. It's what she says while they are preparing—'I'm going to be so lonely in this big house while you are gone'—that makes the kids feel awful about leaving, and that colors our entire visit." The bottom line is that one parent feels sabotaged by the other, but *why* is the key to resolving the conflict. Knowing *why* allows one parent to be validated and also points out what the other parent may be doing to undermine the other's position.

Phrases that will help you listen more actively are:

"Hmmm." (This acknowledges you were listening without judgment.)

"Tell me more. . . ."

"How did you feel when . . ."

"Do you think . . ."

"So, what you are telling me is . . ."

"I see."

All these phrases allow the other party to feel heard and therefore validated.

Neutral Territory

If you were to approach this interaction with your ex as a business relationship, as previously suggested, where would you hold the meeting? Not out in front of your house when exchanging children. Not in your living room. Not in the hallway. A business meeting would be planned—both of you would be formally invited, the agenda would be known, and you would discuss things in a neutral meeting room at the office. That's exactly what I suggest you do when talking to an ex.

You want a neutral playing field—not one of your homes. Even if a friend or relative offers their digs, decline the invitation. Neither you nor your ex should feel that the other has an unfair advantage when you are negotiating. I suggest a public place such as a restaurant or coffee shop. People are less likely to get angry in public and will therefore take more time looking for solutions. So make that appointment, remove all your negative thoughts, and come prepared to listen. It's very important that you and your ex drink soft drinks or coffee, not alcohol. Alcohol removes the inhibitions and easily stirs up bad memories. It might be a good idea to put a picture of your children on the table. If you start to get a little angry, take a sip of water and look at the picture. Then, after the discussion is over, go home and have a drink with friends to celebrate the compromise.

Tact and Timing

When you bring up the subject has a lot to do with how it will be received. If you are an hour late for picking up your child and your ex is seething, it's probably not the best time to ask for extra time with your child. Before you open your mouth, stop and analyze the situation. What have you been talking about previously? Will she be receptive? What is her mood? Is she tired and crabby? Use your head. If your ex just lost a job and is concerned about making ends meet, that is not the time to ask about child support. It does not eliminate the need for child support and you have a right to ask, but be smart about when you ask. It will make a big difference in terms of your ex's response and desire to be cooperative.

Talking to Your Ex

"I've left all the animosity behind. I try to talk to my ex, but it seems like everything I say just makes her angry. I push buttons that I really have no idea I'm pushing."

Here's a news flash: men and women are different. They look at life differently, they process information differently, and they make decisions differently. Therefore, it's not surprising when, for example, a man says something to a woman that he thinks will smooth things over, and it only makes things worse. In my work I commonly hear, "I have no idea what I said to her that made her so angry."

Much of what various relationship gurus suggest when trying to keep couples together also works when trying to help divorced couples communicate. If what John Gray, author *of Men Are from Mars, Women Are from Venus*, says is true, men crave approval while women crave validation. We cannot imagine a less likely camp to look for approval and validation than divorce court. Ex-husbands constantly feel disapproval from their ex-wives, and ex-wives rarely feel validated by their ex-husbands. This is the reason why approaching your co-parent as a business partner works so well. In a business partnership, you are likely to respond less emotionally. You are not in a state of approval, disapproval, or validation. In business, you simply identify the problem, weigh the obstacles, offer a solution, and then listen for the compromise. And that's exactly what you should do when talking to an ex. We call this the ex-etiquette four-step plan to problem solving.

1. Identify the problem.
2. Weigh the obstacles.
3. Ask for help finding the solution.
4. Listen for the compromise.

Let's put the plan into action. Louise and Jack have been divorced for a year. They had a turbulent two years before they decided to separate. Now when they talk to each other it almost always ends up in a fight. Jack pays child support and feels that all of their son's expenses should be covered by the child support he pays. He was recently laid off from his job and is looking for another one in his field. Their son has grown out of the soccer shoes that his mother purchased for him three months ago. Money is tight on both sides, but the kid needs new shoes.

Which conversation gets the job done?

Conversation #1

Louise: Billy needs new soccer shoes and they are very expensive.

Jack: His old soccer shoes are just fine.

Louise: He wears a size 4! The shoes he has now are size 2!

Jack: I pay child support! And besides, I just lost my job!

Louise: "You frickin' deadbeat. You lost your job again. This is so typical of you. You could never keep a job when we were married, either. Everything is always on my shoulders. You better send me that check or else I'm going straight to the D.A."

Conversation #2

Louise: Billy needs new soccer shoes.

Jack: He can wear his old ones. I just lost my job.

Louise: I know you must be concerned about money, but I am confident you will be on your feet soon.

Jack: Thank you. I have an interview next week with a good company.

Louise: I'm sure like me, your main concern is our son's welfare. How can we address this now that you are out of work? He does need new shoes. In three months he has gone from a size 2 to a 4!

Jack: Can we split the expense of the shoes?"

Louise: Money is tight for me, too, but that would really help. They cost $40.

Obviously the second conversation produced the desired results. Louise followed ex-etiquette's four-step plan to problem solving.

Identify the problem: Billy needs new soccer shoes.

Weigh the obstacles: Loss of job, expense of shoes.

Ask for help finding the solution: "How can we address this now that you are out of work?"

Listen for the compromise: "We can split the cost of the shoes."

There were two other helpful tools Louise used in her simple approach to asking her ex for help. First, she showed *empathy* for the loss of employment, which helped to get Jack on her side and reinforced their working relationship. Second, she asked herself the question, "Is this for the welfare of my child or for me?" She expressed that the need was for her son, not a whim of her own. Putting the ex-etiquette four-step plan for problem solving into play gave Louise the desired results. Billy got new soccer shoes.

Language to Avoid

The key to any compromise is to get your ex to see the benefit of considering an alternative to her original position. You can't do this if your opponent, in this case your ex, is on the defensive. One of the many ways to put an ex on the defensive is to accuse her of something. This often depends on the language that you use. Using the words *always* or *never*, and mistakenly interchanging the phrases *could you* and *would you*, are not good choices when going into negotiation. Let's use the same background information as in the previous example. Louise and Jack are discussing soccer shoes.

Louise: Billy needs soccer shoes and they are really expensive.

Jack: He can wear his old ones.

Think about this next sentence and consider what your own response might be.

Louise: You always say that.

Do you feel defensive? Are you ready to agree or disagree? Most likely your reply would be: "I do not *always* do anything." To reaffirm, Louise may restate her case:

Louise: Yes you do! You *always* say that to me, and Billy is the one who suffers.

Now Louise is hitting below the belt. She's using Billy as a pawn to hurt Jack. That simple statement tells Jack, "You're stupid and a failure. You have never stood up to your responsibilities." *She disapproves of him.* Jack will have no desire to look for a compromise after that comment. His only reply will be to defend himself.

Jack: I do not!

Because of Louise's choice of words, she and Jack are no longer addressing the important question, Billy's need of new soccer shoes. The original premise has gotten lost in a sea of *you never* and *you always.*

When asking an ex for a favor, try to use the phrase *would you* rather than *could you. Could you* is merely a way to compile information. It's like asking, "Is it possible?" *Would you* implies a request for help.

For example, if you ask an ex, "Could you please pick up Billy at six o'clock on Friday?" you are asking "Is it possible to pick up Billy?" As a result, you may get a response like, "That may not be convenient. I might have to work late." This answer may frustrate the parent asking for help and may be the catalyst for yet another argument. Asking "Would you please pick up Billy at six o'clock on Friday" is asking for a favor, and you are more inclined to get a simple yes or no answer.

Helpful Language

"I" messages provide a positive avenue for communicating feelings under difficult circumstances. Unlike the negative *never* or *always* interaction, using "I" messages actually helps to ease tension and conflict and reduces defensive responses in the ex. A tool frequently used in conflict resolution, "I" messages foster better listening in the opposition and set the stage for positive feedback. Using "I" messages tells your ex how you feel without a lot of emotional embellishment that may turn her off. It allows you to talk to her without harboring hidden emotions that will complicate communication in the future.

There are three basic steps to using "I" messages successfully when communicating with an ex-spouse:

1. State the feeling.
2. State the offending behavior.
3. State the effect it has on you.

After you state the effect it has on you, request the change in behavior that you would like to see. Don't embellish it. Just state the case. This is an excellent tool to break the negative thought/negative behavior chain reaction.

A very common topic for disagreement between divorced parents is when a parent is late—either to pick up the kids or to drop them off. No one likes to wait, and it can be especially irritating for divorced parents who hate the fact that they have to share their child with someone who infuriates them. Let's see how using "I" messages promotes good ex-etiquette when a parent is late.

"I feel (state the feeling) when you (state the specific behavior), because (state the effects it has on you)."

Then state how you would like the behavior changed.

"I feel angry (feeling) when you are late (behavior) because others may be waiting for me after I leave you (effect). Please be on time (change)."

You have told your ex how her behavior makes you feel. You have not accused her of anything. Using effective "I" messages promotes a positive response from your ex.

An ineffective "I" message is:

"I feel angry when you are late because it is insensitive and makes me late, too."

The goal behind ex-etiquette is good behavior after a bad divorce. Including the words *because it is insensitive* just adds fuel to the fire. You do not have to reaffirm your rightness in each interaction with an ex. It does not make you more right. Each time you feel the necessity to get in a dig, go back and read the section on letting go of negative emotions. Until you can do that, you will not move forward.

2

EVERYDAY EX-ETIQUETTE

"Opportunity is missed by most people because it is dressed in overalls and looks like work."

—THOMAS EDISON

In the previous chapter I laid the groundwork for the principles behind ex-etiquette. I explained how to change your mind-set in order to change your behavior. In this chapter those principles are put into practice. Specific problems and concerns often encountered by divorced or separated parents are addressed using the basic ex-etiquette rules.

"You just make me so mad! I'm not going to budge until you apologize!" Those words have brought untold numbers of co-parents to a standstill. If the ultimate goal is to get along and co-parent the kids, all arguments, no matter who is at fault, are just bumps in the road. If the ultimate goal is to get along and raise the kids, then it really doesn't matter who is to blame.

This doesn't mean that divorced parents should never apologize to each other. It means they shouldn't wait for an apology before looking for solutions to end a disagreement.

Here's an analogy that will serve to clarify this concept. You are driving from Los Angeles to New York City, and you have to be there in a week. It is storming. You come upon a tree that has blown down across the road, and you can go no further. You have several options as to your next move. You can find the person who owns the tree, knock on the door, and demand that the tree be removed so you can continue on your original path. If the person refuses, however, or doesn't accept ownership of the tree, you may have to go to court to make sure the suspected owner legally accepts responsibility. That would take far longer than a week and could be quite costly and unpleasant. On the other hand, remembering that your ultimate goal is to get to New York City in a week, you might look for creative ways to remove the tree so you can reach your final destination on time. One alternative is that you could go around the tree. Or you could move it to one side. You could break out that chain saw you carry in your trunk and cut it into firewood. Or, crazy as it may seem, you could ask the person who owns the tree to help you remove it from the road. That's what good ex-etiquette suggests you do. If you can't solve the problem by yourself, ask for help.

Let me explain what asking for help really does. When you ask someone for help, he has to look at the problem, analyze it, and then offer a potential solution. Waiting for an apology before you begin looking for a solution to a disagreement is just one more tree in the middle of the road. If your final goal is to co-parent the kids, then it stands to reason that when there is a disagreement *both* of you have to look for solutions. Arguing about whose responsibility it is just wastes time and colors all future attempts at positive communication.

Playing One Parent Against the Other

"But we don't have to do that at Mom's."

When you're married, you and your spouse have a mutual interest in supporting one another. When the two of you are divorced or separated, however, that mutual interest is no longer there. Even divorced parents who are committed to cooperating may inadvertently sabotage each other. They may not openly disagree in front of the children, but if one disagrees with the other's disciplinary tactics, for example, the more lenient parent may not uphold the stricter parent's rules. If one home is substantially more lenient than the other, and the parents make no attempt at consistency, they are setting themselves up for failure. Children are constantly sizing up their environment. The child will eventually gravitate to the more lenient lifestyle.

Of course many divorced parents understand this, and that is the reason behind their leniency. But not keeping the rules consistent between the two households teaches the kids to play one home against the other. When parents are not consistent, they are putting the children in the middle just as much as they would by fighting in front of them. The kids will eventually feel they have to make a choice—do I agree with Mom or Dad?

Although you cannot impose your rules on the other home— one of the rules of good ex-etiquette is that you respect each other's turf—you can make it clear what you expect in your home and can hope, through suggestion and a spirit of cooperation, that the other home follows suit.

"This is insane. You want me to cooperate with someone I hate."

Let's say it's just you and your family on a ship in the middle of the ocean. You are on one end of the ship, your spouse is on the other, and your children are in the middle. It is a sunny day and everyone is enjoying life. All of the sudden the sun disappears and it starts to storm. As the wind pounds the ship, it springs a leak in your partner's end and the ship starts to fill with water. The ship lists to one side and the kids tumble toward the end of the ship filling with water. Let's stop this story for a second. In the midst of the chaos, someone hands you a piece of paper that says you are no longer partners with your spouse. Now do you say, "Cool! Since we are no longer partners, that hole is your problem. It's on your side." Or, with your ex-partner's help, do you start to bail to save your kids? The second solution is ex-etiquette in a nutshell.

Good ex-etiquette is a whole new way of life. From this point on you are changing from an attitude of dissent to one of cooperation. Your new mantra is now "Put the children first. Put the children first. Put the children first."

Different Parenting Styles

Although you and your ex each have a unique parenting style, it may take a while for that style to emerge after a divorce. As time goes on you will know if you are too lenient or too strict. If you are conscientious and watch the reaction of your kids and your ex, you will understand what works and what doesn't in terms of discipline. Hopefully, you will be wise enough to adjust your approach.

Here's a typical example of the problems that can arise as a result of different parenting styles. Monica and Matt have been attempting to co-parent their children for two years now. Their relationship has broken down, and they can no longer be in the same room together. Monica explains, "Matt's parenting skills suck. I always have to take up the slack."

Matt, on the other hand, complains that his ex-wife has always tried to control how he deals with the kids. He feels this is an invasion of his privacy, and he wants to be left alone when his kids are with him. He also wants Monica to know that he is and always has been fully capable of taking care of his own chil-

EVERYDAY EX-ETIQUETTE   39

dren. He tells her, "The kids are clean. They have a bedtime. What's the problem?"

Monica simply does not like anything Matt does when it comes to parenting the children. When I ask if the kids complain about being with Matt, Monica's response is very telling.

"Are you kidding? They can't wait to get to their dad's house. No one bugs them to clean up their room. They have pizza for dinner every night. It's a party over there! I'm the one who always has to be the disciplinarian. The kids probably hate me."

Because Matt is a little more lax in the discipline department, does not cook on a regular basis, and isn't a fastidious house-keeper, Monica feels she has to compensate by playing the responsible parent. She expects Matt to follow suit, and when he doesn't, she takes it personally. Matt says, "Being Suzy Homemaker is not required for the children to be healthy or safe."

As much as she hates to admit it, Monica agrees that Matt's right. And that's when she breaks down. Through her tears she explains that she has been afraid that the kids would see Matt as "the fun one" and therefore they would prefer to be with him. She says that because of the divorce she hasn't felt she could influence Matt's parenting decisions, and her frustration has been making her into someone she never wanted to be—bitchy, condescending, and never satisfied.

Matt then confides that the kids have felt Monica's frustration, too, and he worries that they could never satisfy her. In turn, Monica admits that exactly what she feared so much is now in fact happening—the kids seem to prefer to be at Matt's. She is deeply hurt; however, her family perceives her hurt as anger and the children are rebelling. "Mom is always mad," their daughter complains. I ask Monica to consider the following, and answer with a simple yes or no:

Are the kids in danger when they are with Matt? Monica's answer is no.

Do you both accept the responsibility of childcare, and coordinate bedtimes and such things as carpooling to sports practices? Monica's answer is yes.

Is child support paid on time? Monica's answer is yes.

Are the kids clean? . . .

Monica starts to see the real issue. "He gets to have all the fun. I'm the bitch around the kids," she explains.

Now we're getting to the heart of it. Monica feels powerless, and the only way she has felt she would be heard has been to appear unsatisfied. The squeaky wheel gets the grease. "I just want the kids to love me, too," she confesses. As we talk, she realizes that her constant interference when the kids are with Matt is actually preventing both of them from moving forward.

We think when we get older and have children of our own that we will automatically become more secure within ourselves, that we will no longer have feelings of jealousy and inadequacy. But the fact is that if you've ever had an insecure bone in your body, divorce will find it and shake it until it really hurts. That's what happened to Monica.

What does Matt and Monica's story really tell us? It's a perfect illustration of the importance of learning to respect the ex-spouse's turf. Employing good ex-etiquette acknowledges that you cannot govern the other parent's home, you can hold up your end of the bargain and hope, for the sake of your children, that your ex follows suit. As difficult as it might sound, you must learn to trust your co-parent's judgment—or at least not question it on a regular basis. Of course, if you feel the child is in danger, then it is your obligation to call that to the attention of the other parent, or possibly the authorities if necessary. Generally speaking, however, you cannot dictate policy from afar. So if you don't want to have very confused children, it's important to do everything you can to coordinate efforts.

The Things on Which You Must Agree

All the philosophy aside, there are some things that parents *must* agree upon to make co-parenting easier on everyone concerned. They are:

Religious training
Public or private education
Extracurricular activities (sports, music, drama, etc.)

Religious training, private education or tutoring, and extracurricular activities usually cost additional money. Aside from morally agreeing so the co-parents can back the child by attending religious services or performances, they may have to also make an agreement as to how the extras will be funded. Sometimes these extra costs are covered by child support. More often than not, child support does not cover the extras and is just one more thing on which divorced parents may disagree.

One concerned father told me, "My wife has sole custody of our son. Now that he is thirteen, I would like him to go to a parochial high school, but my ex-wife is Jewish and prefers him to go to public school. We have been fighting about this for three weeks straight. My son will be raised Jewish even though my family is Catholic. I feel like he is being denied part of his heritage."

When couples marry outside their religion, they often agree how the children will be raised before they are born. If this agreement is sincere, then divorce should not change the decision. In cases such as this, when the philosophic or religious views are diametrically opposed to one another, the parent with sole custody has the final say. However, when parents share custody and disagree on religious beliefs, the only tie-breaker is compassion for the child and staying true to the original agreement. That's good ex-etiquette.

In the past, the religion of the mother predicted the religion of the child, and this often prevented interfaith marriages. Today, if people of the Jewish and Christian faiths marry, they may use both a priest or minister and a rabbi to perform the ceremony. The loving commitment of marriage makes the philosophical differences seem tolerable. However, divorce removes tolerance, and parents may no longer be committed to supporting each other's faith after the divorce is final. A good alternative is that children are exposed to both religions, and as they grow they can then make the choice which religion they choose to follow as an adult. Unfortunately, it's not uncommon for children put in this position to follow no specific religion later in life. I say, "unfortunately" not because I necessarily believe in organized religion, but because many children in this position view the subject as an allegiance or betrayal issue. "If I choose Mom's religion, Dad will be offended. If I choose Dad's religion, Mom will be offended." And so they choose no religion, and the religious heritage of the family is lost.

Moral Differences

"I share custody of my sixteen-year-old daughter, who is dating a boy with some serious problems at home. When the boy's parents kicked him out, my ex-wife let him move in, and I'm concerned that my daughter and he may be left unsupervised on occasion. I think this is just asking for trouble. My ex says I'm overreacting."

Ultimately the best way to handle this kind of problem is with a proactive approach—both co-parents anticipate it and agree about what to do if it happens. Co-parents are rarely that organized, however, and will more than likely be faced with one going forward with a decision that leaves the other feeling angry and betrayed.

Cheryl and Marty ran into just this sort of situation—and Cheryl's decision was to let her daughter's boyfriend move in. Marty was not consulted, and when his children went back and forth from house to house, the boyfriend was left to fend for himself at the mother's home. Of course the daughter wanted to stay at the mother's rather than go back and forth between parents. All hell broke loose. Marty's perception was that this was just a ploy to make the daughter prefer the mother's home. A custody arrangement that had worked for years was in jeopardy of falling apart.

In Cheryl's defense, her decision was not just a way to sway her daughter's loyalty. It turned out that Cheryl had had similar trouble when she was young, and a friend's parent had taken her in. They had grown to have a lovely lasting relationship, and she now regarded the friend's mother as her second mother. This is what Cheryl had envisioned when she allowed the boy to move in. She did not anticipate the moral dilemma it would propose.

In this case, all the father can do is register his discontent. Ex-etiquette says both parents must respect the other's turf. You cannot control the moral decisions of the other parent. To rectify this situation it took some creative thinking. When the mother explained her true motivation, although the father was irritated that she had not asked his opinion, they made *finding a solution* their main focus rather than assigning blame. Ultimately, both parents wanted to help the troubled child; rather than fight each other, they joined forces. Until the boyfriend could make other arrangements, the father offered his home when the daughter spent time at the mother's. This appeased the father's concern that his teenage daughter would occasionally be left unsupervised with her teenage boyfriend. The boyfriend soon patched things up with his own parents and moved back home until he turned eighteen.

It is not likely that problems of this sort will be rectified so easily. Both parents want their children to adopt their moral code. If one parent is stricter than the other, this is bound to confuse the kids and cause arguments. By the way, this problem is not unique to divorced parents. Married parents often disagree over different disciplinary tactics, and children learn quickly which parent can be swayed most easily. Unless *all* parents are honestly committed to putting their children first, it's the children who are going to suffer. Divorce is not an excuse for poor parenting.

Keeping Secrets

"For weeks my son and I had been planning to see a special movie, but my ex-wife got sneak-preview passes and took him to see it a week before the official release date—and then instructed him not to tell me. When I took him to see it later, my poor son started to cry in the middle of the movie. I led him into the lobby while he sobbed about how bad he felt, but he had already seen the movie and was instructed not to tell."

This is a tough one. Good ex-etiquette recommends that first you comfort the child. One tactic would be for the father to help his son calm down by suggesting that they both return to the movie so the son can point out the upcoming funny parts. The father might also suggest to his son that if this ever happens again he should tell the other parent that he doesn't want to keep secrets. Then father and son could enjoy their time together—and the father can take the issue up with his ex when their child is not around.

The next step would be for the father to be honest with his ex. Following the rules of ex-etiquette, he would stay calm while explaining the child's reaction and then add something like, "I know your intent was not to hurt Billy, but that's what happened." Even if he knows the whole thing was a manipulation on his ex-wife's part, it does no good to be confrontational at this point. The ex is in the middle of a game. The only way to stop it is not to play.

The father should take the opportunity to clarify his position: "I would rather not do this again. I would rather work together to raise Billy. He will be the one who is hurt if we don't." To prevent an argument, he should not accuse his ex of anything but instead simply clarify his observation and future intent.

Parents who attempt to alienate their children from the other parent rarely stop at one try. If this is happening to you, it will be necessary to stay on your toes. If the attempts at alienation get more aggressive—or if you notice your child pulling away—get professional help immediately.

Back-and-Forth Logistics

Very Young Children

"I am a recently divorced father with two kids, aged four and two and a half. Their mother has full custody. The oldest seems to be adjusting fine, but the two-and-a-half-year-old is not. When my ex and I are together and we walk away from the kids for a minute, he cries because he doesn't know which of us to go with. It just breaks my heart."

It's difficult to know how to approach very young children who are confused by divorce. They can't articulate what they feel, so what parents often see is how they themselves feel—and they feel angry! To complicate the issue, very young children do not understand the concept of time, which makes it difficult to explain when Mommy or Daddy will return. If this young boy's mother, as the custodial parent, says, "Honey, don't cry. You're going to see Daddy next Tuesday," what does that mean? When is next Tuesday? If the mother says, "You will see Daddy in a week," what does "a week" mean to a toddler? The child probably does-n't even know how to count, so it's understandable that he is confused. He doesn't know what to expect, and he probably feels disconnected and maybe a little scared.

Divorced parents often think their children are too young to understand divorce and therefore don't need an explanation. In truth, children need to hear over and over about what to expect and what their life will be like when mom and dad no longer live together. In as elementary language as possible, parents need to explain to their young children that they are both there for them, and they shouldn't be surprised if they have to revisit the same problem in years to come. As children grow their understanding increases, and they will want more sophisticated answers for these same questions.

A consistent schedule will help very young children grasp the changes they will face when they live in two homes. It also helps when very young children learn to count and understand the days of the week so that they have a time reference to help them understand when their parents will return and how long it will be between visits. This is why many experts don't suggest joint physical custody until the child reaches at least three years of age. It's just too difficult to explain, and therefore too difficult for them to understand why Mommy and Daddy come and go as they do.

To help very young children grasp the back-and-forth life, get colorful children's calendars for both homes and make a game out of coloring in boxes that represent the days as they pass. *Both* parents need to work with their children on a regular basis so that the children will clearly understand what to expect.

It's not uncommon for divorced parents to view divorce as the end of the road with no need to work on future communication with the ex. Your divorce doesn't mean your work is done. You are still co-parents; therefore you have to talk to each other. Use the rules of good ex-etiquette to keep arguments to a minimum. If you need extra help, counseling is a good idea not only for parents who live together, but also for divorced parents. Talking on a regular basis to an expert that knows your family and can guide you through difficult transitions will help both you and your ex make better decisions for your children.

Separation Anxiety

"My ex and I have been divorced for eighteen months. I know research points to kids faring better when both parents are active in their lives, but I'm afraid my kids are suffering from separation anxiety. Whenever it's time to change houses all hell breaks loose. And to make matters worse, I think I go into mourning the day before they are scheduled to leave. What can I do to help my family—and me—adjust to our new life?"

Unfortunately, separation anxiety is not exclusive to kids who go back and forth between parents on a regular basis. Even children who live primarily with one parent and visit the other after their parents divorce go through a certain amount of separation anxiety when it's time to change digs. And it's not uncommon for caring parents to experience the same feelings when they anticipate their children leaving. Everyone is in a state of flux and looking for a way to cope.

Using many of the rules of ex-etiquette will help in this case. However, one that may not be obvious is "no preconceived notions." This rule is normally used when anticipating an ex-spouse's negative reaction. However, it's just as useful when anticipating a negative outcome to *any* co-parenting situation, not just an interaction with an ex.

The best way we can help our children is to set a good example for them. They know when we are happy, sad, or worried, and they feed off the way we act. If a mother or father who must share custody openly worries as the time approaches for the child to leave, the child will also get anxious. Therefore, monitoring your attitude, or not forming a negative preconceived notion about your child leaving, will ultimately help your child.

Here is a list of dos and don'ts to help make transporting kids between mom's house and dad's easier on everyone.

DO keep your good-byes short. In so doing, you will reduce your child's anxiety about leaving you behind.

DO develop loving good-bye routines. A secret handshake or a simple thumbs-up every day before you leave each other is a great way to say, "I love you, always."

DON'T bribe or bargain with your child to behave if he balks at going to your ex's house. It undermines your ex's parenting skills, which will ultimately interfere with your child's adjustment after the divorce. In other words, don't bribe children by saying things like, "Be a good kid and go to Daddy's (or Mommy's) without crying and we will go to a movie together when you get home." Going to see the other parent is not something your child must endure—it's not torture that he must submit to now that his parents are divorced. If you present it as such, you are doing your child a huge disservice.

DO send clear messages. Your child needs to know that you see his time with your ex as a positive experience. When you see your child adjusting well, make sure you don't send mixed signals by saying something like "But Mommy (or Daddy) will miss you."

DON'T tell your child that you will come get him if he is unhappy at the other parent's home. Part of adjusting to co-parenting after divorce is learning to trust your ex's parenting skills. The goal is for your child to trust and feel secure with both parents. If your child is upset when he or she is with the other parent, allow the other parent to comfort the child. Respecting the other parent's turf is ex-etiquette in action. A truly loving parent helps his or her child feel loved and secure at all times. Hopefully, your child has *two* loving parents.

DON'T discuss problems with the other parent when you are dropping off or picking up the kids. Better to keep that time upbeat and positive. Save serious conversations and questions for a private meeting or phone call.

DON'T be surprised if your child again becomes anxious about leaving you after a holiday or a bout with an illness. Illness or holiday celebrations make us all feel a little vulnerable, and it's not uncommon for children to become overly sensitive and clingy during these times—even if they live in a conventional two-parent home. Consistency is the key to coping with a setback.

As a parent you no doubt have a goal to form a strong and loving bond with your children. Be careful not to turn that close bond into a disability. Reinforce the love of both parents and your child will grow to be a loving and secure human being, even if his parents no longer live under the same roof. To ensure that you don't go into mourning each time your child leaves, have a plan for your time alone. Meet friends, work out, play tennis, go shopping, or spend time with your new significant other. Use the time to *live* your new life, not mourn your old life. Then when your child returns, you'll both have something new to share.

Splitting Up the Kids

"I have two kids, a boy, sixteen, and a girl, thirteen. My kids go back and forth between their mother and me, living at each home for a week and switching on Wednesdays. This was fine when they were younger, but now it appears that my son wants to live with me, while my daughter wants to live with her mother. I hate the thought of not seeing my daughter for such a long period of time, but if this custody agreement is really not making her happy, I want to do what's best. Do you have a solution other than simply separating the kids?"

As children get older, it's not uncommon for them to suggest a change in the back-and-forth custody agreement that seemed to work so well when they were younger. And the time you will most likely hear the rumbling is when they anticipate the added chaos of returning to school.

Organization is the key to success when divorced parents choose the fifty-fifty lifestyle. When a child is young, parents do the scheduling. They make sure the homework is done and the clothes are clean and ready to go with the child to the other parent's home. As the child gets older, more and more of these organizational responsibilities fall onto his shoulders. By the time they reach their teen years there's so much more they have to jam into a day that the week just seems to zoom by. They just get comfortable in their room—they accumulate just the right amount of dirty clothing on the floor—and it's time to go back to the other home. The child may become frustrated that he can't seem to get a handle on where he is before he has to pick up and move. If this is the case, the original custody agreement isn't doing its job. It's time to take another look at it.

Sharyl and my husband share physical custody of their children, so the kids go back and forth between their homes. Sharyl lives right around the corner. This makes it very easy for the children. However, not all children respond the same way to the back-and-forth life. While Sharyl's son floats easily from house to house, her daughter, at sixteen, began to have trouble with the week here/week there lifestyle. For her sake, we had to find another solution.

Most parents, and most courts for that matter, don't like to split the kids up when their parents divorce; therefore, a new solution must be found that satisfies the children's needs. There are a variety of ways to address this problem.

First, I suggest switching after school on Fridays rather than Wednesdays. Switching in the middle of the week means children have to get their clothes together and reorganize their lives right in the middle of the week (something teenage girls *hate* to do). Switching after school on Fridays gives kids two days to get adjusted before returning to school on Monday. They have a night to just veg out with a parent, plus a night for dates with friends. This schedule makes the transition feel much less hectic.

Another alternative to splitting up the kids is to try *lengthening* the time at each home. This may sound like an improbable solution. Let me explain.

Sharyl and my husband shared equal custody of their children. The kids spent one week at Sharyl's house, and one week at our house. When the week here/week there scenario became a burden, Sharyl suggested three weeks at her home, one week at their dad's. Their dad did not like that idea; he suggested two weeks at either home with a Monday night dinner in between just to touch base. Everyone agreed to it grudgingly, but we soon found it to be the perfect solution for our family. Two weeks gave the kids enough time to feel settled, and the Monday night gave everyone the necessary touchstone to stay connected.

Switching on Fridays, at two-week intervals, wouldn't have been the answer when the kids were small, but for older teens, it was just the right solution. Thankfully, everyone adjusted quickly, and we never had to visit the possibility of splitting up the kids.

As the kids grow, you may have to revisit problems you thought you solved long ago. When Sharyl's daughter turned eighteen and was no longer bound by her parents' custody agreement, she chose to live full-time with her mother. This time it was a logical choice. Sharyl lived by herself, while we had six people living at our house! Even though Sharyl's daughter made that choice, her son continues to go back and forth at two-week intervals. He will do this until he is eighteen. Where he goes from there will be a moot point, however. He's moving 200 miles away to attend college.

I have found that as an ex gets used to the idea of cooperating, things get easier. Exes are not used to getting along, and at first they may hate the idea of feeling vulnerable again. It takes time to work up to a divorce; it also takes time to build a new working relationship after divorce.

What About Pets?

*"My ex-wife and I decided early in the divorce that
we were going to try the fifty-fifty thing with the kids
living in both houses. It's worked out for the most
part, but I have to admit, there is a lot of anxiety
when the kids have to leave my home because they
miss their dog (I got custody of Rusty, our golden
retriever)! My ex and I are now contemplating having
the dog go back and forth along with the kids. What
do you think? Have you ever heard of the dog going
back and forth along with the kids?"*

Both Sharyl and I have dogs and know how much the kids
love them. These divorced parents are looking for every way possible to help their children adjust to the back-and-forth life. But
the organization it takes to make joint physical custody successful is just too complicated to add a pet to the mix.

There is a period of adjustment after any divorce. To allow a
pet to go back and forth and then have to stop it because the
logistics are too complicated may set the kids back and therefore
extend their period of adjustment rather than ease their pain.
Maybe the pet can come for a visit after school—and even stay
over occasionally—but I vote against going back and forth on a
regular basis.

I am sure that professionals who find joint physical custody
problematic will think it's ironic that I say yes to the kids having
two separate homes, but no to the dog. My response is that when
a couple chooses divorce they must work within the perimeters of
that choice—they can explain what's happening to their children,
but they can't explain things to the dog. If the kids must have a
pet in both homes, a kitten may be a good alternative. A cat uses

a litter box and has no trouble being inside all day. Plus, the excitement of getting a new kitten may take the children's minds off of the fact that the dog has to stay put. And, no, the kitten shouldn't go back and forth, either.

Comparing Mom's Home to Dad's

"When my kids return from their mother's home, they complain that my car isn't as nice as hers, my rugs are ratty, and my furniture is old. I'm doing the best I can. What do I say to them? Right now, I'm angry and insulted and I yell—which I know isn't the right thing to do. Help!"

Everyone feels the financial effects of divorce. While some make out better than others, it's rare that both walk away satisfied. The good news is that most divorced parents are doing the best they can, and every other divorced parent can identify with their plight. The bad news is the children in question are doing more than just comparing two homes. What is really happening when children respond this way is that they are voicing their frustration about their parents' divorce—and that's what needs to be addressed.

Good ex-etiquette suggests that parents address this sort of problem together. Your ex may be delighted that your child prefers her home, but it's not helping the child adjust if an ex is subtly sabotaging your lifestyle. Rather than accuse her, utilize the rules of good ex-etiquette and ask for help. I know this is a different approach than you would normally take, but if you are truly co-parenting after divorce you must make sure the rules are the same—or as similar as possible—and then stick to them. This isn't about which parent wins. It's about how well adjusted your child is after your divorce, and you need your ex's help for that.

Don't be afraid to present it to her in exactly that way. One of my favorite bits of advice is, "People who ask for help usually get it."

Not only should you start a dialogue with your ex, but if she has remarried, you will also need to start communicating with her new husband. When you share custody, your ex's new spouse spends a lot of time with your child. His opinions greatly influence your child's outlook on life. I am not advising you start hanging out together, but you do need to start talking to him—and listening, too. He can be your biggest enemy, or your greatest ally. I talk more about this in chapter 4.

Tell your children the truth about how hard you are working to make the situation work. Don't make them feel guilty—it's your job to help keep their spirits up—but don't be afraid to let them see that you are driven, organized, and independent. Let them know you have goals for your life. It is a huge accomplishment to start over. Your kids need to understand that. When they do, they will be more supportive.

On a more practical note, a great way to help your child take pride in his home is to let him fix up his room just the way he likes it. Since money is a concern, a little paint in the color of his choice will go a long way toward a new look. Take him to the paint store and let him pick out the color. For children who share a room, let each of them fix up a corner, or perhaps paint one wall the color they like—whatever it takes to instill in them that this is their home and their space. Your house may look like a checkerboard, but the goal is for your kids to be settled, and if it takes a green wall to make them feel good in their space, paint the wall green.

To personalize a room using very little money, give your child one of those disposable cameras. Have him take pictures of his friends, his dog, you, and don't forget his mom (yes, his mom and his life at his other home). Buy some inexpensive bulletin boards and let him arrange the pictures. This is a great project to keep a kid busy on rainy weekends.

Get the picture? Be creative. Encourage kids to fix up their own space, and they will take pride in their home.

Communication Problems

Different Parenting Values

"I can't talk to my ex. He thinks it is perfectly fine to let our ten-year-old son, Brian, ride on the back of his motorcycle. Brian is small for his age and I'm afraid he'll fall off the back. And my ex takes no precautions for his safety. When I tell my ex how worried I am he just laughs it off. Then I lose my temper, usually right in front of Brian. What can I do when my ex doesn't take me seriously?"

When people are angry they say things they probably wouldn't have said if they'd had time to think things through. But when anger takes over for reason, the argument becomes more about the insults hurled than about the original issue.

If you are so angry you can't talk to your ex in person, there are logical alternatives. You can send letters or e-mail or use the telephone—all of these work well to defuse emotions until you can once again address things in person.

The next step is to graduate to the "I" message model mentioned in chapter 1. The "I" message allows you to remove the emotion from your request, which will help you focus when you speak. It will also enable an angry ex to hear you. The "I" message offers a specific solution to the problem when you state the way you would like things to change:

"I" Message Model
State the feeling.
State the offending behavior.
State the effect it has on you.
Then state how you would like the behavior changed.

For example, this is how using the "I" message model would play out in the case of the co-parents' feud over the motorcycle. The ex-wife would say, "I feel worried (feeling) when you take Brian on the motorcycle (behavior) because I'm afraid he will fall off (effect). Please install the sissy bar so he will be safe (change)." It's important to realize that some disagreements you will have with your ex may just boil down to a difference in parenting values. This particular ex-wife knew that. Her solution was not to forbid the child to ride, but to look for a way to make the child safe. She practiced good ex-etiquette and looked for the compromise—the sissy bar. This may not have been the ultimate answer the mother was seeking, but she knew going in that she and the father had a fundamental moral disagreement about riding motorcycles. They disagreed about this issue, but the wife knew that her ex's feelings had to be taken into consideration.

The key is to look for alternatives *before* communication breaks down. For example, this father and mother may want to educate their child in motorcycle safety so that he can make his own good decisions about riding. Attending a motorcycle safety course is something father and son could do together.

Of course your children's safety is always of primary importance. If you truly believe your ex's actions jeopardize your children's safety, the courts can help you protect them.

Kids as the Go-Between

"My ex feels that she no longer needs to be involved in discussing visitation plans directly with me, since our daughter "is now old enough to speak for herself." Jessica is eight years old, and in my opinion, still way too young to organize things."

When parents take this hands-off approach it's usually because they are tired of arguing and it just seems a lot easier to let the child do the negotiating. Quite frankly, that line of thinking is a cop-out. If co-parenting is to be successful, the parents must do the negotiating without the child's knowledge and then present the issue to the child as a united front. To do anything else checks the child's allegiance at every turn. It's hurting the child and not affecting the ex. The child in question will learn that she can manipulate her parents whenever she wishes, and it's not uncommon for children in this position to pit one parent against the other to get what they want. As a result, the parents, both hoping for the child's favor, do not discipline the way they should, and it becomes a vicious cycle. Then, when the child becomes a teenager, the parents are surprised that they have trouble controlling her. They shouldn't be surprised; after all, they gave up control years ago when it became too difficult to communicate with the other parent.

You can't blame divorce for anything. The way you act after separation is your choice. As a parent, you can't control the past or the decisions you made back then; you can only control the present and the decisions you will make in the future. This is a good thing! It means you're not condemned to make the same mistakes over and over. You can start right now by putting your kids first—not in the middle—when you and your ex make decisions. This will ensure that your children form positive relationships with *both* parents—which should be the ultimate goal, whether you're divorced or not.

Ironically, if Jessica's parents were still together, this problem of communication would never have come up. Parents who live together rarely allow their eight-year-olds to make even the simplest decisions for themselves, let alone something of this magnitude. Therefore, what made this an issue is the fact that the parents no longer live together and have chosen to parent separately.

I bet if I were to ask these particular parents if they co-parent, they would, like so many other divorced or separated parents, say yes. Most divorced or separated parents who share custody believe they co-parent. But power struggles and refusal to deal with each other is not co-parenting. Co-parenting is making decisions together based on the best interests of the child.

Many anticipate that divorce or separation will be the end of confrontation, disagreements, and responsibility to an ex-partner. But if you are bothering to read this book you already know that's just plain not true.

Badmouthing

> *"I am a divorced dad with a thirteen-year-old son. In the last few months my son has refused to visit his mother but wouldn't say why. He finally told me that she badmouths me so much when he is with her that he no longer wants to see her. What can I do?"*

Parents who badmouth their ex in front of the children may not understand the negative effects of their behavior. They just know they are angry and they want the child to identify and understand their anger. They forget, however, that children have shared loyalties. The inner conflict that badmouthing creates in children can be devastating for them—and at times it backfires on the parent doing the badmouthing.

This may be what is happening in this home. The child loves both parents. When his mother badmouths his father, the child takes it personally. He didn't want to tell his father what his mother was doing because he also identifies with his mom. Rather than take sides, he clammed up and chose not to visit her again.

Here are some steps you can take if you find that you are the victim of your ex's badmouthing:

Ask your child how he feels about what he heard and *listen* to his explanation.

Empathize with him by saying that you understand how disturbing it must be to hear those things.

If the child has been told something that is untrue, explain that the other parent was *mistaken*, and then clarify the misinformation immediately.

Do not retaliate by saying cruel things about the other parent. It only makes matters worse.

"How do I make my ex stop badmouthing me?"

In the past, the recommendation was to stay quiet and avoid retaliation, but experts are now saying it may be best to address the issue formally to put a stop to it. Often the parent doing the badmouthing simply needs to realize that she is doing it. But she may not receive the news gracefully if it comes from you. You may want to ask a trusted relative to call it to her attention. Or, you could suggest a meeting with a counselor or mediator to discuss the subject. The Bonus Families Web site (www.bonusfamilies.com) has a service in which we will send an anonymous e-mail invitation to a badmouthing parent to visit the Web site. Sometimes that's all it takes to alert a parent to what she is doing.

If this is not enough, you may have to take a more proactive approach. Teach your children to make judgments based on what they know is true—not on what they hear. For example, to protect a child from being swayed by an ex's badmouthing, a divorced father may say something like, "Sometimes when you hear something bad over and over again, you may start to believe that it is true, even if you knew in the beginning it wasn't true. I know Mommy often says I don't care about you, but that doesn't mean it's true. Make your own judgments, and if you are afraid or worried, we can talk any time. I will always tell you the truth."

As most children get older they automatically question inappropriate badmouthing without being prompted by their parents. An eighteen-year-old child of divorce confided, "The last time my mom said something bad about my dad I told her to stop it. I came right out and told her it made me feel uncomfortable when she did it. I told her that my dad never said anything bad about her, and I wanted her to act the same way."

Badmouthing doesn't necessarily have to be done with words. Actions may be even more hurtful, as in the following example.

"My thirteen-year-old son told me that his mother (my ex-wife) was cleaning out the garage and found several old family pictures. Right in front of my son, she proceeded to cut my face out of all the pictures and glue pictures of celebrities where my face had been. This hurt my son very much. He even said she put some of those pictures on display in her home. Isn't there a way that a parent conducting themselves in this manner can be held accountable?"

The truth is, this mother probably thought what she was doing was funny—and it probably would have been to anyone other than her children. It is not uncommon for divorced parents to forget that their children have the same love and affection for both parents. Even if kids don't understand the scientific basis behind DNA, they have a keen awareness from a very early age that they are half mom and half dad. When mom puts down dad or dad puts down mom, the child takes it very personally.

It's also not uncommon for an offending parent to believe that her children will side with her when making a joke or to assume the put-down will be accepted in a lighthearted manner. At Bonus Families many children of divorce have confided that parental put-downs do not make them side with the perpetrator—as is apparent in this case. The child did not walk away thinking it was funny, and he did not prefer his mom. As a matter of fact, the whole thing may backfire on her. The boy could begin to identify with his father as the underdog and reject his mom's bad taste. This mother misbehaved, not only from a custodial position, but also from the standpoint that her flip attitude may be eating away at her son's self-esteem and personal identity.

What to do? This mother obviously does not realize the impact her behavior is having on her children. But who tells her? Rule number 8 of basic ex-etiquette says, "Be honest and straightforward." In other words, when faced with a problem of this sort, the offended parent should take it up with the offender parent. If she will not listen to you, you may want to ask a therapist, mediator, or clergy to speak on your behalf. The key, however, is to build your own communication with your ex so that you will not have to rely on others to convey your message. Remember, stay as logical as possible. Avoid subtle put-downs. I suggest you say something like this: "Kathy, the boys came home with a story of you removing my face from old pictures of us and replacing it with the head of Brad Pitt. As funny as that may seem, it hurt Will's feelings. He was very upset about it, and I respectfully ask you to remove those pictures when the boys are in your home. And when you do, I promise I will remove the ones of Carmen Electra and me whenever the boys are at my house."

Just kidding . . . but you get the idea. No value judgments, no trying to make her feel guilty. Just the fact: "It hurts our son's feelings." If she scoffs at your insight, try not to allow your son to be the messenger. No, "Oh yeah? Well ask him, then." At that point say, "I am trying to communicate that our child was upset. You have been informed." Leave it at that.

Parental Alienation Syndrome

Parental alienation syndrome (PAS) is the result of a deliberate effort on the part of one parent to alienate the child from the other parent. It is quite a complicated syndrome with deep psychological roots; it merits a much more in-depth discussion than I can give it on these pages. PAS and good ex-etiquette are at opposite ends of the spectrum in terms of an approach to parenting after divorce. If your co-parent is attempting to alienate your child, it's unlikely that following the rules of good ex-etiquette will stop the behavior. You may need the courts to decide.

Parental alienation syndrome is insidious and it takes time. Why do parents engage in this type of behavior? The answer is that their emotions have so clouded their reason that they stop putting the children first. It's the supreme form of revenge—brainwashing a child into rejecting the other parent. In some cases, the alienation is extreme enough to sever the ties between child and the alienated parent. However, most of the time this is not the case. The most common scenario is that the offending parent so colors the child's attitude that the child questions his devotion to the nonoffending parent. The child doesn't stop seeing the parent, but he does become less devoted, less affectionate, and less trusting because he has been exposed to a constant barrage of negativity against one parent from the other parent.

Although many parents can see this happening, most don't know what to do about it. Professionals once warned that retaliation was even more damaging to the parent-child relationship, so rather than mirror the same bad behavior, many parents sat in silence as their child slowly pulled away from them.

I am of the new school that believes something must be said to children who are in the midst of a parental war of alienation. The statement "Your mom (or dad) is mistaken" can be an excellent preface when a clarification is needed. At least it can be said that you are utilizing the rules of ex-etiquette, even though your ex is playing dirty pool. The following is a typical scenario.

Tom and Christine have three children, ages nine, six, and four. Christine divorced Tom, but after about a year and a half, she decided that she wanted to reconcile with him. Tom, however, had moved on to dating Joyce. Tom and Joyce are talking about getting married. The kids love Joyce, and Christine is furious. She will not accept her hand in the dissolution of the marriage, and she thinks that Tom's first priority should be to try to reconcile with the mother of his children. She believes that the only reason Tom isn't getting back together with her is because he is now dating Joyce. In Christine's mind, Joyce is preventing the reconciliation, which is exactly what she tells the kids. If Christine tells them this enough times, the children will eventually accept that Joyce is the reason for mommy and daddy's breakup. The children then become distant from daddy and hate Joyce— which may have been Christine's intention all along.

Here's a likely conversation and a possible way for Tom to handle the attempted alienation. His youngest child asks, "Daddy, why are you and Mommy not married anymore?"

"Daddy and Mommy didn't agree and decided it would be better to live apart. But we both love you very much."

"Mommy said the reason you're not married to her anymore is because of Joyce."

"*Mommy is mistaken, honey.* I met Joyce after Mommy and I decided to get a divorce."

Notice that Tom did not say, "You're mother is a liar. It was her idea to get a divorce. She was sleeping with that other guy and now that he dropped her, she wants to come back!" He gently explained that mommy was mistaken and then clarified the misconception. He should keep patiently reiterating that mommy is mistaken each time the subject comes up. The goal is to clarify, not criticize.

When an Absentee Parent Resurfaces

"My ex and I were married when we were very young. I was twenty-one and he was twenty-three. We had a child soon afterward, but my ex left us, and we were divorced a year later. I remarried a wonderful man who has been the only father my son has ever known. Today I got a phone call from my ex's mother. She tells me my ex got

married last year and now wants to see our son again. My husband is furious and so am I. I'm thinking about saying no to protect my child."

This is a fairly common scenario. A young couple has a child, but the young man is not ready to be a father. He abandons the biological mom for years. In his late twenties or early thirties, he meets someone, has another child, and all of the sudden the light-bulb goes on. He is more mature, he realizes how selfish he has been, and he sincerely wants to make amends for his immaturity. He attempts to reenter his first child's life. This presents problems on a couple of different levels.

First, the child in question is seven or eight years old by now and has probably been greatly affected by his father's previous lack of interest. He may have bonded with another father figure, and the reappearance of the biological dad can be upsetting for both.

Second, a very resentful ex thinks to herself, "He made my life miserable, and look how well he treats his new wife and her child. I hate him for that, and now it's *my* turn to make *his* life miserable." The resentful biological mom then makes it difficult for dad and child to communicate, and although the father wishes to make amends, the father-child relationship is affected forever.

Ex-etiquette rule number 5 is "Don't be spiteful." Ex-etiquette rule number 6 is "Don't hold grudges." Both apply in this instance. Of course the mother is angry, but being spiteful and preventing the father from seeing his child will ultimately hurt the child, not protect him, and will most likely cause resentment when the boy gets older and realizes that the mother contributed to the alienation. There is another school of thought: the child already has a father who loves him (the mother's second husband), and to disrupt that trust would be detrimental to the child. But the truth is that if the biological father wants to reconstruct his relationship with his child, most courts will support him in his request. Considering the stress and frustration a court battle will cause your family, it would be best to allow the ex to right his wrong. And that means all parties must work to make the reintroduction as stress-free as possible for the child.

Staying Close

"Do you have any tips how to stay close to my kids even though I don't see them as much as I would like?"

Sharyl and I have different custody agreements with our ex-husbands. Sharyl has joint physical custody where the kids go back and forth every other week. I have joint custody and my daughter lives with me and visits her dad every other weekend. But at Bonus Families we have worked with thousands of couples with a variety of custody arrangements; therefore, we both understand how important it is to stay close to your kids when you can't live with them on a full-time basis. Here are a few tips to make the transition easier on both you and the kids.

Listen to your kids. You may feel like you need a crystal ball, but make a special effort to stay up on their likes and dislikes. That way you aren't suggesting a trip to the bowling alley when they really want to roller-blade. And don't be afraid to call your ex to check the kids' likes and dislikes. This is a good way to stay in touch with everyone concerned.

Plan activities before your children arrive. I sometimes hear from a noncustodial parent, "I don't want to give my children a false idea of my life. I want them to be part of my family and understand what my life is really like." Such a parent just goes about her daily routine whether her children are visiting or not. It's the right idea, but the wrong execution. If the parent spends all her designated time with her children cleaning out the garage, the children will eventually stop wanting to visit. She should clean out the garage on one of the days, but do something special the next. Having fun with her children is equally as important as teaching them responsibility. So make plans in advance. It saves precious time and prevents the dreaded "I'm so bored" syndrome.

Suggest the kids occasionally bring friends to your house. I know many may frown on this one because the goal is to spend quality time with your child, but I suggest this for two reasons: First, if your child lived with you full-time and you were going somewhere special, I promise you he would ask you if he could bring a friend. Your goal should be to keep your home as normal as possible. Second, if you are a noncustodial parent, it is rare that you will meet your children's friends unless you make a concerted effort to do so. Allowing your children to bring friends lets you meet the kids to whom your children are attracted.

Write letters or e-mails. Kids love to get letters in the mail. Although they may regard it as old-fashioned, sending letters is a good way to get them used to the fact that not every letter necessarily has a check enclosed. E-mail is another great way to stay in touch. Exchange instant messenger addresses and you can be online live and chat about the day in real time. Don't forget to send lots of *framed* pictures of what you did together on your last outing. When you frame a picture your child is more likely to display it. If you send unframed snapshots, they will probably end up in a drawer.

Make your house their home. I cannot stress the importance of this point. Noncustodial children often feel as if they are visiting; it's rare that they feel completely at home at the noncustodial parent's house. Have lots of pictures around your home of your excursions together. Make sure your children have their own space that no one touches so they can stash their backpacks, clothes, toys, etc., without fear of someone invading their space.

Phone calls. Phone calls are a great way to stay in touch with your kids, but they can become a bone of contention for an uncooperative ex, who may feel you are invading his privacy. That's when it is time to have an honest heart-to-heart to explain how much you miss the kids. Set up special times to call so both the kids and your ex can expect it—and then make the call!

A noncustodial parent can run into trouble when her ex feels as if her time and desires are not being respected. Using the rules of ex-etiquette will help. They specifically ask you to show respect when you interact and to be as open and honest as you can with each other. As time moves on and you all get used to your new life, things will fall into place and you will soon see the rewards of your labors. Have patience, and remember the final, unwritten rule to good ex-etiquette: "If at first you don't succeed, try, try, again."

The Underinvolved Parent

"My ex promises that she will take our child to the movies. My son waits for her, but she never shows up. What do I say to my ex? What do I say to my child?"

I hear this all too often, and it is distressing every time. In response, there's not much you can do with flaky parents. You can't change them. You can address the problem mentally by using what you have learned to break the negative thought/negative behavior chain. But while that may help *you* cope, it doesn't make your child feel better when mom doesn't show.

Unfortunately, flaky parents are more concerned with themselves than with the welfare of their children. Based on that, my concern is not for the parent, but for the child who may feel unloved and unworthy as a result of the flaky parent's negligence. If this happens, tell the child, "Just because we are your parents and all grown up doesn't mean we don't have things to learn. You are a wonderful kid with amazing creativity, great ideas, and lots of love to give. Aren't you lucky that you already know how important it is to share how you feel with people that you love?

Remember all the people in your life who *do* show you love on a daily basis. Let's name them all." Then start naming them together—grandma and grandpa, friends, teachers, and most of all, *you*. Now your child is thinking about the people who love her rather than the one she fears may not. Although there isn't much that can fill the gap left by a parent's insensitivity, this is a step in the right direction.

Many parents in this position feel they must make excuses for the offending parent to protect the child. After years of covering, they finally get fed up and tell the child to ask the other parent about the constant broken promises. I hesitate to suggest that the child confront the offending parent because I have run into parents who blame their poor behavior on the kids, as in "I would come around more if you were a better kid." It takes someone very strong to know how to respond to a statement like that, and most kids are unprepared. It may set your child up for even more hurt. Therefore, I usually suggest that custodial parents work to build up their children's self-esteem and reaffirm their own relationship. Leave the flaky parent to his or her own resources.

That said, what do you say when a hurt child cries, "But I miss Mommy. I love her." Sometimes being a good parent means being a good actor, and as a divorced parent you must put on the best possible performances in the name of sparing your kids. Put your arm around your child and say, "Of course you do. I understand." Then let him know he can share anything with you, because *you* love him. Do your best *not* to compare your love for him to the other parent's love for him. Here are a few additional tips:

Find something at which your child can excel so that he learns to feel good about himself. Sports are good, but if your child is not athletically inclined, try music, drama, singing lessons, arts and crafts, or even volunteering—anything to help him learn to see his own worth.

Be there when you say you will.

Spend time with him. Set aside a "fun day" on a regular basis for just the two of you. Make it a regular outing he can count on. And don't cancel.

Flaky parents often blame their absences on the child's mistake or misunderstanding. Make sure you personally confirm all meetings between your children and their noncustodial parent.

The Vengeful Parent

Stacey, a mother of two, has been divorced from Bill for two years. "Why am I the only one who is miserable?" she asked me during one session. "I figure he can be, too!"

I asked Stacey what that meant. She explained, "When I have to deliver the kids, we meet at a McDonald's just off the highway. I'm usually forty minutes late—just enough to make him crazy. And he always brings his new wife. That ticks me off. I might not feed the kids on purpose so *he'll* have to pay for their lunch. That way they are nice and whiney when they arrive and he can deal with them."

"You purposely don't feed the kids before you leave?" I asked.

"I *always* feed the kids. He can do it for once. And since he's late on his child support, a buck or two for a Happy Meal is expected."

"So, you're angry that your ex is late on his child support?" I asked. "And that's the reason you are late in returning the kids?"

"He does it on purpose. I know when he gets paid. I was married to him for six years. I know when he has money, and he always says he doesn't have it."

To get a clearer picture, I asked Bill why he is late on his child support.

"Because she pisses me off!" cried Bill. "She does things just to make me angry. She's late all the time. I know it's on purpose, and the kids are never fed. She can just wait for an extra week. Maybe two weeks if she *really* pisses me off."

Stacey and Bill's exchange is pretty typical of the circular behavior that goes on between divorced parents, but who is really getting hurt here? If Bill doesn't pay his child support on time, it's the kids who will do without. If Stacey is late and doesn't feed the kids, the kids are hungry and crabby and yes, that may upset Bill, but it's the kids Stacey is hurting.

How can you stop this cycle? Apply the golden rule to getting along with an ex. I have said that putting the children first is the key to good ex-etiquette. But there is another unwritten rule that is just as important: never ask your ex to do something you wouldn't do. If you wouldn't drive two hours to drop your child off to meet a visitation schedule, don't ask your ex to do it. If you hate your ex to be late when dropping the kids off, don't be late when it's your turn. If you are responding in retaliation for what you perceive as a past offense, rethink your approach. Consider the fact that even if you win this round, in the long run, your kids will lose the main event.

3

REMARRIAGE OR INTEGRATING A NEW PARTNER

"Most folks are about as happy as they make up their minds to be."

—ABRAHAM LINCOLN

Many people find that just when they finally begin to settle into a routine of co-parenting, that's when the other shoe drops—in the form of a new partner. Your ex may meet someone and want to bring him or her around the kids. Or, you have met someone and you are not sure how to introduce him or her into your co-parenting lifestyle. This chapter discusses good ex-etiquette when a new partner arrives on the scene.

How and When to Tell Your Ex

"The kids came home from a visit at their dad's with the announcement that his girlfriend is moving in (or he is getting married)."

Good ex-etiquette dictates a well-orchestrated transition from single life to life with a partner. If you are seeing someone seriously, it is not your children's responsibility to break the news to their other parent. It is the responsibility of the parents to treat each other with the respect due them as co-parents. This means, if you find yourself considering moving in or marrying someone else, your ex-partner should be well aware of this fact before you announce your intent to the outside world. Upon the decision to move in together or marry, you should tell the mother or father of your children at or around the same time you tell the children. That way her response to the announcement "Daddy's getting married!" can be "Yes, honey, I know." Your goal, for the children's sake, is to appear as a united front.

If possible, you should schedule a gathering so that all the adults can meet without the children present. If you anticipate this being awkward, nothing more than introductions need happen at the first meeting.

If you live miles, states, or even countries away from your ex, a letter or phone call is in order. It makes no difference which one you use, the goal is to inform your ex that you are involved with someone with whom you plan to make a life.

What should you say? The truth. No embellishments. No "You were so stupid, you didn't see my worth. Well, I finally found someone who does!"

Here's an example of an appropriate letter:

Dear Lucy,

I wanted to tell you first before anyone else that Michelle and I plan to marry soon. I will be telling the children within the week. I want to assure you that my goal is to make the transition as easy as possible on the kids and to continue to co-parent alongside you in the best interests of our children.

Sincerely,
Dave

If you are talking on the phone the language need not be so formal, but you get the idea. You are notifying your ex first and reassuring her that your children will always remain a priority.

When to Introduce the Kids and Your New Love Interest

"Using good ex-etiquette, is there a good time to introduce my children to a new partner?"

It's important that divorced parents learn to distinguish between a new love interest and a potential partner. One does not necessarily become the other, therefore, it is *not* necessary to introduce your children to every date you have. It's best to wait until you know where the relationship is going. Then introduce your potential partner *slowly*, as a "new friend." You could do this during a day at the park or while out for pizza or a movie.

It's not uncommon today for new couples to move in together to see if things will work out. But if you have children, you should know exactly where the relationship is going before moving in with a new partner. If the relationship breaks up, the kids are once again going to be dealing with separation. Therefore it's best to maintain appropriate boundaries during the dating process to protect your child from getting too attached to someone who may just be passing through.

Young children look to the adults in their family as their primary role models. When parents change partners often, young children may secretly wonder, "Why did he leave? What's wrong with *me*?" If the mom or dad continues to break up with new partners, the child may blame herself every time someone leaves. She may not know how to formulate feelings into words and consequently may carry the blame, unchecked, well into adulthood.

For the sake of the kids and for the sake of the new relationship, proceed slowly. Do not assign boyfriends or girlfriends parenting responsibilities until there is a clear commitment to the relationship and potential for marriage. Remember, your date is not just a potential lover; he or she is a potential parent figure. Keep that in mind when you are making your choices.

"What do you mean by 'maintain appropriate boundaries'?"

Here's how one single mother established appropriate boundaries between her three-year-old daughter and a man she had been seeing for a little less than a year. The adult relationship had become a committed one, and the boyfriend had become quite a good friend to the child. They spent time together watching TV, reading stories, and occasionally flying kites at the park. One Sunday morning, the mother was talking to her daughter about the importance of going to church together. She explained that family members are special to one another and that worshiping together was a way to show respect and demonstrate how much they care for each other. The little girl's natural response was, "Is Michael (the boyfriend) part of our family?" The mother knew this was a very important question and used the opportunity to clarify the difference between family and friends by saying, "No, honey. Michael is a good family friend."

Although this mother and her boyfriend were committed to each other, they had not decided upon a future together. The mother did not want to give her daughter false hopes about a future with Michael, and her comment clearly defined the boundaries between friendship and family. It explained that when and if she *did* commit to a future with Michael, he would then be part of the family with all the benefits of full family membership.

If your family does not attend church, then you might want to use eating dinner together or taking family trips together as an alternative example. The objective is to pick a situation that your child sees as a family event and then use that situation as a way for her to distinguish family members from friends of the family.

When There Has Been an Affair

The previous examples are based on the assumption that a reasonable amount of time has passed between the divorce and the new relationship. If there has been an affair, anger and resentment may be high, and the interaction between ex- and new spouses is less likely to be civil. In this case, an introductory meeting is not in good taste, but the ex-spouse should still be made aware of the impending nuptials before—or, at the very least, around the same time—the announcement is made to the children. Any mention of the circumstances surrounding the breakup should be kept to a minimum, especially when the children are present. Even though you are dying to tell your children what a terrible person their other parent is for running off with someone else, you must truly consider whether that information will benefit your child in any way. Is this too much to be expected from people in the midst of such an emotional experience? No! Once you are parents, you do not have the luxury of only hurting yourself when you make a decision. If past behavior was questionable, good ex-etiquette dictates that you not compound your or your ex's indiscretions by talking about them in front of your children.

Dealing with the Affair

Perhaps the most difficult thing to do is to have a civil relationship with an ex who cheated on you. On top of trying to go it alone, you are dealing with betrayal. You don't have a desire to cooperate when you feel betrayed. You feel you were wronged, and it is up to the other person to compensate for the bad behavior by abiding by your wishes. Unfortunately, you do not have the luxury of such thinking. Although your mind is reeling and your heart is broken, you still have children wondering what the heck happened. To complicate things further, you are not allowed the grieving time one normally requires to cope with the pain of a breakup because you are forced to co-parent with the very person who caused you the pain. The object of the affair may later become your ex's permanent partner, which only adds insult to injury. It may seem unfair that you are expected to pick up, move on, *and* cooperate with them. All you want to do is crawl into bed and pull the covers over your head, hoping that everyone will go away and just leave you alone…. But then your child tugs on the covers and wants breakfast.

> *"I was shocked and devastated when my forty-one-year-old husband ran off with our twenty-three-year-old au pair. This was after the au pair befriended our four-year-old to the point that my little girl does not understand why mommy is so mad at daddy and Bianca. I feel my life as I knew it has been yanked out from under me. I don't know what happened. I didn't deserve any of this."*

Betrayal is devastating, but it is possible to come back stronger, more loving, and ultimately more appealing than before. I mention "appealing" because after a betrayal, many people question their own desirability. Betrayal has nothing to do with how desirable *you* are. To betray someone is a decision the betrayer makes alone. The woman whose husband ran off with the au pair asked me some wise questions about coping with the affair. Let's look at them one at a time.

"How do I deal with my ex-husband's toxic behavior toward me?"

Of course I don't know the specifics of this marriage before the affair, but it sounds like this ex-husband is going through the classic midlife crisis—a forty-one-year-old man running off with the twenty-three-year-old au pair. If he is now toxic toward his wife, and she doesn't feel she did anything to bring it on, it's probably because he feels guilty. If he is behaves badly toward her, she may retaliate by behaving badly toward him. Then he can say, "Look how awful she is! That's the reason I left. It wasn't my fault. I had no choice!" This alleviates the guilt he may harbor for tearing his family apart. This is his problem. Don't take it on as your own.

"How do I find out what, if anything, will make him civil?"

Good ex-etiquette means you acknowledge that you can't change anyone's behavior; you can only change how you respond to their behavior. When you stop reacting to his poor behavior he will have to face his own demons, and he will not be able to shift the blame on to you.

"How do I keep my own life positive and productive?"

Ah, this is the best question you can ask, because *this* you *can* control. Stand up straight. This was about his inadequacies, not yours. Be proud of who you are. Live your life joyously and concentrate on being a good role model for your child.

"How long will it take to stop being angry with both my ex and his new wife?"

Again, this one is within your control. It's true that you have been wronged. This will be a journey. Believe it or not, finding forgiveness for them may be the key to your own happiness. I know it sounds difficult—especially now when you are hurt. However, once you release the angry feelings you harbor, they no longer have a hold on you, and neither will your ex. Forgiveness is a very important part of moving past your anger so you can successfully co-parent.

But how do you forgive? Keeping a journal of your thoughts and feelings may help you work through some of the negative emotions you feel right now (see "Journaling: Therapy in Book Form" on page 80). You will be surprised how releasing your anger onto the pages of a journal will allow you to better utilize the basic rules of ex-etiquette. Go through the list of rules in chapter 1. When you are angry, it's difficult to put the children first, ask for help, have no preconceived notions before you speak to your ex, use empathy, avoid grudges, look for compromises, be flexible, and so on. When you have forgiven, your mind is then open to looking for solutions, and ultimately you will become a better co-parent.

> ### *"How can I protect my child from turning out to be the slut/home wrecker that her stepmother is? Or the liar that both her father and his wife are?"*

You can start by employing ex-etiquette—good behavior after a bad divorce. Set the example. Make sure your child knows the importance of love, honesty, fidelity, and allegiance by demonstrating them in your own life.

> ### *"Is there any way to find respect for my ex or the slut he married?"*

Respect? Maybe not. Tolerance may be a more reasonable goal—and you should get out of the habit of referring to her as "the slut"! Each time you use such negative language, it reinforces your pain and anger—and it also keeps you in a defensive or reactive state. You can't move past the pain when you are stuck in a defensive mode, asking yourself, "What's wrong with me? What does she have that I don't have? Studies have shown that most people do not have affairs because they no longer love their partner. They have affairs because they fear their partner is no longer impressed with them, so they look for someone who is. They feel good when they look good in someone else's eyes. You knew all of your husband's secrets, all his insecurities. He may have known you loved him, but he feared he no longer impressed you. Someone twenty-three years old is impressed merely by his age. Notice that none of this has anything to do with you. Only you know what you have to change to be the person you want to be. Make those changes based on how you want to grow as a person. Chances are that your husband's defection had nothing to do with you and everything to do with how he feels about himself.

Making Amends

"OK, I'm the one who had the affair. I admit it. But my ex is so furious that we can't even talk, let alone co-parent successfully at this point. She bites my head off every time I see her, and our child is really mixed up."

If an affair is the reason for your breakup, one of the first steps toward making amends is to apologize to your ex for your misdeed. Even if you have met the love of your life and you think the affair was a necessary evil, you have still betrayed someone's trust. Showing that you are remorseful for your contribution to the

JOURNALING: THERAPY IN BOOK FORM

One way to work through the emotions that prevent you from moving on after divorce or separation is to keep a journal. I find it's a tool more women utilize than men; this is unfortunate. When you are so angry that you are embarrassed by the intensity of your thoughts, it can be a great relief to put those thoughts down on paper. In a private journal you can do the necessary soul-searching and venting to work through a problem. A journal is a great tool to help you gain distance from your problems so you can move past what is bothering you.

If you are having trouble getting started with your journal, use the "I" message model to begin to express your feelings. Don't censor anything. No one else is going to read this. This is your place to vent.

State the feeling.
State the offending behavior.
State the effect it has on you.
Then state how you would like the behavior changed.

Here's an example:

I am so pissed off (feeling) because my ex lies to me about everything (behavior) and it makes me crazy (effect). I wish she would just fall off the face of the earth and then I wouldn't have to deal with her anymore (change).

Granted, these feelings and wishes are not necessarily productive or possible, but you have to move through them to get to the place where you can forgive. So, start with how you feel right now. Write it down. Get rid of it so you can move on.

Many people keep a journal with the belief that they can gain strength by rereading their words. This may be true, but just as important, you have to learn to close the cover, walk away, and leave those angry words on the page. When you throw the garbage out you don't go outside every half hour, open the can, rummage through the filth, and examine what you have thrown out. You throw it out, close the top, and forget about it. Use the same premise when you are writing in your journal. To move through the negative emotions you may have to learn to leave those thoughts on the paper. When you stop checking the garbage you take your first step on the road toward forgiveness and moving past the pain.

demise of the relationship will help your ex to rise above the hurt. I know that offering a simple apology for something as huge as an affair may sound ridiculous. Nonetheless, it is a necessity. You must openly make amends for the pain the affair created.

This will not be easy. Affairs have wide ramifications. The betrayal and the breakup of the family are only the beginning of the repercussions. You must also take responsibility for how your actions affected your ex-spouse and children's emotional health and your family's financial situation.

There are three very important points to remember. First, your ex-spouse and children will be justifiably skeptical of your motives, and it will take some time for them to trust you again. If you seriously want to co-parent from this point forward, you must approach every issue with the utmost integrity. Second, you may have to apologize many times before they hear you. Third— and this is a big one—neither parent should ever discuss anything concerning the affair with or in front of the children.

Moving In with Your New Partner

"My children do not like my partner. Should we still move in together?"

In a word, no. At least not immediately. Although you may be ready to move on to your next relationship, your kids may not be. They may view getting close to your new partner as a betrayal of their other parent. We will talk more about this in chapter 6, "Ex-Etiquette for Bonusparents." Until then, understand that often children do not accept a new partner simply because not enough time has passed since their parents' breakup. They may dislike anyone you take on as a new partner because they just aren't ready to move on. If this is the case, the only answer is to slow down and remember that your timing may not be your kids' timing. That may mean that you don't move forward with your relationship until your children are ready.

Addressing Feelings of Competition

"I always want to feel like I am my partner's first priority."

When you marry someone with children, you should recognize that he will constantly be juggling allegiances to others and to you, his new wife. It's better to acknowledge the struggle and work with your partner to deal with it than to place yourself in competition with his children, his ex, or anyone else.

By now you have read these words a number of times: "Control your thoughts, and your life will be in control." You have the power to feel any way you want to. Your feeling that you are your partner's first priority is not up to your partner, it's up to you. With this in mind, a more positive thought than "I always want to feel like I am my partner's first priority" is "The love my partner and I share is our family's stabilizing force." That is a positive affirmation of your family's origin—love for each other.

Establishing the Primary Parental Figures

"I'm a twenty-two-year-old father of a two-year-old daughter. Her mother and I met as freshmen in college but never married, and we have joint custody. She recently got engaged to somebody else, and I have no clue how my daughter is going to distinguish me from her stepfather at such an early age. I see her often and would never give up any custody or visitation rights, but with somebody else having the day-to-day contact at such an early age,

I can't help thinking that she will see him as the primary father figure."

It is true that the stepdad will probably be a very strong father figure in this child's life. This fact is likely to hurt the biological dad, but it is a reality. Situations such as these are exactly why ex-etiquette, a code for good behavior after a divorce or separation, is needed.

Many of us dream of a conventional two-parent family with a mom and a dad and two-point-however-many babies. That dream does not necessarily die because there is a divorce. Many continue to want the conventional family unit. That's when some divorced parents, still consciously or unconsciously longing for that big happy family, undermine the parenting efforts of the non-custodial biological parent and reinforce the parenting efforts of the new partner. For this reason, it is imperative that the non-custodial parent—in this case, the father—maintain a good relationship with the mother, or he may find himself pushed to the periphery while the mother and stepfather raise the child.

Normally after separation, the biological parents are in the primary parenting roles and the stepparent is integrated into the mix. In this case, however, the stepfather will probably be the primary father figure because he lives with the child. But openly integrating the noncustodial biological parent from the beginning will ensure his continued interaction with his child. This can only be done if the father works very hard to keep an open line of communication with the mother. He must do his best not to resent the stepfather if he wants to remain active in his child's life.

It is important that each of these relationships—mom, dad, and stepfather—are clearly defined right from the beginning. The best way to do this is for these three parents to have regular meetings to discuss the child's upbringing. They must stay in touch and support each other's parenting efforts. If they undermine each other, they will have one very confused little girl.

Coordinating Efforts

Two Against One

"I always feel it's two against one—my ex and his new partner against me—whenever there's a disagreement about the kids."

When a divorced parent remarries, he has a new ally, and the ex-partner often worries that her opinion will no longer matter. Ex-etiquette rule number 4 is "Biological parents make the rules; bonusparents uphold them." By this I mean that the parents of the children establish policy. I am not making a blanket statement saying that exes should necessarily exclude the new partner when making decisions for their children. As a matter of fact, there are times when the opinion of the new partner is extremely relevant to establishing household policy. For the children's safety and to maintain their respect, the stepparent must be able to make disciplinary decisions on her own. However, if the parents have made an agreement and established rules for the children, then it is up to all the parental figures to work together to maintain those rules.

Mediation and negotiation tactics work quite well when dealing with co-parenting problems of this sort. One of these tactics is called reframing. There's a fine art to reframing, and it takes some practice, but it will help you release your emotions and solve problems together.

Reframing means redirecting the other side's attention away from personal preferences and toward the task of identifying common ground. It allows you to find creative options and discuss fairly methods for problem solving. Just as a new frame around an old picture makes the picture look different, a new way of looking at your co-parenting problem may help you to find a solution.

Reframing in Action

Tim and Jennifer have been divorced for four years. Tim has been remarried for a year to Maryanne. Tim and Jennifer share custody of their daughter, Jessica, who is now ten. Jennifer is pretty strict. No TV until chores and homework are completed. Bedtime is at 9:00 sharp. Tim and Maryanne lead a different life. They are more laid-back, no specific bedtime, and if homework doesn't get done, it's not a big deal. Jennifer is looking for some consistency for her daughter, and she asks Tim and Maryanne for their cooperation. Tim and Maryanne do not see the importance of consistency at this point in his daughter's life and so they pay lip service to Jennifer's request for a bedtime and homework completed on time. Jennifer whines; Tim and Maryanne laugh. Meanwhile, Jessica is failing.

Instead of arguing with Tim and Maryanne and taking an offensive position, Jennifer can reframe the problem and make a very persuasive case. Sitting down together, Jennifer takes the floor: "Tim, I understand that you do not see the need for Jessica to do her homework every day, and I know that you and Maryanne enjoy watching TV with her until 11:00 at night, but when I talk to her teachers and explain that the reason Jessie is behind is because her dad doesn't see the big deal in a ten-year-old doing her homework, they will not be persuaded. I truly value your opinion. How would you advise me to respond to their concerns?"

When Jennifer says, "How would you advise me to respond to their concerns?" she is doing two things to help solve the dilemma. First, she reframes the problem and presents it in the form of a question. In order to answer the question, Tim and Maryanne first have to analyze the situation and then offer a suggestion. Second, she asks for help, ex-etiquette rule number 2. Asking for help in solving the problem makes the opposition analyze the problem and suggest a solution. She also prefaces her request with, "I value your opinion." Most people will not be able to resist the compliment; instead of automatically rejecting a position they will openly offer a solution.

In this case, Tim starts by offering a flip answer to Jennifer, "Just tell the teacher Jessie's only ten years old and homework is no big deal." But even as he speaks he realizes how ridiculous his words sound. Up until now he's felt his house was the fun house and Maryanne and he were the fun parents. "Leave the rules to that mean old mom," he has often said. But hearing himself suggest something that a teacher would obviously find ridiculous makes him realize that his previous point of view was not in Jessica's best interest. It was merely a way to infuriate Jennifer.

Reframing the problem enabled Jennifer, Tim, and Maryanne to find common ground—their daughter, Jessica—and they solved the problem together.

"If you are grounded here, you're grounded there."

As my own kids grew up, there were times when my husband and I disciplined them that they did not feel were fair, and for a while we faced them sneaking to the phone to complain to their mom about their dad and me. It caused a lot of backbiting and dissent for a while, and Sharyl admits that she often felt it was two against one. But the children's attempt to divide and conquer was short-lived. The adults quickly learned how important it was to coordinate our efforts if we didn't want the kids running us. Using the best ex-etiquette we could muster, when we felt it necessary to discipline, we worked out a procedure that has served us well:

1. Call the other parent.
2. Explain why the children are being disciplined.
3. Ask if they understand the decision or need clarification.
4. Ask if they have any suggestions.

You may not believe we are this organized. We are. But, in all fairness, it was something we learned to do. We did not start out like that. In the beginning it was chaos. I do have to say that our basic disciplinary philosophy is the same, and this made it easier for us to establish boundaries for the children. Using the approach above, I can't remember one time when Sharyl said, "That's too severe and I cannot uphold that at my home." I did overhear her

REMARRIAGE OR INTEGRATING A NEW PARTNER 87

say, "I'm sorry, Steven (my bonusson), but I have to support your dad and Jann on this one." No parent—married, divorced, or remarried—could ask for more. Steven quickly learned that if he was grounded at one house, he was grounded at the other. Sharyl does have the reputation among the kids as being more of a softie, which meant if the kids acted up at her house, there were fewer consequences than if they acted up at ours; however, we were always notified of the offense, and their father then had the option to discuss the misconduct directly with the kids.

Discipline

> *"My ex's boyfriend just moved in with her. We share custody of my six-year-old daughter. I'm not crazy about the idea of her boyfriend disciplining my daughter!"*

Do not assign boyfriends or girlfriends parenting responsibilities until there is a clear commitment to the relationship and the potential for marriage. Only then should you consider deepening their involvement with your children.

New-Partner Resentment

> *"My husband is the custodial parent of his twelve-year-old son. His ex-wife has standard visitation rights; the problem is that she won't use them! She won't come to pick her son up unless the child calls her and asks, and then she has to consult her husband's work schedule before she gives her consent. On many occasions she will just tell him that she is too busy to pick him up. She is a stay-at-home mom*

who has remarried and has a three-year-old daughter from that marriage. I am worried that she makes this child feel unloved and is distancing him from his little sister. Finally, it isn't fair to my husband that he has to be the full-time parent and his ex takes no responsibility in raising their son."

It's obvious that the writer of that statement is frustrated and therefore resentful about the life she has chosen. Her frustration has clouded her reason, and she cannot see what is really important—that the child needs to feel loved and secure. Where did I get this impression? She started out discussing her concern for the child, but ended up discussing the true reason behind her frustration: "It isn't fair to my husband that he has to be the full-time parent and his ex takes no responsibility in raising their son."

Divorce and remarriage does not reduce our parental responsibilities to part-time. We are always full-time parents. It's not uncommon, however, for new partners to react as this writer did, and become frustrated by what they see as time being stolen from their new family because of old obligations.

The father she describes was doing exactly what he should have done. Using good ex-etiquette means that sometimes one parent must pick up the slack simply because it's the right thing to do. This father loves his son and so he followed through in the child's best interests. He put the child first.

This stepmother cannot see this because she is right in the middle of the negative thought/negative reaction chain discussed in chapter 1. Her anger is making her concentrate on how the inequities of the father's responsibilities affect her life rather than look for solutions to help the child, the father, and, yes, even the mother, better raise the child.

It's important to note that all the issues of concern the stepmother initially mentions are truly important for her stepson's development; she is right to be concerned about his well-being. However, good ex-etiquette reminds us that we cannot control the other home. The writer cannot change the biological mother's behavior. She cannot change the father's behavior. She *can* follow the father's lead and put the child first. When she does that, she will probably be amazed by how everything falls into place.

Lack of Privacy

"I have no privacy. My wife and I are in bed and my ex-wife is banging on the front door because my kid left something behind. It's embarrassing! There has to be a better way. "

One of the primary rules of good ex-etiquette is to respect each other's turf. You would never just drop by a friend's house and bang on the door if one of your kids left something behind. Why would you treat the father or mother of your children with any less respect than you would treat a friend? It's good manners to call someone before you visit. That same courtesy should be extended to your ex-spouse if you expect courteous behavior in return.

Good organization is the key to successful co-parenting. When it's time to pick up or drop off the kids, don't be afraid to show up at the door with a checklist if that's what it takes to keep everything straight. Make copies, and both households can use the same checklist so everyone knows exactly what's coming and going. This will ensure that you don't leave things behind and you won't have to show up unannounced.

More Privacy Issues

"A few months ago my adult stepdaughter, who was living in our home while my husband and I were on vacation, asked some very pointed questions about exactly when we would return

home. About the third day of our vacation, we returned home unannounced, and upon walking in, found her mother (the ex-wife) hiding in the guest closet trying desperately to call the daughter and ask what she should do. My husband was furious. Neither the daughter nor the ex-wife has shown any remorse, nor have they apologized. My husband and I are disappointed, hurt, and angry. We feel violated and cannot seem to get over it. Do you have any recommendations that would help us? Should we go to counseling?"

Things like this happen far more than you think. I have heard some crazy stories. One ex was caught red-handed in the closet with steaks from the freezer! A new wife related a story of paintings being "stolen" off the wall—only to show up in the living room of her husband's ex-wife.

I would never say counseling is not in order, but it sounds to me like the new wife's feelings are perfectly natural. Of course she feels violated; people were snooping around her home. The ones who need counseling are the ex and the daughter. They are obviously in cahoots about something and have an agenda known only to them.

Waiting for an apology before going forward does nothing to help find a solution to the problem. If the goal is to continue communication, good ex-etiquette suggests that this stepmother not hold grudges and move forward. She might consider meeting with her stepdaughter and her spouse's ex in a public place over coffee, talking about their motives, and clearly outlining the behavior that she expects in the future.

Then, she might change the locks. There's a fine line we walk when we want to stay cordial after divorce. They obviously crossed it.

Dealing with the Past

"I was rummaging around the closet last night, and way in the back on the top shelf I found my wife's wedding album from her first marriage. I asked her to get rid of it, but she insisted that she keep it—for her children she said, but I'm not so sure."

Both Sharyl and I have our wedding albums from our first marriages safely tucked away for the exact same reason. They're a record of our children's heritage, and we know they will want them when they get older. These wedding albums contain not only pictures of us with our exes, but also pictures of grandparents that may no longer be living or favorite aunts or friends we haven't seen since high school. My sister-in-law passed away a few years ago at the age of forty, and some of the best pictures we have of her are in Sharyl's first wedding album. My sister-in-law looks young and vibrant in them. When I look at the pictures, I find I can barely remember how sick she was before she died. I'm grateful we have them.

We all have a past. The past is just that—the past. It makes each of us who we are today. There might be room for concern if the partner in question had the pictures prominently displayed on the mantel or tucked away in the top drawer of her chest of drawers where she could see it every day. Under those circumstances, it would be time to have a serious discussion about leaving the past behind, and maybe even getting counseling so that the partner in question could move on unencumbered. But a wedding album "way in the back on the top shelf" is very likely symbolic of exactly where the woman in question mentally categorizes her first marriage. It's something she wants to remember from time to time, but it's not in the forefront of her life. Her new partner is.

Understanding the Co-Parenting Relationship

All this striving to cooperate after divorce can be quite disconcerting for a new love. Rather than interpreting the cordial relationship between divorced mom and dad as in the kids' best interest, a new partner may interpret that the parents are not ready to sever their ties to each other. She may grow skeptical of the time the parents spend together, and as a result become insecure in her new relationship. I have found that new female partners question their feelings of insecurity and wonder if they are a little nuts for having such feelings. Many new male partners, on the other hand, consider the close contact to be a desire for continued sexual activity; they worry that their new love still pines for the ex.

Can you go too far trying to be an amicable ex? Sometimes co-parents *are* too close. I often get questions from new partners asking, "Is it appropriate for my boyfriend to stay overnight at his ex's house when he is visiting the kids?" or "My wife can spend up to an hour talking to her ex on the phone. She says it's about the kids, but it bothers me."

Let's look at this logically. If there is a new union, that's where your allegiance lies. Discussing the rules and maintaining them for the sake of the children can be done without chatting for hours and sleeping overnight. Some people have told me that they feel trapped in the intimate exchange with their ex, but if they abandon the status quo they fear their ex will be less likely to cooperate when co-parenting the kids. If you feel this way, examine your relationship with your ex very carefully. The co-parenting relationship after divorce should be based on trust and the mutual love of the children, not fear. Parents should be respectful of each other when they interact for the sake of the children; however, respect should not be confused with an obligation to continue an intimate relationship if one is not desired. Once divorced, both your ex and you have the right to seek intimacy elsewhere—and the new partner deserves to be able to depend on the new union.

That said, most divorced couples that are sincerely trying to co-parent already have a routine in place by the time they remarry. If a new love comes into the mix, is intimidated by the routine, and makes it difficult for the parents to co-parent, the new love is setting the new relationship up for failure.

If you get involved with someone who has children, it is your obligation to assimilate into the parenting circle. Do not try to reorganize it or establish policy. By the same token, if you are co-parenting after divorce and start a new relationship, it is your obligation to set clear boundaries for everyone concerned. The following is a cautionary tale about what can happen when an ex does not establish clear boundaries.

"My fiancé has fifty-fifty custody of his son, age twelve, and therefore he interacts quite a bit with his ex-wife. She left him for another man three years ago, and now she wants him back. She recently purchased three season tickets to a local football team—one for her, one for him, and one for their son. I feel this is inappropriate. My fiancé doesn't agree and says he is doing it for their son. His own divorced parents fought constantly and he does not want that for his son. I don't think this situation is right. Is there a healthy limit to their contact?"

An amicable split is always the goal for the sake of the children, but when the breakup is friendly it's even more important that parents follow a clear set of limits. Most children harbor a secret wish that mom and dad will someday reconcile. If mom and dad get along well and hang out together, the kids will naturally begin to wonder when the reconciliation will take place. When they find out there will be no reconciliation, it can be even more devastating than the original divorce.

This is where many would say, "Wait a minute. We are talking about the mother and father of this child. Can't they be together any time they want to?" But there's more to it than that. In this case, the ex is trying to entice the father back into her life while he is committed to another. In a situation like this, the father must make his intentions very clear. If reconciliation is not his intent, he's sending the wrong message by attending the football games without his fiancée. If he wants to continue to spend time with his ex and his son—and he has definitely decided to marry another—then he should purchase another season ticket for his fiancée and she should accompany the group to the games. Once a couple has become engaged, that's the primary relationship—and it must be respected.

The fundamental idea behind good ex-etiquette is "put the children first," and that is exactly what this father thinks he is doing by maintaining an amicable relationship with his son's mother. But let's look at what the father's actions are saying to his son. His father loves his fiancée and they plan to marry, but he also gets along very well with his ex-wife, his son's mother. The three of them—the father, mother, and son—have a fabulous time together. To a child of twelve who doesn't understand the intricacies of adult relationships, the fact that his father is engaged to another could appear to be the reason his parents are not getting back together. It's very possible the child could become resentful because it looks like his mom and dad would be together if it weren't for his father's fiancée. Based on that, it will be next to impossible for the fiancée and the child to build a healthy relationship in the future.

This is all new ground, staying cordial with an ex after divorce and remarriage. The rule of thumb, I always like to say, is "be cordial and cooperative, not cuddly." It is important to respect an ex as the mother or father of your children, but there are no social obligations after divorce implied by the relationship. This father does not have to spend leisure time with the ex, and if he is doing it just because he wants to, then of course this is sending conflicting messages to the ex, the fiancée, and his son.

The best way for the father to practice good ex-etiquette is to make his intent obvious to everyone. If he has a fiancée and plans to marry, then that is the primary relationship. His fiancée should be at his side. If he wants to reconcile with his ex-wife, then he should not be engaged to another.

Let's look at a similar problem.

"My wife has stayed very close to her first husband, and that's hard for me to deal with. Before we were married they would go out for dinner at times, just the two of them. He was remarried and she was single. They have adult married children. Now that we're married I asked that she not have any contact with him. Am I wrong on this?"

As I mentioned earlier, once you are divorced and remarried, you pledge your trust and companionship to your new spouse. When you interact with an ex, it should be done in the best interests of the kids—usually with the kids, and even the new spouse, present. Once children are grown and out of the house, the parents' interaction is diminished, but their responsibility to their children doesn't stop. On the contrary, once their children have children, the life of divorced parents is again intertwined because of the grandchildren, birthdays, holidays, etc.

Although this can be intimidating to new spouses, they should not attempt to dictate policy between divorced or separated parents. By the same token, if the divorced parents are meeting for casual lunches or dinners that do not include their current partner or children, this could be the cause for some concern. When divorced parents who have remarried express a specific desire to meet in private, that's a red flag. Intimate meetings are inappropriate once either partner has remarried.

Alcohol or Drug Addiction

Many have asked me how to deal with an ex or an ex's new partner who is addicted to drugs or alcohol. I always remind co-parents, you are not dealing with your ex if he is addicted to drugs or alcohol—you are dealing with the drug. Addicted parents cannot co-parent effectively. They put the drug first, not the child, so trying to rationalize behaviors or plan co-parenting meetings is just spinning your wheels. The main concern is always the children. If there is proof that the parent is addicted to alcohol or drugs, don't be afraid to look into altering the custody agreement for the sake of the children. I would strongly suggest that parents who must interact with an addicted ex refer to the resource guide at the back of this book for information on support groups and organizations. Taking a proactive approach to dealing with a family member who is addicted is the only answer. Take care of yourself, your new partner if you have one, and your children.

Mental Illness

A mental illness is a disease that causes mild to severe disturbances in thought and/or behavior, resulting in an inability to cope with life's demands and routines. If a divorced parent is mentally ill, his ability to parent and communicate with his ex may be impaired. Many mental illnesses can be controlled with a combination of medication and therapy, but if the mental illness goes undiagnosed or the affected person does not take his medication, things can get quite unpredictable.

Some of the more common mental disorders are depression, bipolar disorder, schizophrenia, and anxiety disorders. Symptoms may include changes in mood, personality, and personal habits and/or a desire to withdraw from friends and family. Studies show that certain mental disorders seem to run in families, so if a parent is diagnosed, it should not be surprising if his child eventually displays similar symptoms. In older children and pre-adolescents the symptoms may include the following:

Substance abuse
Inability to cope with problems and daily activities
Change in sleeping and/or eating habits
Excessive complaints of physical ailments
Defiance of authority, truancy, theft, and/or vandalism
Intense fear of weight gain (eating disorders)
Prolonged negative mood, often accompanied by poor appetite or thoughts of death
Frequent anger

In younger children symptoms may include the following:

Changes in school performance
Poor grades despite strong efforts
Excessive worry or anxiety
Hyperactivity
Persistent nightmares
Persistent disobedience or aggression
Frequent temper tantrums

Unfortunately, family members and professionals often pay more attention to the mentally ill parent and ignore the suffering of the children in the family. Staying attentive to the children of a mentally ill parent is an important way to help prevent mental illnesses from passing from one generation to the next. There are some things a co-parent and bonusparent can and should do to aid a child in their care that is dealing with a mentally ill parent.

Teach the child that her parent is ill and that the parent is not to blame if his behavior is erratic.
Offer sound information about the parent's illness.

Supply a calm and predictable home environment.
Facilitate counseling for the child.
Promote the child's self-esteem through involvement in posi-
    tive extracurricular activities.
Maintain a strong relationship with a healthy parent figure.
Make sure the child knows the ill parent also loves her.
Promote the child's healthy friendships with peers.

Fear for your life or the life of a family member is not a by-product of practicing good ex-etiquette. If an ex or a spouse's ex is manifesting symptoms that you think may be associated with mental illness, do not try to diagnose them yourself. Get help from a professional. Check the resource guide at the back of this book for help in finding counseling, support groups, and medical advice.

4

GETTING ALONG WITH YOUR SPOUSE'S EX (OR YOUR EX'S NEW PARTNER)

"We must be the change we want to see in the world."

—MAHATMA GANDHI

Many people regard maintaining a cordial relationship between parental counterparts as going against human nature. They expect jealousy, anger, hurt feelings, and territorial behavior—all of which they consider part of "just being human."

Co-parents can't use "just being human" as the excuse for bad behavior. The evidence clearly shows what negative interaction between parental figures does to children. It's time to take some responsibility.

Becoming a *counterpartner*, rather than merely a counterpart, may be the answer. Yes, it's a play on words, but when analyzed, it does describe the change in mind-set necessary to raise well-adjusted kids after separation or divorce. Getting along with an ex starts with the proper mind-set. The same holds true when dealing with a spouse's ex or an ex's new partner.

To clarify, the *American Heritage Dictionary* defines the word *counterpart* as "one that has the same functions and characteristics as another; a corresponding person or thing." Another definition goes on to say that a counterpart is "one of two parts that complement each other." Custody arrangements often call for bonusparents to perform many of the same functions as biological parents. Therefore, biological parents and bonusparents who are sincerely interested in putting the children first will strive to become partners in raising the children in their care.

Old-school divorce did not require a word to describe a relationship between past and present partners, but today's lifestyle certainly does. For that reason, thinking of yourselves as counterpartners, two people in similar roles who cooperate while sharing responsibility for the care of the same children, rather than merely counterparts, gives everyone a mutual goal to work toward. Plus, the word *counterpartner* describes the biological-bonus relationship without having to specify gender or label (for example, "ex" or "new partner's ex").

I have been married to Sharyl's ex-husband, Larry, for fifteen years. Naturally she no longer refers to me as her ex-husband's *new* wife. For some people, an even more distasteful label is "current wife" or "current husband." That gives the impression that the person is just one in a long line of spouses. Even if that is true, it is not polite and exhibits poor ex-etiquette. The term *counterpartner* just seems to make everything a lot easier.

This is where some parents get riled. "Wait a minute," they say. "These are *my* kids. No stepparent has equal weight. Partners? Be serious!" In principle, I agree. In most cases, parents should make the rules, and bonusparents should uphold them. Still, if your children spend any time at all with your remarried ex, it would be naive to believe your ex's new partner has no influence on them. Knowing this, it makes more sense to cooperate with each other so you can offer the same morals and ethics to the children than to compete with each other. Whether you like it or not, you are all in this together.

But You're Different

Because Sharyl and I are friends now, people often believe us to be the exception to the rule. "Yeah, but you get along," they say. "What about the people who hate their partner's ex or their ex's new partner?" The truth is we did dislike each other very much in the beginning. We faced all the common pitfalls—she thought I was controlling and plotting to take away her children. I thought she was needy and insecure. Since I was the one who handled the family finances, I often wrote her alimony and child support checks. After my husband and I were married, we lived in the same home in which they had lived while they were married. Although this was done to offer the children stability through their readjustment period after the divorce, the transition Sharyl and I were forced to make from "my home" to "your home," and vice versa, was traumatic for both of us. Basically, we were hoping one of us would just give up and go away.

On a personal level, we liked many of the same things. One day I was picking up her daughter to return to my house, and while helping Melanie gather her things, I walked by Sharyl's bedroom. The door was open. On her bed I saw the same bedding I had chosen for my bedroom. Sharyl sometimes tells the story of sitting down to dinner with her children, only to watch her daughter pick up a new plate from the table and say, "Daddy and Jann have these same dishes, Mom. Cool!" And then there's the fact that we live only eight houses away from each other. Anytime we wonder what the other is doing, all we have to do is look down the street.

Biological–Bonus Conflict

During my work as a mediator, I have more commonly seen conflicts between biological moms and bonusmoms than between biological dads and bonusdads. If you think about it, it's easy to understand why. In most families, the mother is regarded as the nurturer and the keeper of the family schedule. Although many divorced dads play an active role in their kids' lives, usually they don't do the scheduling or organize the play dates. Strange though it may seem, I have found this to be true even if the parents share equal custody. If the father remarries, it is quite common for his new wife to take on the primary nurturing and scheduling responsibilities when the children are in their father's care—and that's when interpersonal problems can occur. A newly divorced mom who may be feeling insecure about being on her own and a new stepmom who may be feeling insecure about her newfound parenting responsibilities can be a volatile mix. Both may struggle for control. Without an open line of communication between them, this can lead to disaster.

Like divorced mothers, divorced fathers may feel insecure, but for a totally different reason. Many divorced fathers feel guilty that they do not live with their children and resent that their ex's new partner does. While mothers appear most jealous when someone takes over the day-to-day mommy responsibilities, fathers fear the loss of status as protector, provider, and primary male influence on their children.

To drive this observation home, let's look at an exchange between a biological dad and a bonusdad that was discussed at one of our Bonus Families workshops. It will explain their different points of view and help to illuminate their inherent animosity.

Bob (biological dad): The divorce nearly broke me, and I could barely make ends meet. Then Sally moved in with Mark, a guy with money, and although my son had everything he wanted, I wasn't the one who was buying the things for him. I felt like a failure. Every time I tried to save up for something special, this guy went out and bought my kid something bigger and better. I could never compete.

Mark (bonusdad): I knew Bob was having financial problems. His child support payments were often late, and Sally felt bad asking him for the check each month. Rather than wait for the money, I just bought Jason what he needed. I didn't realize it was undermining Bob. I thought I was helping.

Bob: It's not so much the things that are purchased, but the value put on the things. Mark makes a lot more money than I do. He drives a newer, bigger, faster car. Everything is designer label. My son is so swayed by the glitter—our values are now completely different. How can I say, "Mark, I think you are very materialistic, and now you have made my son just like you." I can't.

And so Bob said nothing to Mark, but all the while he was feeling inadequate as a provider and worrying about the values that were being instilled in his child. Every time he saw Mark he was reminded how he no longer had control over his son. And Mark, just living his life, had no idea what he'd done to make Bob so angry.

Parents want to control their children's environment, but it's difficult to do when your child lives for weeks or months at a time with your ex and her new partner. The values imposed at the other home have just as much influence on your children as your values do. As a result, the competition can become so intense that the competing parties lose sight of their original goal—instilling positive values and raising a well-adjusted kid—and spend most of their time trying to undermine each other's influences.

To further complicate the issue between Mark and Bob, Mark was beginning to see why his partner and Bob were divorced.

"Who could get along with him?" he wondered. "Look at what I do for his child, and he never has a civil word to say to me."

There's a reason for this misunderstanding. We all come to relationships with a past and a separate point of view. If left unquestioned, our separate point of view will also be the root of our misconceptions. Bob and Mark did not talk to each other. Even though Bob's child lived with Mark half the time, Bob rarely spoke to the man that served as a father figure for half of his son's life. They had no idea how the other felt.

Bob and Mark's behavior is not reserved for men. Women are guilty of the same avoidance behavior. It's not uncommon for the maternal counterparts to go for years without talking to each other. They bathe the same child, feed the same child, tuck the same child into bed, but they avoid talking to each other.

Building a Working Relationship with Your Counterpartner

The answer to this problem, of course, is to put your issues behind you and build a working relationship for the sake of the children. As usual, it sounds good in theory—a business relationship to co-parent the kids, everyone cooperating for the sake of the children. It is our experience, however, that the counterpartner relationship can be even more volatile than the ex relationship. Angry divorced mothers and fathers may compete with each other for their children's time or for their children's affection, but their roles as mother and father are different and clearly defined. Counterpartners are in the same parenting role, so they are competing with each other for the same rights and duties. Mother against mother figure. Father against father figure. That's competition at the most basic level possible.

You don't choose your counterpartner, your ex does. This can automatically set you up for an adversarial relationship. Very few exes celebrate their ex's choice of new partner. Very few new partners rejoice in their partner's ex. Because there is so much mistrust and resentment in the beginning, any sort of communication is very difficult. However, difficult doesn't mean impossible. If your mutual goal is to work together in the best interests of the children, you can do it. That mutual goal is the key.

Here's an example of our personal evolution from counterparts to counterpartners. One of Sharyl's favorite stories is about the day she found out Larry and I were going to be married. She took him aside and said, "So help me God, if she's mean to my children, I'll make your life miserable!" Fast forward to about a year later, when we had settled into a routine of attempting to co-parent the kids. We live in a small town where everyone knows everyone else, but the children's doctors, dentists, and teachers were not privy to our back-and-forth schedule. Understand, this was in 1990, and the thought of joint physical custody was new to everyone. Sharyl would make a doctor's appointment for the kids, but the doctor's office would call me to confirm it. Or I would make an appointment for a dental checkup, and the dentist would confirm with Sharyl. Neither of us ever let the other know; we just took the children to their appointments. Then we called the other to let her know that the children were just fine. It looked like we were cooperating, but we really weren't.

Rather than simply make appointments or plan for sports practices, counterpartners should call one another with a heads-up. But we didn't know that back then. Larry, Sharyl, and I came from old-school divorce. We thought we were pretty progressive just because we didn't argue when we dropped off the kids. The thought of cooperating with each other further than that just never occurred to us. There was no model to follow.

We finally realized that the children were not benefiting from our inability to communicate. They were coming down with illnesses—such as stomachaches—that could only be attributed to stress. Sharyl and I began to make an effort to coordinate medical appointments and to show up at Little League games together. At first we did not sit together; we stayed on opposite sides of the field. But as the days went by and our mutual goal, the kids, became obvious, we slowly closed the gap. Now and then there was a glitch, but once we admitted that we had all been contributing to the communication problems, we made the necessary changes. And that's when things began to smooth out. Don't get me wrong; this process took years.

I knew we were OK when Sharyl called one day in a panic and asked me to pick up her son because she was stuck in traffic. "I didn't know whom else to call," she said, "and I knew you wouldn't want him sitting at school without a ride either." That was a huge step for her. That one sentence acknowledged that she approved of my being in her child's life; she was comfortable asking for help. And I was grateful that she had called; she was absolutely right that I would have felt terrible if Steven had been left at school with no ride. Sharyl and I had become partners in his upbringing.

Before You Start: Check Your Attitude

Any exercise I offer always starts with mental preparation. This is because I believe you must organize your thoughts to organize your feelings. Good choices are a natural outcome once you have cleared your mind of negative thoughts and become focused on a positive goal.

Every day I work with divorced or separated parents and see the impact that a positive attitude can have on the quality of relationships. I believe that if people want to make their lives work, they will. It is their attitude that ensures their success.

Each day we make a choice. We can choose a positive thought or dwell on what has hurt us, what has angered us, and what we feel we deserve because we are angry and hurt. That thought choice is our outline for the whole day. There's an old saying, "I woke up on the wrong side of the bed," but you don't just wake up one morning with a bad attitude. You create it.

Lose the Labels

"My spouse's ex hates me, and I just don't know why."

"My spouse's new partner hates me. He won't even look at me when I pick up the kids."

When people say things like this to me I usually ask, "Do you think it's *you* this person hates, or is it just your label? Would the person hate *anyone* in your position?" Everyone I have ever asked this question has answered, "It's the label. The person doesn't even know me."

In the beginning it's hard to think about your partner's ex with anything but animosity and mistrust. You might think, "That's the ex. They shared love and intimacy. They shared hopes and dreams." And now, as the new partner, you might worry: "Can our relationship ever be as special?"

Your partner's ex may look at things in the exact same way, but from the opposite standpoint. "That's the new love. They share the love and intimacy we once shared. They have hopes and dreams. Look how easily I can be replaced. I guess our relationship was never that special after all."

And so these two begin to hate each other without really knowing each other. The label "new" or "ex" is all they know about their counterpart, and every day they hate each other a little more.

When they put aside the labels and start relating to each other as parents—people who want the best for the same kids—it makes it easier to let go of the anger they automatically associate with the label. They release the anger or resentment, and they can relate more civilly. Some parents comment, "I'm not so sure I want to act civilly. Why do I have to? Kids are resilient. They will be just fine." Maybe they will, but if so it will be in spite of their upbringing. Do you want someone to be well adjusted *in spite* of your behavior or *because* of the example you have set?

Ten Tips to Help Build the Counterpartner Working Relationship

People looking for ways to cope with a partner's ex or an ex's new partner don't want long-drawn-out explanations of the psychological reasons behind the arguments. They don't have the time. "Just tell me what to do," they plead. "How can I get her to _____ (change, act like an adult, take responsibility, let me have my kids back)?"

Following are ten tips to help you build a working relationship with your counterpartner. Read them with the understanding that you can't make anyone do anything. You can only control your own turf, your own thoughts, and your own behavior. When you make a commitment to do that, you will see a change in the other person's behavior. It's inevitable. Because as you concentrate on your own behavior, you will no longer be reacting to something the other person has done to upset you. You will finally be in control of your own life.

1. Have a goal. How do you see your interaction with your ex's new partner? Visualize it. Do you see yourself arguing? Do you avoid interaction? Does jealousy affect the way you communicate? Then that is the sort of interaction you will perpetuate. Decide upon the relationship you want. You are the only one who can break the negative thought/negative behavior chain. Picture yourself getting along. When you prepare for a conversation, anticipate a *positive* interaction. Don't dwell on past interactions that have not been productive. The goal you set for yourself is the relationship you will have.

2. You do not have to be friends. Being friends is not the final goal. Sometimes there is just too much residual hurt and anger. But that doesn't mean it's impossible to

be polite and cooperative. In the beginning, look for common ground, and discuss only problems you need to solve. If the kids are the only common ground you share, that's what you talk about. You do not have to play tennis or have lunch together. The goal for both of you is to put the kids first when making decisions.

3. Understand that the children already have a mother or father. *For the new partner (bonusparent):* Don't try to be your bonuschild's mother or father. If you try to take over or establish policy, the ex (biological parent) will resent it, which will cause communication problems between the two of you and anxiety in the children. If you support the time the parent can spend with her children, she will appreciate your influence. If you make it difficult for the parent to spend time with her children, or if you fight her on policy, she will resent you. Love the kids, but not so overtly that their parent feels intimidated. *For the ex (biological parent):* You don't have to compete with your ex's new partner. Your children know who their parents are. They *want* to spend time with you. Make positive time together your first priority, and you will have nothing to fear.

4. Find your niche. Many of the counterpartners with whom I have worked don't have a clear idea of their responsibilities. Consequently, they fight, argue, resent each other, and feel usurped. Get clear about your roles. Find what you are good at and offer that to the kids. Don't compete with each other. For example, I am a perpetual student. I am constantly taking classes in something. Therefore, I'm the one who helps the kids do their homework, research their reports, and fool around on the Internet. Sharyl, on the other hand, has instilled in the kids a pride in their appearance. She was

also the one to make sure the kids had regular teeth cleanings, doctor's appointments, haircuts, and trimmed toenails when they were little. The times we unconsciously crossed over to each other's niche, the kid did not get as good a grade on the report, and Steven came home with the haircut from hell (not to mention very short toenails). Each of us was furious with the other. When you find your niche and stick with it, the children get the best of both of you.

Can you ever stray from your niche? Of course, but do it respectfully. Inform your counterpartner of your intentions. One dad told me, "My kid's stepdad tried too hard. He was always the first one to volunteer as the coach for soccer—or any of my daughter's extracurricular activities. Finally, I explained to him that, while I appreciated his enthusiasm, he needed to include me, not ace me out, or we were going to have problems. He appreciated that I just came out and told him what was on my mind. Now he and I have an understanding. This year we are both coaching soccer. So far, so good." This is a good example of respectful communication between counterpartners.

This brings me to a special note to dads. Try not to rely only on sports as your chosen niche. The chances are that both dad and bonusdad like the same sport; therefore, if you seek your niche only within that realm you could be adding to the competition. Access your personal strengths and offer them to the kids. Work toward a time when, for the sake of the children, both dad and bonusdad can coach the Little League team at the same time.

5. Develop empathy. Misunderstandings and breakdowns in communication will happen if you are unwilling to look at a problem from a point of view other than your own. Becoming empathetic, putting yourself in the other's place to understand a particular behavior, may be all you need to get a fresh perspective and move toward cooperation.

Here's an example of how empathy helped Sharyl and me to understand each other's position, and having forged that understanding, make the necessary concessions to get along.

Sharyl: Jann watched my children after school while I was at work and often made arbitrary decisions without consulting me. What really got to me was when my kids had doctor appointments and I had no idea. I didn't like it, and I finally told her how jealous I was that she could be with the kids and I could not. I hated that I had so little control over my own children. After I calmed down and did some soul-searching, I realized that I had to work and that my kids would love me anyway. I decided I would rather have them with someone who truly loved them than at a day-care center.

Jann: When Sharyl told me that she resented that I could be with the kids more than she, but that she realized it was better for the kids to be with me after school than at a day-care center, it sent up a red flag. I knew she was putting the kids first and that I was doing a good job, but I also realized that maybe I was doing *too* good a job, which explained her unwillingness to cooperate at times. When I put myself in her place, I decided I wouldn't like some other woman taking over my children either. I wouldn't like to find out secondhand that my child went to the doctor for a checkup when I hadn't even known about the appointment. Even if the appointment were made on his father's time, I would resent not being informed. So how could I have been surprised by Sharyl's resentment?

Sharyl: When I put myself in Jann's place, I realized I wouldn't want to have to check with my husband's ex-wife every time I wanted to make a decision. She had a child of her own, and I could see she was trying to stay consistent with all the kids. If she'd called me as much as I called her, I would've thought, "Doesn't she think I have any sense?" That's when I suddenly understood Jann's sarcastic remarks when I called to check on the kids. I asked if they had eaten and questioned her about what she fed them for lunch. She probably wanted to sock me.

Developing empathy, mentally putting ourselves in each other's place, allowed us to understand each other's point of view. In that state of mind, we no longer took our disagreements personally. As empathizing became more second nature, disagreements became rarer. We found that we agreed far more often than we disagreed on our approach to parenting. As our newfound spirit of cooperation developed, something else very surprising happened—Larry's relationship with Sharyl improved. When she and I ceased our bickering, there was no one to keep things stirred up, and Larry automatically looked for ways to cooperate.

6. Cultivate respect. Because it is rare to hold one's ex or their new partner in high regard, respecting one's parental counterpart may seem like a tall order. But notice that I say, "*cultivate* respect." The Dalai Lama said, "Try to cultivate respect toward your own enemy, or the people who create problems or harm to you." For our purposes, the word *cultivate* means "to move toward respect by using small gestures." Just as you would plant a small seed, water it, and watch it grow, allow your interaction with your counterpartner to grow slowly into a cordial relationship.

Here's an example of a small gesture between counterpartners.

Sharyl: One day my son, Steven, misbehaved at school and the principal called Larry and Jann's home to say he was suspended for a few days. Steven was eight. He and a friend had found some matches on the playground and were caught lighting them behind the school. Larry could not be reached. At that point in our relationship, Jann and I rarely spoke; however, we recognized the importance of keeping the rules consistent from house to house. That day I got the phone call at work. It was Jann. She explained that she was going to go pick up Steven from school and wanted to know how I would handle the situation if Steven were at my home for the week. Until that time we never consulted each other. I told her what I thought, and she thanked me for my suggestions and politely hung up the phone. My opinion of her completely changed when I heard the words, "What would you do?" I felt like I had my kids back. She wasn't trying to steal them. She was trying to help. I wasn't on the outside looking in after all.

Jann: I knew Sharyl and I would agree on how to handle Steven being suspended, so asking her opinion was not a stretch in the sense that she would want me to do something that I thought was inappropriate. It was a stretch to be vulnerable, however. That was what was difficult. At the time, I resented that I had to deal with her at all, and I didn't want to consult her about anything. However, the parents (all of us) had agreed that we would keep the rules consistent from house to house. If I didn't do my part, I couldn't expect it of anyone else. My calling her was a small gesture—a wave of the white flag. When we hung up the phone my opinion of her had changed. She knew how hard it was for me to make the call and she was very gracious about it.

Respect for someone else's feelings enables you to be gracious and make your judgments fairly. When you find yourself making your decisions based on what is fair, then you respect that person enough to consider her feelings. At that point, you have reached your goal. That's good ex-etiquette.

7. Formally acknowledge his or her good work. *For the new partner (bonusparent):* Almost everyone reacts positively to positive reinforcement. Saying things like "Your kids are great, and I partially attribute that to

your influence on them" helps to break down the walls of resentment. It lets the parent know that the bonusparent has noticed her influence on the children and regards it as positive. Of course, if you don't believe it, don't say it. If you don't feel comfortable saying something like that, then just act as a stabilizing force when the kids are with you. *For the ex (parent):* One of the biggest complaints I hear from bonusparents is that the parents fail to acknowledge bonusparents' devotion to kids that are not their own. Acknowledgment from the biological parent goes a long way toward promoting cooperation. Begin with something like, "I really appreciate how kind you are to the kids." Or you might say, "I want you to know that I see how kind you are to the kids, and I truly appreciate what you do for them." The bonusparent will then be more inclined to repeat the cooperative behavior.

8. Don't compare, don't compete, and don't stew over past intimacies. Comparing yourself to someone else simply undermines your self-esteem and sense of self-worth and keeps you riled up. If you compare yourself to others, you will never find your true self. Strive for your own sense of self and hold your head high. A secure man or woman is the most attractive of all.

Read the following words sent from a new husband who was asking for help in trying to come to grips with his wife's relationship with her ex. He was truly struggling.

"I hate that their history together overwhelms ours. I hate seeing them together at my stepdaughter's events and knowing the familiarity and intimacy that is there. I hate knowing that he knows my wife's body as

intimately as I do. I hate it when their conversation slips from the topic of their daughter to some mutual friend or interest. I know it is not healthy to think about these things but I can't seem to help it."

He's right! It's *not* healthy. Granted, every one of the feelings this gentleman has expressed is understandable, but not one feeling expressed will help him build a lasting relationship with a new love.

For the new partner (bonusparent): Your first priority is to have a goal for your relationships; otherwise you will have nothing to work toward. If your goal is to go forward with your new spouse, then honor what you have together. Make new memories; celebrate new intimacies. Do not undermine your own existence by comparing what you think or feel with what your partner's ex thinks or feels. You are making assumptions based on the love that *you* feel for your partner; you have no idea what the ex-partner feels. *For the ex (parent):* If your ex is nicer or more attentive to the new partner, it's not necessarily because your ex believes the new partner is better or sexier than you. It has everything to do with timing and learning from past mistakes. Resentment will make you a less effective parent and person. If finding a relationship is important, then it's better to put your energy into trying to meet someone who is worthy of you. Or, better yet, put your energy into lifting your spirits and changing your life for the better.

9. Learn to ask your counterpartner's opinion. *For the new partner (bonusparent):* If you are not sure how to handle a situation, don't be afraid to pick up the phone and ask your counterpartner what she would do. Many bonusparents, especially bonusmoms, are afraid to do this because they feel it hands over control to the very person they are struggling with for power. Consider how you feel when someone asks your opinion. Most

likely you feel respected and valued, and that's why I suggest that you use this strategy to break the ice with a counterpartner. It's difficult to admit that you have been rude or that you contributed to a disagreement. Asking your counterpartner's opinion is a simple way to put the relationship on a new and more positive footing. *For the ex (parent):* Many moms complain that they just don't trust the bonusmom's judgment when it comes to the kids' care. "I don't *know* her!" they complain. "And she's got my kids!" Dads complain, "Their stepdad and I don't share the same values. I worry about my children when they are in his care." If your child were spending the night at a friend's house, would you not call the friend's parents beforehand? Wouldn't you talk with the parents long enough to feel comfortable that your child is at their house? If anger, animosity, and jealousy are preventing you from using the same judgment with your counterpartner, it's time to change that. The best way to get to know someone is to ask her opinion. If you are concerned about how someone might handle a given situation, *ask*.

10. Don't add fuel to the fire. Be part of the solution, not part of the problem. If you are attempting to raise children together after divorce, good communication is not a choice; it's an obligation. And if you have married someone with children from a previous marriage, you are in effect saying you will do everything possible to support those children through life. In other words, you didn't sign on to cause trouble.

For the new partner (bonusparent): Some new partners think if they can keep the exes fighting it will ensure that they will never reconcile, so they do things on purpose to keep the kettle boiling. My response to that kind of behavior is that if you are worried about your partner and his ex reconciling, you shouldn't have gotten married in the first place. *For the ex (parent):* Some exes are so angry that the ex has found happiness with someone else that they look for ways to make the ex and the new partner just as miserable. They justify it as payback. If this describes you, I urge you to remember that your inherent dislike of the new spouse has nothing to do with who your ex's new partner really is. It has to do with how you feel about your lot in life. It has to do with your anger at being replaced, or with the fact that you feel your ex never really saw your worth. However, your desire for revenge doesn't do your kids any good. Do what you can to move past the pain toward your own independence. In so doing, you will teach your children an important life lesson.

Putting Good Ex-Etiquette into Practice: Who Goes First?

"I think it's time to call a truce with my partner's ex. According to ex-etiquette, who makes the first move— the ex or the new partner? What's the procedure?"

Calling a truce implies you have known each other for a while but have been at odds. In this case, it doesn't matter who takes the first step. You know each other. You know what the problems are. Either a phone call or a note is appropriate to initiate your first private communication. The key, whether you are the initiator or the receiver, is to be gracious in the attempt.

Phone calls are less formal, but they may also make you vulnerable to a negative response. Writing a letter will give you a way to edit your invitation. Letters also are less likely to put the recipient on the spot. Whatever your choice, the phone call or letter should say something like this:

"Hello, _____.

*This is not an easy call to make/letter to write. I know
we are both uncomfortable with the situation as it is.
That's why I would like to do all I can to make things
easier for (names of the kids) by trying to put our own
issues aside. Would you be willing to meet me so we can
sit down and talk about things? I don't want to argue or
put you on the spot. I would really like to look for a way
to work together."*

Then follow these four steps.

1. Suggest a neutral place. Pick a meeting place that is far
   enough away from both your neighborhoods that well-
   meaning friends will not distract you. Look for a place
   that offers you some personal security. By this I mean a
   place that offers something to sit behind or lean against,
   such as a booth or a table, so that you don't feel too
   physically vulnerable for your first meeting.

2. Suggest a time for the meeting. Include a conclusion
   time. For example, you might say, "How about 1:00
   P.M.? I have another meeting at 2:00, but that will give
   us a good forty-five minutes. Will that be convenient for
   you?"

3. Plan what you are going to say. Don't walk in
   unprepared. Use the techniques discussed in chapter 1 to
   present your case—"I" messages, tact and timing, etc.

4. Give yourself time between the end of the meeting and
   seeing the kids in question. After the meeting is over
   you will probably be preoccupied with what you have
   discussed. Until you iron out all misconceptions, which
   may take more than one meeting, telling the kids that

you just had lunch with their mom or dad or bonusparent may make them worried and uncomfortable. It's best to iron out the difficulties and then demonstrate your new understanding of each other by your actions.

Putting Good Ex-Etiquette into Practice: Approaching a Resentful Ex

"I have been married to my husband for a year. He was previously married and has a daughter, Julie, who will be eight in a week. Julie's mother is throwing her a skating party for her birthday. She invited my husband, but she asked that I not attend. My husband is taking a stand and saying he will not go if I am not invited. If I'm not there I'm sure my bonusdaughter will think something is wrong, and I certainly don't want to ruin her day. I have tried to get along with my husband's ex. She won't budge."

The main objective in situations such as these is for the counterpartners—in this case, the mother and the bonusmother—to forge a working relationship so that, for the sake of the child, they can both comfortably attend the birthday party. Knowing that the mother has requested that the bonusmom not attend, it's the bonusmom's job to initiate communication. She can begin with a phone call. If that is too intimidating, an e-mail or letter might be a better bet. The conversation could begin with something like this:

"I know you don't feel comfortable when I am around, and I am sorry about that, but Greg has asked me to go

to Julie's birthday party. I would stay home, because I don't want anyone to feel uncomfortable, but Greg is rather adamant about this. Plus, your daughter is a wonderful girl. I attribute that partially to your influence, and I would like to feel comfortable asking your opinion on things when Julie is with her father. Concerning this problem, however, if you honestly feel it will make Julie uncomfortable that I attend, I will talk to Greg and explain why you don't feel I should be there. Right now I'm sort of stuck in the middle between the two of you. Isn't there a way we can work this out so your daughter has the great birthday party she deserves?"

Note that when the new wife refers to her husband when talking to the ex-wife, she calls him by name, not "my husband" or "we." This is calculated. Some exes may feel that using the term "my husband" or "my wife" or "we" is flaunting the new relationship. As crazy as it may seem, other terms that may alienate a new ex are "the children's father" or "the children's mother." Exes don't need to be reminded, even subtly, that the children have a father or a mother who also has a say in the decision making. They already know that. (Interestingly, I have found that these semantics pertaining to past relations seem to bother women far more than they bother men.)

Notice also that the new spouse refers to the child either by name or as "your daughter." This again is politics, but it serves a purpose. By using the term "your daughter," the new spouse is offering the first spouse respect by acknowledging that she understands the child in question is not only her partner's child, but the ex-spouse's as well. When a parent is fearful that her child will prefer the bonusparent and as a result favor the other home, the new spouse's acknowledgment of the parent's importance goes a long way.

The letter or conversation ends with the bonusmom asking, "Isn't there a way we can work this out so your daughter has the great birthday party she deserves?" With those words, she enlists the mother's help to solve the problem. Remember the ten rules of ex-etiquette? Number 2 is "Ask for help when you need it." Proper ex-etiquette in this case begins with the mother and bonus-mother working on their communication so that they can peacefully coexist for the sake of the child.

Interacting with Your Counterpartner When There Has Been an Affair

When there has been an affair, both counterpartners have to face issues that are hard to overcome. For the ex, of course, the issue is betrayal. For the new partner, the issue is guilt over having been a part of the betrayal. Both will have trouble putting their feelings aside in order to interact. Ultimately, however, an affair, although probably the most difficult thing to overcome when attempting to co-parent after divorce or separation, does not change your responsibility to your children's lives and future.

If handled correctly, the kids won't know that there has been an affair, and the rules of good ex-etiquette still apply. You must remain polite to your counterpartner even though your interaction will understandably be strained. If emotions have gotten out of hand and the children do know about the affair, it would not be surprising if the children resented the new partner too.

Although this may sound as if I expect you to have superhuman strength, good ex-etiquette is even *more* important in this type of situation. For the children's sake, do everything you can to stay civil when you interact in front of them. For more help, refer back to "When There Has Been an Affair" in chapter 3.

Dealing with Jealousy: They're Having a Baby!

"My ex-husband and I have been divorced for eight years and have an eleven-year-old daughter. We've had our ups and downs, but we have now settled into a comfortable routine. My ex remarried in February, and we all do our best to get along while co-parenting my daughter. I just found out they're expecting a baby boy. To my surprise, I'm feeling jealous, hurt, infuriated, and without any outlet for my feelings. How can I handle my jealousy and keep my daughter positive about her new baby brother?"

No matter how much a person initially wanted a divorce, there are usually conflicted feelings about the failed relationship. This is especially true in cases where couples were married for many years. In this case, hearing that her ex's new wife was going to have a child was the catalyst for this woman to revisit feelings she'd thought were far behind her.

Other women in this position have confided that there is a particular mind-set behind their jealousy. Some have explained that even though they are divorced and both parents have moved on, there has still been one thing that gave the first wife distinction—she was the mother of her ex's *only* child. That position made her feel special. Now that the ex-husband's new wife is expecting a baby, she becomes an equal to the first wife, a peer. That makes the first wife angry, hurt, and jealous.

Men have also confided to me that when their ex has a child, it's the final proof that she has moved on. Some regard this as a good sign. Others have conflicting feelings and wonder how to handle the situation.

This is a great example of how the negative thought/negative behavior chain affects behavior. Because the first wife's feelings are of her own making, the other players—namely the ex-husband, their daughter, and his new wife—wonder if it isn't time for the first wife to consider medication. From the others' point of view, this woman has been cooperative and cordial for years; all of a sudden she is doing an about-face. Too embarrassed to confide the real reason for her behavior, the first wife probably feels quite alone.

In this situation, good ex-etiquette would be for everyone to stay calm and be as cordial as possible when interacting with each other. Ironically, although this first wife is in pain, she could not be in a better place for overcoming the situation. She already knows her actions are a result of her jealous feelings, and she's asking the right questions: "How can I handle my jealousy and keep my daughter positive about her new baby brother?" Good for her.

I am happy to see that she refers to the new child as the brother of her daughter. Many try to convince their children that the other parent's new children are not "real" brothers or sisters. This has the effect of sabotaging the children's relationship from the beginning. Looking for a way to alienate anyone in any way is not good ex-etiquette.

If you are dealing with jealousy, the first thing you need to do is a bit of soul-searching. Be honest with yourself about why you feel the way you do, and then break the negative thought/negative behavior chain. Don't dwell on what you secretly feel are your inadequacies—and certainly don't compare yourself to anyone else. Remember, comparing prevents you from seeing your own worth, and you are actually setting yourself up for failure.

Next, mentally take note of the catalyst for your jealous thoughts, and counteract it with a positive thought. Reaffirm what you know to be true about yourself. If you find yourself drifting into comparison mode, stop! And start the positive thinking process again.

When you adopt this way of thinking, you will find that you can once again think clearly. Your mind will not be clogged by all those negative thoughts that lead you to question your own worth. If you see yourself positively, so will the world around you. It's hard work and a slow process, but if you are diligent, you will wake up one day and find that your feelings of jealousy have disappeared.

Losing Sight of the Ultimate Goal

"I have been married to my husband for two years and am having a terrible time with his ex. My bonusson goes back and forth between both parents' houses. We recently signed him up for soccer and bought him a pair of cleats. His mother has been told that the cleats stay at our house, but she doesn't want to have to buy her own pair. It's something like this every day. I can't take it anymore. What do I do?"

This is what happens when you allow yourself to get caught up in a personal vendetta and lose sight of what is in the best interests of the children. How do I know? Because I have been there. And you will stay there, too, until you remember something very important—the cleats (or the bicycle or the dress pants) do not belong to the parents. They belong to the child.

Let's look at how this bonusmom phrased her explanation so we can understand her mind-set: "*We recently signed him up for soccer and bought him a pair of cleats. His mother has been told that the cleats stay at our house, but she doesn't want to have to buy her own pair."*

Do these cleats fit the parent and bonusparent too?

Notice I have not referred to these two women as counter-partners. That's because they still have a long way to go. They can stop this absurd scorekeeping, but both of them have to contribute to the peace process. Right now they are in a reactive state where they can only respond to each other's bad behavior. They are setting each other up for failure.

Let's examine how this type of interaction evolves into a problem. It's time for the child to return to mom's. As he is packing up his stuff, throwing his cleats into his bag, his stepmother says, "Honey, we bought those cleats, so they should stay here. Tell your mother to buy you cleats for her house." It doesn't sound as if she is trying to be mean. The tone of her voice is perfectly sweet. But think about what she's doing. Now the child is in the middle. He returns to his mother's house. She says, "Honey, you have a game tomorrow and it looks like you forgot your cleats at your dad's." The child explains, "Oh no, Mom. My bonusmom said *they* bought the cleats, so they have to stay at Dad's." Even the most even-tempered person would not be able to hide her discontent. Plus, the child knows he's the bearer of bad news. His mom is mad at his dad and his dad's new partner, and it feels to the child as if it's all his fault. This kind of craziness is not exclusively the province of mothers and bonusmothers. Fathers and bonusfathers can take part in this negative behavior too.

To defuse this particular situation my suggestion is to send the child's cleats back with the child when he returns to his mother's. The *father* should initiate communication with the mother by saying, "You know, I (not we) have been thinking about it, and these cleats are really for Billy. I don't know what I was thinking. To make things easier on him, and to equitably share the responsibility, let's send the cleats back and forth, and when he's ready for the next pair, maybe you can buy them. Then, if he continues with soccer next year, I'll buy them again. Let's just switch back and forth for the extras."

If the biological mom says, "I wouldn't share squat with you!" the dad's response could be, "I was looking for a way to set our differences aside and make it easier on our son. Is there some way you would prefer to handle it? What are your suggestions?"

If she then says, "Stick it in your ear," the ex can say, "I was just looking for a solution to the problem, and I thought you might have some ideas. I guess the ball's in your court."

Then let it go. Hopefully the mother will think about it and realize that she now has the opportunity to do the right thing and have it look like it was her own idea. Rather than set her up to fail, the ex has set her up to succeed—and to save face.

Promoting a Positive Relationship with the Kids

"My ex got married last year, and all of a sudden I feel like I'm in competition for my own child's affection!"

During a workshop Sharyl and I taught years ago, I heard a very helpful bit of insight into the way children view the counterpart-

CHOOSE YOUR BATTLES

If you find that you are arguing about the children's belongings, keep in mind that children grow. They will grow out of their clothes soon enough. Concerning yourself about clothes not returning to your home is a waste of time. In three months the clothes won't fit anyway. Do you want to be upset about something that will quickly be a moot point? Save your energy for the more important issues.

ner relationship. A boy of about sixteen explained that his father had remarried when he was four and that he loved both his mother and bonusmother. He found it annoying that people thought he should compare the two. It was very clear in his mind that his mom and bonusmom each had their special roles; they couldn't be compared. He knew who his mother was and he was very close to her, but his bonusmom also had a special place in his heart. His attitude drove the concept home—when the parents have a clear understanding of the part biological and bonus plays in their children's lives, the children will too. This child was not compelled to compare biological parents with bonusparents because he was raised not to do so.

This child's attitude is also a reminder of the importance of teaching our children to see their relationships with their parent and their bonusparent as two separate relationships—not either/or but *also*. More important, if the child has permission to form a loving bond with his stepparent, or to openly discuss his love for his biological parent, he will not feel caught in the middle. He will avoid those gut-wrenching allegiance issues. When parents and bonusparents truly put the children first, their roles become very clear.

Testing Allegiances

"My wife's ex-husband and I have slowly become friendly, which makes things much easier when it comes to co-parenting the kids. Unfortunately, he confided to me that he recently got cited for driving under the influence of alcohol, and I am sure that he hasn't told my wife this. I know that she will not let the children in the car with him if she thinks he ever drinks and drives, and I agree with this. I feel very

conflicted. On one hand, I'm worried about the safety of my bonuschildren; on the other, I hate the idea of betraying the confidence of a friend and upsetting the cooperative lifestyle we have come to enjoy."

Counterpartners walk a fine line when they become friends. That's because there may be times when they learn things about each other that they wouldn't necessarily have known had they remained simply the "new husband" or "new wife."

One of the ten basic rules of good ex-etiquette is to be honest and straightforward. The best course of action is to create an atmosphere where the two parties in question can tell each other the truth. If it is a safety issue for the children, as in this case, this bonusparent may have to suggest a specific date by which the information must be passed to his wife. He might say something like, "I believe it is your responsibility to tell _____ what you have told me. Please tell her before you are scheduled to pick up the children next week. You have put me in a very awkward situation. I am glad that you and I get along. It's much better for the children. But please don't put me in a position where I have to intercede. The responsibility to tell her is really up to you, and you should do it right away."

Friends with Friends

"In the beginning, it was amusing when my husband's ex and I ended up at the same parties. It's not so amusing now that she has become best friends with my best friend. I don't like this at all."

When you co-parent with a counterpartner, you publicly acknowledge your acceptance of your spouse's ex or your ex's new partner. This may be fine within the realm of parenting, but some counterpartners have a problem with the relationship once it reaches outside the parenting boundaries. Ironically, they work very hard to accept the relationship within their private extended family, but when others, specifically close friends and family members, start to include the counterpartner in social gatherings, some say, "Hey, wait a minute. That's crossing the line!"

"I guess what really bothered me," explained one ex-wife, "is that no one was asking me if it was OK. I felt I was being rather magnanimous accepting my husband's ex as openly as I had. But when my friends started to invite her out to the movies with us, or out for drinks, I was really hurt."

If you openly accept a counterpartner, expect family and friends to follow suit. Although at first it may make you feel a little uncomfortable, just remember, as some consolation, if your friends and family are accepting your relationship, you have done your job well. But, as a note to friends and extended-family members, even if it appears that counterpartners accept each other, as a courtesy to your friend or relative, always ask if she would like her counterpartner to be included before extending an invitation to the counterpartner.

Part II

INTERMEDIATE
EX-ETIQUETTE

Parenting and Family-Building

5

TURNING YOUR STEPFAMILY INTO A BONUSFAMILY

"Accept the things to which fate binds you, and love the people with whom fate brings you together, but do so with all your heart."

—MARCUS AURELIUS

Although there are more people living as stepfamilies than conventional two-parent families, society still looks at the stepfamily dynamic as something outside the norm. Stepfamilies are not the family model we are brought up to expect. Even people brought up by divorced parents don't anticipate living in a stepfamily as adults.

Aside from the normal adjustments all new couples must make when entering a relationship, stepfamily-based unions must also weather constant contact with a past partner. Regular interaction with an ex-spouse can intensify feelings of anger and jealousy, emotions that may plague any relationship. Add a difference in parenting styles, visitation schedules, and a romanticized version of what the future will be like, and life gets even more problematic.

One of the biggest obstacles to overcome is the fact that many stepfamily members view *every issue*, no matter how large or small, in terms of allegiance or betrayal. If the stepchild feels affection for the new stepparent, he may feel he is betraying his biological mother or father. When conflicts arise between the stepparent and the stepchild, the biological parent almost always struggles with where his allegiance should lie. ("Do I side with my mate or with my child?") Constantly having to weigh these choices eats away at the very fiber of the new family. And because the most basic of all emotions are involved—namely loyalty, love, fear, and guilt—they have the power to eventually tear the stepfamily apart.

This chapter discusses the code of behavior necessary to make the stepfamily a comfortable place to live. It is irrelevant who is to blame for any of the problems discussed in this chapter, because the truth is that how you behave is your choice. If you behave poorly, you have *chosen* to do so. Most often, anger is a convenient excuse for bad behavior: "Yeah, well, I know I shouldn't have said that, but he made me angry!"

As a thinking, caring human being you have the power to stop your own bad behavior at any time. After all, good ex-etiquette in a stepfamily simply asks you to take responsibility for your own actions and set the example. Every family needs a leader. In your family it can be you. If you are reading this book with a partner, that's even better. You will have a mutual goal. Finding a mutual goal is one of the key points to establishing a working relationship with an ex. It holds true in any relationship—an ex, your current partner, her ex, your kids, and her kids. In this case, your mutual goal is to make your stepfamily feel like home.

Starting from Scratch

As with every problem we have faced in this book, we will start this chapter with the proper mental preparation. Think of your mind as a slate on which you have written all the bad things that have happened to you in the past—and your justifications for your actions. Now erase the slate. We're starting from scratch.

Step Versus Bonus

Most people acknowledge that the word *step* has a negative connotation. Some well-known professionals prefer to continue to use *step*, hoping to eventually change that negative connotation to a positive one. I believe that's impractical. The word *step* has been with us for more than a hundred years; the negative connotation will continue as long as children continue to hear fairytales such as *Sleeping Beauty, Snow White and the Seven Dwarfs,* and *Cinderella.* In these stories, the stepparent is always the bad guy. Children are programmed from a very early age to accept that a stepparent is unkind, intolerant, and devious.

The first time I knew the word *step* was not right for me was the day after I had stayed up all night with my sick stepdaughter. As I rubbed her shoulders and blotted her feverish face, I felt love for this child. Don't think she hasn't infuriated me at other points in our life together, but at this particular time, we bonded. The next day she was feeling better. We were at a friend's home and introductions were necessary. After being up with her all night taking care of her, calling her my stepchild seemed to diminish the feelings we had for each other. I wanted another word to describe how I felt about her.

At the time, all I had was "daughter," and that's the word I used, but "daughter" is inaccurate. If I use it on a regular basis, it does not give her biological mother her place of importance— and Sharyl and I have grown to understand that giving the biological parent her place of importance is primary to good ex-etiquette—and to being accepted by the stepchild. It was a few years later that Sharyl and I finally came up with the word *bonus.* It was a logical choice. A bonus is something positive, a reward for a job well done. Using the word *bonus* instead of *step* is simply an acknowledgment of the hard work it takes to be a good stepparent, or a good step*anything*, for that matter. And it translates down the ladder from *bonus*family to *bonus*child. The term *blended family* works, but *blended mother*? *Blended child*?

Personally, I regard the word *bonus* as a compliment. It says, "I acknowledge that you are trying, and for that I offer you my caring and respect." So, to me, my stepkids are my bonuskids, and I hope they will always think of me as their bonusmom.

Becoming a bonusfamily does not happen quickly. It takes work and determination and a desire to stop the typical stepfamily cycle of resentment and revenge. This allows people to offer their children a new legacy with a more positive outlook for the future. For that reason, from this point forward, I'll use the term *bonus* more often than *step* when referring to a positive bonusfamily unit or bonusfamily member.

In Search of a Positive Bonusfamily Model

It is important to first lay the groundwork for good bonusfamily behavior. This comes in part in the preparation of a plan, and in part in the implementation of that plan.

There are two parts to the plan I recommend. The first part is always mental preparation. To help you get a real feel for what you encounter when you become a member of a bonusfamily, I'll start with an exercise I have adopted from the Bonus Families Stepfamily Workshop. I call it the "Before Exercise" because it's one you do with your new partner *before* you move in together or marry. You need to have a clear idea of what you will encounter as a bonusfamily member. Hopefully, this exercise will help you to see what is ahead.

The second part is agreeing on house rules. I call it, "Setting Up House." A checklist is supplied as an example of the things you need to agree upon if your home is to run smoothly.

Part One: The Before Exercise

Step 1: Get a pen and paper and write down the relationships you feel you create when you form a bonusfamily.

When I ask this of people who attend our workshops, most write down the names of their new partner and their children. They may possibly include the names of their partner's children, but they stop there. Below is a list of all the relationships you create when you marry or move in with someone with children. It reaches out far beyond your partner and kids.

1. New husband
2. New wife
3. Your child with ex
4. Child of new husband and wife
5. New wife's ex-husband
6. New husband's ex-wife
7. Ex husband's new wife
8. Ex-wife's new husband
9. Child of ex-husband and new wife
10. Child of new husband and ex-wife
11. Child of ex-wife and new husband
12. Child of ex-wife's new husband
13. Child of ex-husband's new wife
14. Extended family of ex-wife's new husband
15. Extended family of ex-wife
16. Extended family of new husband
17. Extended family of new wife
18. Extended family of ex-husband
19. Extended family of ex-husband's new wife

That's quite a list, isn't it? I am always amused by people's shock when I bring their attention to how many potential relationships there are in combined families. I believe that's one of the reasons so many stepfamilies fall apart—the primary couple does not realize that a successful bonusfamily is more than the two people that care for each other and a combination of kids. Most understand that any family extends beyond their immediate relatives to include grandparents, aunts, uncles, and cousins, yet only a small number acknowledge those same ties once the parents no longer live together. Very few enter a new relationship understanding and openly accepting that they may have to interact with, for example, their new partner's ex-in-laws. Nevertheless, those ex-in-laws are your bonuschildren's grandparents, and it's your responsibility as a parent figure to reinforce those relationships. That's part of what it means to "put the children first."

Step 2: Envision the relationship you expect with each one of the people you have listed, then list how you will foster a positive relationship with each one.

Considering each relationship separately and then asking yourself what you will do to make the relationship work puts the quality of that relationship in your hands. You have the power to create the relationship you want. I suggest you start with your new partner, and then work from there. For example:

> *What will I do to foster a positive relationship with my new partner?*
> I will have reasonable expectations about our new relationship.
> I will not place my partner in the position where he must choose between his children and me.
> I will agree on disciplinary tactics and stick to the rules.
> I will do my best not to undermine my partner's authority in front of the children (no matter whose children they are).
> I will remember to set aside some time for just the two of us.

Do the same with the next person on your list. To help you along, I have addressed some of the most important relationships you will encounter. But remember, there are many potential relationship categories. To do this exercise in its entirety, you should take a look at all the relationships listed on page 137 and honestly consider what you can do to make each relationship the best it can be. Watch out for negative expectations that could possibly sabotage your new life together (see "Help with Turning Everyday Negative Expectations for Your Stepfamily into Positive Affirmations" below).

What will I do to foster a positive relationship with my partner's children (my bonuskids)?

How you see yourself interacting with your bonuskids is extremely important. If you resent them or see them as spoiled or contrary, those thoughts will prevent you from building a relationship. Here are some positive affirmations for this relationship.

HELP WITH TURNING EVERYDAY NEGATIVE EXPECTATIONS FOR YOUR STEPFAMILY INTO POSITIVE AFFIRMATIONS

A negative expectation is basically a negative prophecy. You are foreseeing, and therefore expecting, a negative outcome. But you can take that negative thought or expectation and turn it into a positive affirmation. Here is an example of how you can use this change in mind-set in your everyday life as a bonusfamily.

Let's say your new stepdaughter drives you crazy. You see her as selfish, spoiled, and disrespectful. When you walk in the house at the end of the day, do you think you will greet that stepchild with an open mind? Most likely, she will say hello, you will glare at her, and she will wonder what she did this time to make her stepparent so angry.

Rather than dwell on the unproductive relationship you are having with your stepchild, visualize the relationship you *want* to have. Picture yourself talking to her in a relaxed manner. It doesn't matter what she has done or what she might do to reinforce the negativity— concentrate on *your* goal for the relationship and take steps to make that the reality. Do this for every relationship you have, and you will have turned your negative expectations into positive affirmations.

I will have a clear idea of my responsibilities as a bonusparent before I move in.

I will accept my bonuschildren's individuality.

I will respect my bonuschildren's past allegiances.

I will try to listen more than dictate policy.

What will I do to foster positive communication with my new partner's ex?

I accept that I may have to interact with my partner's ex on a regular basis to help coordinate parenting efforts.

I will not compete, on any level, with my bonuschild's biological parent.

I will do my best to support his or her parenting tactics when his or her child is in my care.

I will be as cooperative as possible when interaction is necessary.

What will I do to foster positive communication with my new partner's extended family?

Because extended-family members form strong allegiances to past partners, these are among the most difficult relationships to anticipate. Decide what you will do to foster a positive relationship with people who are related to both you and your spouse's ex by marriage. Even though your husband, for example, is divorced from his ex, your husband's relatives might still interact with the ex because of the children.

Continue this exercise for each relationship. I know that at this point the exercise can get overwhelming. That's the reason I recommend it. I want everyone to realize the commitment they make when they are in a relationship in which one or both of the partners have children.

Step 3: Have a heart-to-heart talk with your partner.

In the movie *Jerry Maguire*, Rod Tidwell (the character played by Cuba Gooding Jr.) asks Jerry if he's "had the talk" with his love interest, a widow with a young son. Jerry admits he hasn't, and Rod takes him to task, suggesting that he do it soon or else disaster will follow. Jerry marries, but never does "have the talk," and he and his wife end up separating. Movies have happy endings, and Jerry and his wife eventually reconcile.

Movies are not real life.

After you have compiled your lists, you and your new partner should "have the talk." Take note of your negative or unrealistic expectations. Then compare lists. Together, figure out the best way to affirm positively what you both expect for your life together. Talk about everything—*all* your worries and concerns and how you will care for each other's children. What will you both do to keep this bonusfamily strong? I have worked with many couples that know there are problems going in, but choose to go forward hoping that everything will work itself out after they are married or move in together. Don't lie to yourself. If you have worries, address them before you bring your children into a questionable relationship.

The following e-mail was sent to our Bonus Families Web site. This is what can happen when you don't do the Before Exercise.

"I have been living with my girlfriend for five years. She has a daughter who is sixteen and is honestly a little wilder than I would like. Drugs and alcohol are not part of my life, and I don't want to live with the problems associated with them. Neither my girlfriend nor her daughter have taken responsibility for the girl's alcohol consumption, and I told my girlfriend that if they don't get a handle on her drug and alcohol use, they are both out of here. I don't see why I have to compromise my lifestyle any longer."

Because there was no plan right from the beginning, the writer, like many others in the same position, did not realize that moving in with someone with children is a commitment far greater than merely agreeing to live in a monogamous relationship with an adult. In these cases it's not surprising that when times get tough angry, unprepared partners think, "Hey, this isn't even my kid. Why am I stressing? It's time for you and your kid to move on."

This gentleman has a lot of work to do if he wants to continue this relationship. First, he has to establish in his mind that there is a primary relationship—his partner and him. Right now it sounds like he has a roommate who has a child.

When you are involved with a parent, at the moment you move in, you are first a lover and a member of the primary relationship, but you also become a father or mother figure to their children. That's two separate relationships, not one. Please note: I did not say "father" or "mother." I said, "father figure" or "mother figure." There is a big difference. Although the title carries the same moral responsibilities to the child, you are not the child's parent. You have made a commitment to be a partner to the child's parent. This does not mean you are free to take over. It means you should look for ways to support the parent's parenting. As a bonusparent you can make suggestions, but make sure they are just that—suggestions—not ultimatums.

If this couple had done the Before Exercise years ago, it's doubtful the writer would have had the same attitude he has today. He would have known exactly what was in store for him. Actually, it's doubtful they would have moved in together—but that's the reason for the exercise.

Considering each relationship and asking yourself what you will do to foster a positive relationship puts the quality of that relationship in your hands. If the responsibility seems overwhelming at the time of the exercise, you should pay attention. It most likely signifies that you are not ready to take on the relationship—so don't do it.

Part Two: Setting Up House

Once you have completed the Before Exercise and have a clear idea of the commitment you are making, you need to agree on house rules. House rules are the everyday workings of how you want to run your home. Things to consider:

Chore assignments
Allowance
Homework rules
Curfews
Sleeping arrangements
Discipline
Conflict resolution
Finances (contributions to each other's children)
Coordination between households

Rules about such subjects as curfew, chores, allowance, and homework are personal decisions you must make for your own home. It may be difficult to assign regular chores to bonusfamily members who go back and forth between two homes. To reduce resentment in family members that stay put, coordinate chores as best you can with your child's other parent's home.

"We would love to coordinate efforts with my ex's bonusfamily, but my ex has no desire to coordinate efforts with ours. We just can't agree."

We each progress at our own speed, and your desire to cooperate may not match that of your ex—or of your spouse's ex. So what do you do when no matter what you say or do, the ex and her new family do not want to listen or coordinate efforts with you?

Good ex-etiquette tells us that you must respect each other's turf. You can only control your own four walls. You can pray that both your ex and your spouse's ex will read this book. Then they might begin to understand that it is their obligation to put their issues aside and coordinate efforts. If they choose not to do that, however, you cannot control their home or parenting style. If you try to manipulate the situation by withholding time with the children or being late or not being receptive to a request for a favor, it will only complicate the issue. It won't hurt your ex as much as it will hurt the children. They will be caught in the middle of your power struggle. Just remember, you cannot establish rules for the other family, but *you can set the example.* Choose your battles. As your newfound attitude of cooperation changes your ability to communicate with each other, a day might come when you can coordinate efforts. Make that your goal.

House Rules Between Parents

"One of the things that attracted me to my husband was the fact that he took an active role in parenting his children. But then I moved in, and everything changed. I'm tired and frustrated that I have to do everything, and all these kids aren't even mine."

Our parenting roles are deeply engrained into our psyches—even if we have never had children, when put into a parenting position, men and women fall into traditional parenting roles.

If there is anything positive to be derived from divorce, it may be that joint custody places a divorced father in a role of being self-sufficient when caring for his children. As a result, he cooks—or at least provides—them dinner, washes their clothes, tells them a bedtime story, and puts them to bed.

He then meets someone, she moves in, and because the traditional roles are so engrained—plus she may have children of her own that she has to manage—she starts to cook the dinners, wash the clothes, and coordinate play dates, and the man backs off. The woman gets overwhelmed and looks for help, but rarely gives up the authority, and the man is thinking, "Hey, you're doing it all just fine. This was your idea anyway."

Frustrated, the woman then decides she can't do it all on her own and lets her partner do a little bit. He doesn't do it the way she likes, so she decides it's easier to do it herself and takes back the responsibilities. But she's exhausted and resentful.

I confess. I, too, fell into this role. I moved in with my husband, and suddenly he was sleeping through the stuffing of Christmas stockings. Ironically what initially attracted me to him was that I walked into his kitchen and found him cooking dinner for his children. Not just frozen pizza, but pasta and salad and garlic bread. He had made the sauce from scratch! I thought, "What a great dad!" But now here he was, snoring away while I stuffed the stockings.

The first year, I thought it was funny. He was so cute snoozing by the fire. The next year the behavior was still amusing. By the third year, it was irritating; fourth year, aggravating; fifth year, infuriating. The sixth year, I finally had an epiphany: I had created the problem. Rather than disengage, which some say works, I sat down with him and told him I was sorry I'd robbed him of parenting the children. I explained it was unintentional, and I asked what parenting duty he would like to resume first. My thoughts were that we had agreed to parent each other's kids, but he must also remember to parent his own kids. "I think I'd like to take Steven dirt bike riding," was his answer. I said that was fine, but I suggested that when he got home perhaps we should cook dinner together and let the children see our cooperative effort. His next choice was that he would pick up our daughter from after-school sports. Slowly things got better. Rather than run defense for him and anticipate that he just wouldn't be able to be as efficient as I like, I began to wait until he asked for help. And when I let him do what he was supposed to do, he was fine.

This is not the answer many bonusmoms are looking for, but it's a good assessment of what happens if you don't take the time to clarify your responsibilities as "parents" in the home. Discuss the specifics. Come to an agreement, and work to let each other parent without interference.

DISENGAGING

Disengaging is a process by which the stepparent stops parenting her stepkids due to the lack of support from her partner, the biological parent. Disengaging is a last resort for a frustrated stepparent who has become angry after years of family discord and disrespectful stepchildren. It is based on the premise that the less the stepparent does in terms of parenting her stepchildren, the more the biological parent steps in. Although there are aspects of the disengagement process that are useful in theory, it is not something I advocate. Good ex-etiquette should negate the need for disengagement.

Stay Flexible

Sticking to the rules is important, but bonuschildren will be more apt to respect you as a parent figure if they see that you are also listening to their concerns and making judgments based on the information before you. This does not mean if the child is whining, you give in. It means that stepchildren, especially older stepchildren, view many issues within the family as "fair" or "unfair." If they perceive you, the stepparent, as being unfair, then you will seem wicked to them. If they know that you will honestly assess the situation based on the rule in place, and make your judgments accordingly, they will be more willing to accept your decisions. The key here is to let them in on your reasoning and be flexible within the framework of your house rules.

Sleeping Arrangements

"How do we decide who shares a room?"

There are two things to take into consideration when deciding who should share a room: gender and biology. Let's look at how one bonusfamily solved the sleeping-arrangement dilemma.

When Mitch and Dee Dee combined families they suddenly had six children living in the same house—one boy and five girls. Mitch had a boy and a girl. Dee Dee had four girls. They all moved into Mitch's three-bedroom house. Their first priority was to find a bigger house, but until they could, they had to make do with the bedrooms they had. Logic would dictate that girls share with girls and boys share with boys, but in this family's case, that would mean one boy would have his own room, while five of his female siblings (some biological and some bonus) crowded into the other room. In this family's case, gender could not be the tiebreaker. They decided that Mitch's daughter and son would have one bedroom, while Dee Dee's four daughters slept in two bunk beds in the other room.

The most important aspect of bonusfamily room sharing is to make sure that each of the children, no matter how small the room, has a wall—or at least a shelf—that is all their own. This is especially important if the child has a room of her own at one house, but has to share at the other. In these cases, privacy becomes the issue, and families must take special care to be respectful and allow family members private time if they want it.

"My husband has a six-year-old daughter from a previous marriage, and together we have another, three-year-old daughter. My bonusdaughter sleeps over twice a month and shares a small room with two single beds with her half-sister. The room is really too small for two beds, so I suggested buying an air mattress that could be stored away for my bonusdaughter. But my husband won't hear of it; he thinks she'll feel slighted. My feeling is my stepdaughter has her own room at her mom's house, why does my daughter's room have to be cluttered with an extra bed that only gets used twice a month? I love my family very much

and want everyone to be happy and comfortable."

I am going to speculate about the battle this father may be waging on a subconscious level. It would not be uncommon for him to go out of his way to include his first daughter in just about everything that concerns this family. Although his new wife may feel this to be an intrusion, at the same time he feels that this shows his oldest daughter that he loves her as much as he loves his "new" family. He may want to make sure that his daughter knows that she holds a permanent place in his heart. Therefore, this bed is symbolic of more than just where she sleeps while at his home.

Let's take another look at the original inquiry; the language is very telling. The writer says, "my stepdaughter has her own room at her mom's house, why does my daughter's room have to be cluttered with an extra bed that only gets used twice a month?" Something new partners often forget is that their partner, in this case the husband, is father to *both* girls. It's impossible for him to choose between the two. A bed may seem like a small thing to the stepmother, but in his heart, this daddy is juggling babies. He may feel guilty that his daughter has to *visit* instead of living with him. He could be struggling with guilt about the divorce. Like so many other divorced fathers who do not have custody of their children, he may secretly fear that he abandoned his child when her mother and he divorced. There are lots of things he may not be voicing, so this new wife needs to be as sensitive as she can to his concerns.

I was in the exact same situation and can pass on what we did at my house. We went the bunk-bed route. The little one slept on the bottom and the older one slept on the top when she was at our house. We tried a trundle bed first, but this type of bed is not all that sturdy with prolonged use, and it's rather heavy for a child to maneuver. My bonusdaughter kept scraping her shins (and so did I), so we progressed to the bunk bed, which served as a great place for the girls to hide out, bond, and giggle.

Sharing

"My husband and I were recently married. We both have seven-year-old daughters and there is a lot of fighting over ownership of the stuffed animals. What do we do?"

Anticipate this sort of thing before you move in together. With an indelible marker, in very small letters, write the owner's initials— or some identifying mark—somewhere on the toy to let them know which animal is which. I do not suggest that you give your children the marker, and tell them to do it—even if they are older. I have had the experience of children initialing the other child's belongings and then claiming them. If you do it, in your handwriting, there will be no question of to whom the toys belong.

Who Disciplines and How?

"Should stepparents discipline their stepchildren?" is one of the most common questions I am asked. That's the reason I included "Biological parents make the rules; bonusparents uphold them" as one of the ten rules of good ex-etiquette. Unfortunately, it's the only rule that requires an amendment, because there are certain times when you cannot take this rule literally.

In a bonusfamily, one parent is the parent while the other is the bonusparent. Being careful to stick to this rule as stated may automatically put the bonuscouple in an adversarial position— the biological parent is the boss and the bonusparent isn't. When both adults have children, then they are both parents and both bonusparents. Following this same line of reasoning, they are both bosses.

A crucial part of forming a bonusfamily is for the adults to decide upon and then present the rules in a fashion that lets the children feel safe and secure. If you and your partner have no set plan and openly contradict each other in front of the children, aside from undermining each other's authority, this also undermines your children's feeling of security in their new family. I have noticed that when there is open hostility between the parent and bonusparent or between bonusparent and bonuschild, the family has a tendency to split into factions based on blood relations. Once that happens, it is very difficult to rediscover the middle ground.

In most cases, biological parents do make the rules for their children, and the bonusparents should uphold those rules. But there are definitely times when bonusparents need to be able to offer input into establishing policy. One example is when the bonusparent is the primary caregiver and must have the authority to make decisions *for the safety of the children in his care.* The second example is when the bonusparent is also trying to coordinate house rules and disciplinary tactics with an ex of his own.

Problems arise when the bonusparent establishes policy without consulting the biological parent and then is unwilling to compromise when confronted. As a result, the biological parent feels threatened, and power struggles ensue that are difficult to solve unless everyone stops, takes a deep breath, and remembers once again to put the children first.

Keeping Discipline Consistent

"My husband and I have been married for a year. We both have fourteen-year-old children—he has a boy, and I have a girl. My husband shares custody of his son with his ex-wife. Recently when school report card time came, my daughter presented hers

to me, but my bonusson told his father that report cards were coming out a week later. It appears that my bonusson got bad grades and was afraid to tell us. My husband did not punish my bonusson for lying or for the bad grades. This would not have been the case if my daughter had acted in the same manner."

It's not uncommon for noncustodial parents, especially non-custodial fathers, to feel guilty about their divorce—and their inability to live with their children full-time. Parents who feel this way tend to be extremely lenient whenever their children visit. To further complicate the issue in this particular case, there is a child who lives in the home full-time and follows the rules. She sees the inequality in the way she and her brother are disciplined. Soon her bonusdad will wonder why his relationship with her has deteriorated. What often happens next is that the spouse calls her husband's problematic parenting to his attention. He then tries to change his ways, but he's inconsistent because he's fighting his guilt. His son gets angry because he can now only manipulate things some of the time; he may even threaten to move in with mom full-time. The father panics, punishes poor behavior even less, and ends up with a flaky kid with bad grades and no direction.

For the child's benefit, the husband has to acknowledge that the divorce is done. He cannot make things better by not confronting his son's poor behavior. Guilt-ridden or not, he needs to stand his ground and do the best he can to coordinate efforts with the biological mom for the sake of the child. And that lesson does not stop with the son. The bonusdaughter is watching too. If the husband wants to maintain a loving relationship with her, he must be as consistent as possible with *all* the children in his care. No one said good ex-etiquette was going to be easy.

Discipline When Only One Parent Has Children

"I have a seven-year-old son. My partner has never had children. When we first started to date, he was polite to my son, but recently my partner seems to discipline not out of love, but out of a need for control. I want this relationship to work, but I'm ready to leave. I don't know how to make my partner see he's approaching this all wrong."

A difference in disciplinary techniques is one of the biggest problems plaguing stepfamilies, and the turmoil this causes seems to be exaggerated when only one parent has children. To complicate the issue, it sounds like this new stepparent has fallen into a very common trap—attempting to discipline far too soon.

We never know how we will act when we become parents, but it seems biology could be the determining factor. Biology allows us to forgive many of the mistakes our children make along the way, whereas stepparents tend to look at things more objectively—they form their allegiances through acts and deeds. If there is turmoil, stepparents are unlikely to take it in stride unless they have had practice and have built a bond with the stepchild. This takes time, which is something that biological parents have on their side. The stepparent-stepchild bond usually builds at a more accelerated rate, and when adults are forced to move too quickly, they often resist.

To demonstrate this point, let's look at a typical stepfamily scenario and examine the different ways a biological parent and a stepparent approach the problem. Let's say the house rule is no eating in front of the TV. The biological mom comes home from work very tired, sees her teenager eating in front of the TV, and assesses that it's no big deal—there's no food on the rug—so she decides to take a shower and relax. The stepparent walks in, sees the teen eating in front of the TV, and goes crazy. "You are breaking the house rules!" the stepparent cries. The child says, "Wait a minute. Mom saw me eating in front of the TV and didn't say a word. Who the heck are you? You're not my parent."

The only alternative the stepparent then has is to confront the biological parent. The biological parent is thinking, "Look, I'm exhausted. I've had a terrible day at work. All I did was let the kid eat in front of the TV. So shoot me." But the stepparent sees it as betrayal: "You aren't supporting me! You are letting your child break the rules, and it makes me look like the bad guy. You are choosing your child over me."

This example demonstrates the different attitude of the biological parent and the stepparent. Biological parents learn to pick their battles with their kids. Everything doesn't have to be a big deal, and they may simply let some of the small stuff go. Stepparents view this as inconsistent parenting and often try to step in to compensate for what they feel are the biological parent's failings. This is the quickest way for a stepparent to appear "wicked." The kids resent the stepparent's interference because they are being disciplined when their own parent would not have disciplined them. The biological parent resents the interference because it implies the stepparent does not respect her parenting skills. The stepparent, simply trying to help organize the household, feels frustrated, angry, misunderstood, and worst of all, betrayed by his partner.

There's something else to consider. Arguments between biological parents and their kids are soon forgotten, whereas stepparents often view arguments with their stepchildren as "disrespectful." Respect is very important to stepparents, but this issue is often taken for granted by biological parents. Biological parents don't see arguments as a direct affront; stepparents often do.

In the end, hugs, kisses, and "I love you" or "I'm sorry" are great ways to end disagreements. These signs of affection occur more naturally and freely between biological parents and their kids than between stepparents and stepkids.

Because of these differences, it is imperative that the biological parent and stepparent agree on disciplinary rules and tactics before they move in together. Remember the Before Exercise.

Establish your house rules together, and then *stick with them*. All rules should apply equally to all family members—even the adult family members. If you are blending a family when only one parent has children, then obviously the biological parent has the final say, but it must be consistent with the morals of the stepparent, or the situation will never work. A stepparent who morally disagrees with a biological parent's rules will not uphold them.

By the same token, if a new partner wants to be accepted as a parent figure, he must move slowly into his new position as authority figure, taking the biological parent's lead and working to refine the rules if need be.

How Will Your Bonusfamily Solve Conflicts?

We learn how to communicate with our partners by watching how our parents interact with one another. If you manipulate with hurtful words, or slam doors at the end of a disagreement, or refuse to talk, or are unforgiving, your children will mimic your behavior in their relationships. And don't think you are off the hook if you are a stepparent. *All* parent figures are role models for the children in their lives.

We all know we aren't supposed to argue in front of the kids. Yet even the happiest of couples catch themselves occasionally raising their voices enough for the kids to hear. To make matters worse, when these couples realize the kids are watching, they might move to a private room to finish the argument and make up behind closed doors. The kids don't see the concessions the parents make to end the argument. They see the final outcome— the parents are no longer fighting—but the kids have no idea how their parents got there.

This sort of approach gives your children a model for conflict, but no guide to successfully solve problems. For this reason, when offering tools to help stepfamilies resolve conflicts, I have gone so far as to suggest that parents stage an apology for their children after a disagreement. While cooking dinner or just watching TV, go through the motions of apologizing again when you know the kids are watching. While I don't suggest you bare private matters or try to justify your position, offering the words "I'm sorry" and "I accept your apology" or "I'm sorry too" teaches children something positive they can use in every relationship throughout their lifetime.

"My mom and stepdad were arguing, and my stepdad was really mad," a twelve-year-old child recently volunteered at a Bonus Families Stepfamily Workshop. "First he was yelling at the top of his lungs, then he wouldn't talk to my mom. She saw me watching them and went over to my stepdad and said, "I'm sorry I lost my temper." I could tell my stepdad was still mad, but they hugged and a little while later they weren't so mad."

What did this mother's simple apology teach her child? It taught him to look for unselfish ways to solve conflict. It taught him compassion, empathy, love, caring, and the ability to assess a situation and make a positive decision rather than merely react out of hurt feelings. It taught him to accept the responsibility for his actions and to respect another's feelings; the list of positives is quite long.

What if this mother had taken the opposite approach? What if she had noticed her child watching the argumentative behavior and then stomped out of the room? What would that then say to her child? It would say, "I can control the situation with my anger. If I withhold communication and affection, I can manipulate this person into feeling bad enough to give me my way. Anger gives me power. When I am angry, I will win."

Retaliatory behavior promotes resentment and teaches our children to be vengeful and unforgiving. Furthermore, it makes family members less likely to want to apologize to us in the future. No family, nuclear or combined, can survive with such feelings at its base.

Does this mean that we should teach our children to shrink in the face of conflict? To shy away from their partner in the face of an argument? Of course not. Apologies are important, but there's more to it than that. The bigger lesson may not be the apology, but the gracious acceptance of an apology when we are angry. Accepting an apology teaches our children the power of forgiveness—perhaps the most important tool we have to make our bonusfamilies a happy, safe, loving place to live.

Family Problem Solving

If someone asked me for the most important single tip that I could give to ensure a successful transition to becoming a bonusfamily, I would have to say that it is to establish a form of family conflict resolution before you move in together.

From talking to thousands of people over the years, I have found that the bonusfamilies that really work have a forum for conflict resolution in place from day one. A problem arises, there's no guesswork, and family members know exactly what to do to solve the problem. This prevents the family from breaking into factions. No one teams up. Each member of the family understands firsthand the steps that the family members must take to resolve conflict.

The principle behind family conflict resolution is to look for mutually agreed-upon compromises. This negotiation goes by many names—the family discussion, the family meeting, decision time—each family should pick a name that means something personal and evokes a feeling of resolution from within the stepfamily unit.

Parents attempting to combine families have expressed a concern that a cooperative method to resolving conflict may force them to give up their parental power. They are leery of offering an open forum to solve family problems. On the contrary, because stepfamily members are often overly sensitive about issues of fairness and parental favoritism, having a forum to end misunderstandings offers family members an equal opportunity to air their differences. Children of divorce often express that they feel powerless. Their parents have made the decision to split up and then become involved with someone else, all without consulting them. Teenagers, especially, find this to be extremely presumptuous on the part of their parents. Family discussions, when approached correctly, give children a forum to be heard; therefore, they feel as if they can once again have some control over their own lives.

There's conflict in every family. But conflict is different in bonusfamilies than in conventional families. Although resentment, allegiance, and betrayal are all issues that are addressed in conventional families, they are magnified in bonusfamilies. While kids hate to be disciplined in traditional two-parent homes, generally speaking, they feel it is appropriate when either mom or dad disciplines them. It is understood that both parents have the children's best interests at heart. This is not always the case when two parents combine their families. If the proper bonds have not been made between stepchildren and stepparent, when the stepparent attempts to set rules, the kids resent it. They simply are not ready to accept the stepparent as an authority figure.

When handled properly, family discussions can serve as problem-solving vehicles to air differences without assigning blame. By setting up rules for these discussions, families can often avoid the allegiance and betrayal issues that are so common to stepfamily disagreements.

Rules for Family Discussions

The following outline is the Bonus Families Model for Family Conflict Resolution. They set the guidelines for a successful bonusfamily discussion.

1. Make an appointment to talk things over. Family problems are too important to be left to spontaneous outbursts. Conflict resolution works best when family members are calm and come to the table with an open mind, ready to look for solutions to problems. Asking family members to make formal appointments for family discussions demonstrates the significance of constructive conflict resolution within the stepfamily unit. Suggesting that any family member, no matter his or her age, may call a family discussion promotes feelings of equality and fair play. When something is bothering a family member, she should make a formal appointment to meet: "I am calling a family discussion for 5:00 P.M. on Sunday afternoon." She should give family members ample time to reorganize their plans so that they can attend the mandatory family discussion. Social events come after the family discussion.

2. Come prepared. As time decreases a family member's anger or resentment, she may forget the original motivation behind requesting a family discussion—but the problem will arise again if it is not addressed. Family members should come prepared with a list of points they want to cover so that topics can be addressed once and for all.

3. No outbursts, no interruptions. Anger may be the catalyst for the family discussion, but if yelling or insulting other family members is allowed during the meeting, the discussion will not teach children how to solve problems in a respectful manner. Nor will the problem be solved. Require those who have the floor to be direct, but not insulting. No interruptions from those who are listening.

4. Teach family members to use "I" messages when speaking. "I" messages provide a positive avenue for communicating feelings in difficult circumstances. "I" messages also foster better listening in the opposition and set the stage for positive feedback. Following the model in chapter 1, remember the three basic steps to successfully using "I" messages:

> State the feeling.
> State the offending behavior.
> State the effect it has on you.

After you state the effect it has on you, request the change in behavior that you would like to see. Don't embellish it. Just state the case: "I feel (state the feeling) when you (state the specific behavior), because (state the effects it has on you)." Then state how you would like the behavior changed.

Let's look at the interaction between two stepsisters, Teresa and Amanda. Their constant bickering was causing considerable tension, and out of frustration Amanda's mother called a family discussion. Rather than fight back and forth, they were instructed to use "I" messages during the meeting. Amanda said, "I feel angry (feeling) when Teresa wears my clothes without asking (behavior) because I may want to wear them the next day and they will be dirty (effect). I want Teresa to ask to borrow my clothes so I can plan accordingly. And I want to be able to say no if I don't want her to wear them (change)."

Teresa's excuse for the behavior was that she didn't know it bothered Amanda, although Amanda explained that she had discussed this problem with Teresa on many different occasions.

By expressing herself in a calm fashion, Amanda was finally able to get through to Teresa and change her offending behavior. Until that point, Amanda's ranting had no affect on her stepsister's actions. Something else reinforced the power of the family discussion—every family member was a witness to Amanda's polite request for the behavior to stop. Teresa could no longer pretend to be unaware of Amanda's discontent.

5. The family searches for a solution to the problem—together. The culmination of the successful family discussion is that family members feel comfortable working together to find solutions to perceived problems. When family members openly consider each other's suggestions as solutions it reinforces family unity and mutual respect. In the case of Teresa and Amanda, the solution is obvious; Teresa stopped borrowing clothes without asking. However, if the problem is not as simple as that, family members must collectively figure out a solution that they can all agree upon.

Family discussions can turn into shouting matches when family members, specifically the parents, use them as a forum for discipline or blame. That's not the purpose of these discussions, and family members will be reluctant to sit still while others point fingers. In successful family discussions there is no boss. The person with the grievance calls the meeting. She is the one to begin the discussion once all are in attendance. If the discussion goes off track, someone, again usually a parent figure, may suggest that the discussion be redirected to the problem at hand. Family discussions are a way to solve problems. When used for that purpose, they work.

Here's an example of a family discussion with positive results. It shows firsthand how such discussions can truly help resolve conflict within a stepfamily.

The Browns had been a stepfamily for approximately two years when Greg, the father/stepfather, went into business for himself using his home as an office, a situation that required his wife, Pam, to help him. Theirs was a combined family that included two children from Greg's previous marriage, ages ten and six, and two children from Pam's previous marriage, ages nine and eight.

The Browns had used family discussions as a form of conflict resolution from the beginning of their relationship, and the children had grown to depend on them.

Greg and Pam devoted long hours to their new business, trying to offer the children the same lifestyle they'd enjoyed in previous years. Completely engrossed in the new business, the parents missed a special awards assembly for one of the older children and a parent-teacher conference for one of the younger children. Greg and Pam did not realize that they had missed these two events until the older children called a family discussion. Up to that time, it had always been the parents who initiated family discussions, but the Browns' rule had always been that anyone in the family could suggest a family discussion if there was a problem to be solved. The children took it upon themselves to assign a date and time, and they made invitations to ensure that all family members could be at the meeting.

Greg and Pam were amused that the children had called the discussion, but they went along with it because it was the model they had created. At the appointed time, everyone sat down around the dining room table. Then the two older children, stepsiblings, announced the reason for the family discussion: they felt Greg and Pam were working too much. The children made it clear that they missed their parents and they wanted them to cut back on their hours. In a very orderly fashion, the children explained to Greg and Pam that they had missed two important meetings— which had never happened before—and changes had to be made.

Greg and Pam had attended one of our Bonus Families workshops; they understood the necessity for a forum for conflict resolution early in the relationship. As they relayed this story, they explained that they'd had no idea the children felt they were working too much. They were grateful that they had raised their kids to feel that a discussion with the whole family can solve family problems. Greg and Pam cut back on their hours.

This story proves that when you raise children within a step-family to accept conflict resolution as a way of life, and give them positive tools with which to work, they will become equipped to solve family problems.

The key to successful bonusfamily conflict resolution is that each family establishes its own rules and then sticks to them. They stay open and flexible and mold the method of conflict resolution to their family's individual needs.

Financial Support of Each Other's Children

To be a good bonusparent, you must accept that child support is always less than what's actually needed. It pays for necessities but it doesn't cover the extras—and there will be extras. If you want a well-rounded child, you have to expose her to as much as you can. That means you must make available to her such things as soccer during soccer season, horseback riding in the warmer weather, and drama workshops. As the child gets older, the demands only increase. Child support does not cover prom dresses, tuxedo rentals, yearbooks, senior pictures, or car insurance. Therefore, the bonusparent may have to pitch in with finances—or the biological parent may have to pay more than just the court-ordered child support. It's important that bonusparents understand this when they move in or marry someone with children; otherwise, there is likely to be resentment.

Many stepparents feel helpless when it comes to this situation. So let's address the mind-set necessary to be a *bonus*parent.

First, to avoid feelings of anger and helplessness, it's important to mentally separate the child from her other parent (the counterpartner). Many times if there is conflict between past and present partners, the bonusparent runs the two together in her mind. Every time she sees the child, she sees the parent that makes her angry. Bonusparents must remember that the other parent and the child are two separate people.

When you pay child support, it's for the child, whether the ex spends the money or not. Therefore, to stew about the ex is a waste of time. The other parent is part of the past, and how she supports herself is not part of your life. It may make you angry that she has control of the child support money, but let that go. You can only control your four walls, and your spouse's ex does not live within them. The child, on the other hand, is part of the present and the future. How she leads her life is not only part of your life, but your shared responsibility now that you have married her parent. You can have a positive influence on her or a negative one. It's up to you.

Remember that when you control your thoughts, you control your life. Anger and resentment are very intoxicating—especially if you feel justified in your feelings. You will find, however, that they work like a cancer. They eat away at *your* self-confidence, *your* happiness. Eventually they ruin *your* life. If you continue to brood over "fairness," it will continue to evade you. Something else will come up, and you will be faced with the "fairness" issue again. It's not the situation that affects you—in this case brooding about the extra money that must be spent on a bonuschild—it's what you *think* about the situation. When you feel something is unfair you are acknowledging that you have no control to change things. That's when you may become resentful. The only thing you can control is your attitude.

Empathy can give you some insight into these situations. At least that's how Sharyl and I have gotten through it. Put yourself in your partner's place. *Feel* the love she has for her child. Based on that, it's not a question of fairness; she is making the choice to pay more than is required because as a parent, she wants what's best for the child. She doesn't care if it's court ordered or not. And when you consider that, would you really want it any other way?

Empathy offers a whole new perspective. And sometimes that's all we need.

6

EX-ETIQUETTE FOR BONUSPARENTS

"Each problem that I solved became a rule which served afterwards to solve other problems."

—René Descartes

Bonusparents share a unique and complicated perspective. Although they are not biological parents, they often find themselves in a parental role. To complicate the issue, some bonusparents have children of their own, and this means they must constantly juggle parental responsibilities with stepparent responsibilities.

"Part of my problem is that I really don't know what I'm supposed to be doing," a confused bonusdad once explained to me. "Am I supposed to treat this child like he is my own, or am I his pal? Everywhere I turn I feel like I'm stepping on someone's toes. I'm doing the best I can."

These words echo the sentiments of many bonusparents. Now that joint custody is the most common custody solution, meaning both parents see the child on a regular basis, more stepparents are questioning their roles. "How much should I interact with this child?" they ask. "Should I be strict or a buddy? What are my rights? How much authority do I really have?"

Bonusparent Rights and Responsibilities

Does the stepparent have any legal rights as far as the stepchild is concerned? Not really. Technically, the only legal rights you have as a stepparent are those bestowed upon you by the parents. They are the legal guardians. Even if the bonusparent is the primary caregiver, the legal rights still remain with the parents. For this reason, letters of permission should be on file at the children's school and any other place where a stepparent's authority may be questioned.

"My husband and I have decided to divorce. He had a daughter from his first marriage with whom I have developed a close, loving relationship. What are my responsibilities to this child now that her father and I are splitting up?"

Once parents and bonusparents divorce, bonusparents do not have any legal obligations to the children of an ex-partner. They are not responsible for child support, nor are they automatically granted visitation rights. But your moral responsibilities are another matter entirely. Many bonusparents do not realize the impact they have on the children they leave behind. Their emotional attachment to the children is through the biological parent, and once they leave the parent, they move on with no thought for the kids. But the kids are affected all the same. The bonusparent is a parent figure. Those who think the kids don't care are only fooling themselves.

Of course there are the kids who are glad to see the bonusparent go. The relationship may have been turbulent from the beginning; when that's the case the kids usually rejoice when it's over. But more often than not, the child has bonded with the bonusparent, and when the bonusparent leaves, the child suffers another divorce. In fact, it may be that the bonusparent and child are so emotionally bonded that it is detrimental to the child if contact is interrupted. If this can be proven in court, a bonusparent has a chance for visitation after the breakup based on two possible determinations:

1. Psychological-parent status
2. Equitable-parent status

What's the difference? A bonusparent can be deemed a psychological parent in the eyes of the court if he is seeking visitation with a child after having established an emotional bond that, if terminated, is ruled to be detrimental to the child. Psychological parent status does not grant joint custody to the bonusparent; it merely recognizes the impact of the bonusparent-bonuschild relationship and declares that severing that relationship would be detrimental to the child's well-being. Sole legal custody remains with the biological parent, and no child support is ordered. The court merely recognizes that the child will be affected if he is not allowed contact with the bonusparent. It ensures the legal rights of a bonusparent to visit his bonuschild.

In some states, custody has been granted to a person who is not the biological parent if that person is found to be of great emotional or psychological support to the child. For example, a man who has been married to the biological mother and raised her child as his own but is not the child's biological father may petition to be regarded as an equitable parent. If someone is granted equitable parent status by the court, he receives partial custody, but with that right comes the duty to pay child support. When same-sex parents split up, they often seek psychological- or equitable-parent status.

To my knowledge there is no formal legal statute that enables a person to petition for visitation with a child without having been married to that child's parent. Custody and divorce laws differ from state to state, so it's a good idea to check your state's specific statute. If you were never legally married to the child's parent and you want to continue interaction with a child, the best approach is to continue to maintain a positive relationship with the parent after the breakup.

There's one more very important thing to consider: the feelings of the child in question. Does he want to continue contact? If the child is very young, he may not know how to express that he wants to continue a relationship with a bonusparent after a breakup. If he is a teenager, however, you will likely hear in no uncertain terms whether or not the child wants to continue the relationship. All *three* parent figures—his father, mother, and bonusparent—must listen very carefully to the child, and then act accordingly. That's good ex-etiquette.

"What are my responsibilities regarding going to the kids' extracurricular activities?"

Many bonusparents regard attending the kids' school events as part of their responsibility as a new partner. They feel that being involved lets the children know that they are interested in the kids' lives and want to be close to them. It is a good rule of thumb to expect bonusparents to offer their support at the children's special events.

Keep in mind, however, that this may not coincide with the children's other parent's point of view regarding bonusparent responsibilities. Many bonusparents live with their bonuschildren 50 percent of the time. If they assume the primary caregiver role, they actually see their bonuskids more often than the kids' own parents do. This may be why some parents balk at the bonusparent attending special events. The biological parent may ask,

> ## HEALTHY BONUSPARENTING CHECKLIST
> Put the children first—all the kids, not just your own.
> Parent figures appear as a united front.
> Parents interact respectfully at all times.
> Keep rules consistent for bonus and biological children.
> Parents give their children permission to care about *all* parent figures.
> Parents stay open to suggestions from the other parent figures.

"Can't I just spend some time with my kids without him around?" The answer is yes, but sports events and other activities are when a child may need *everyone's* support. It's a better idea for parents to plan special alone time with their children for another time.

Bonusparent Names

"What should my bonuskids call me?"

Finding a name that suits a bonusparent can be difficult because there is not one definitive answer, like "Mom" or "Dad." The goal is to find a name that is reflective of the relationship between the parent figure and child—or just a nickname the child feels comfortable using.

If a child's parent is living and takes an active role in his or her upbringing, it is inappropriate for the child to call his bonusparent Mom or Dad unless the parent feels comfortable with that choice. It is inappropriate under any circumstances for a child to be forced to call his bonusparent Mom or Dad.

If the biological parent has died, then the bonusparent becomes the primary parent figure, and Mom or Dad is appropriate. Ultimately, it's up to the child. If the child feels comfortable calling his bonusparent Mom or Dad, follow his lead.

Keeping Names Consistent

"I am engaged to a man who has six-year-old twins. I love my bonuschildren-to-be very much, and I want to do whatever is best for the two of them. We are at a point where they are both starting to call me "Mommy." My fiancé and I are planning on having babies after we marry, and we do not want to have any distinction between what the twins call me and what my own biological children will call me. I feel that it is very important that they never feel they are outsiders or that they are loved less than their half-siblings. We have discussed coming up with a name that both the twins and our own babies can call me. Any suggestions?"

This bonusmom has added a new dimension to the dilemma of what the kids should call her. She would like all the kids to call her the same thing, no matter their origin. That's a tough one. I understand the desire for family unity, but I find that most biological parents feel the title of Mom or Dad is reserved for them. If the biological mom is part of the child's life, she probably won't be happy at the thought of her twins calling someone else Mommy.

At our house, where compromise was the name of the game, this was the one issue on which Sharyl would not budge. It was confusing for the youngest one. Being only three or four at the time and hearing my biological daughter call me Mommy, it was only natural for him to follow suit.

Our family therapist's perception was that Sharyl was being unreasonable. That only infuriated Sharyl more. She felt that she had lost a lot in the divorce, and the one thing she was not going to give up was her title as Mom to her children. A compromise was necessary. In the end, we asked Steven to make up a special name just for me. He wasn't that creative. After all, he was only four at the time. He simply added an *a* to my name and calls me Janna. But it was his special name for me, and I cherish it. Steven loved that he could make up a special name, which took the attention off the disagreement and on to resolution.

I have heard quite a few variations of the words *mom* and *dad* over the years that are suitable for bonusparents. Some use variations on the word *auntie* in various other languages. The Spanish word *tia*, for example, is a fairly common bonusmom moniker (French, *tante*; Italian, *zia*).

The best name suggestion I have heard so far was from a new bonusmom who told me that all the kids at her house call her "Mimi." The bonuskids were the first born, and that was the name they chose for her. When she had kids of her own, they were prompted to call her Mimi, too. The way she put it was, "It's close enough to Mama, and cute enough to be tolerated by all."

Other names I have heard for bonusmoms are:

First names, sometimes with *-ie* or *-a* added to it as a sign of affection.

Initials, for example, M.J. (Mom Jennifer) or J.J. (Jennifer June)

Smom (This doesn't always float with biological moms. Most prefer that *mom* not be any part of the name chosen for the bonusmom.)

La La

Mère or Belle Mère (French for mother or stepmother)

In Portuguese, Spanish, and Italian, the term *Padrasto* is used for "stepfather." In Dutch it's *Stiefvader* and *Beau-père* in French. Here are some other names I have heard for bonusdads:

Initials, for example, J.T. (John Thomas)

Buddy or Bud

Pops

Papa

Bubba

Biggy Guy (which eventually became Biggy, which later
• became Mr. Big)

Don Don (an affectionate name a little boy made up for his
bonusdad whose name was Donald)

There's one thing you should watch out for: the name a young
child makes up for a bonusparent may become inappropriate later
on. I have heard from quite a few teens who called their bonusparents endearing names when they were young, only to be
embarrassed about it as they got older. I remember one twelve-
year-old girl who was mortified when her friends teased her about
calling her bonusdad Sneezy (after one of the seven dwarfs). So
be aware that the name is something you may have to revisit as
time goes on. You may treasure the special name your bonuschild
bestows on you, but there may come a time when he chooses to
abandon that name in favor of your first name. If that happens,
good ex-etiquette says to be gracious.

Adding a Baby

*"We have lived in a bonusfamily for three years now.
My wife has two children from her previous marriage,
and we are now expecting our first child together.
What can we do to ensure that the children see
adding a child to the family as a blissful event?"*

While some children may be ready for a new child in the family, others may see it as just one more person to steal away mom
or dad's attention. Some children will not share their fears, and it
may turn out that even though the parents think they have covered all the bases, they really haven't.

This is what happened in my home. A year after Larry's and my baby was born, my daughter, Anee, confessed she'd had a secret fear all during my pregnancy that I would love the new baby more than I loved her. At nine years old, Anee's reasoning was that since I was no longer married to her father, but married to the new baby's father, I loved the new baby's father more than I loved her daddy; therefore I would love the new baby more than I loved Anee. I remember my sadness as I heard her confess her fears. Actually, I was surprised that she felt my affection for her was related to how I felt about her father. This was proof to me that children personalize their parents' feelings about each other. Anee's response came even though we strove to do everything the experts suggested. I had never badmouthed her father. We included all the children in the preparations for the new child— we even asked them if they wanted to add to the family before we considered it.

I was grateful that as my daughter spoke, she confessed that after the baby was born she realized her fears were unfounded, but I still felt like a supremely unconscious parent. Anee and I are and have always been very close. How could I not have known how she felt? How could she have hidden her fears so completely that I had no idea? I pass this experience on as a warning to all parents who are considering adding a child to their bonusfamily. Don't take it for granted that your children are as excited about the new addition as you are. Like my daughter, they may harbor secret fears that they are afraid to talk about.

My bonusdaughter confessed that many of her adult role models actually colored her opinion of having a new baby brother or sister. She was warned that everything would change once the baby was born. She was told that I would not have the time for her. Like my biological daughter, she only confessed this after the baby was born and she could see that my affection for her had not changed.

The following points will help you help your children adjust to the addition of another child.

Before the baby is born:

Don't keep the arrival of the baby a secret. Have open discussions with your children about adding to the family. Emphasize the positive ways a baby will change the dynamics of the family.

Include your children in the planning for the new baby's arrival. Good ways are to ask them for name suggestions or let them help in decorating the baby's room. Older children can be a great help with planning and giving baby showers.

Anticipate what will upset the existing children most and make changes before the new baby arrives. For example, if the new baby has to share a room with an existing child, make sure the existing child has a space of his or her own. Set aside a wall for artwork and a shelf for personal belongings. A closet organizer for older children's clothes can help to make a closet that must be shared into one with two personal spaces.

After the baby is born:

Promote a feeling of acceptance from the start. Many new parents buy a special welcoming gift for the new baby from the existing children, such as a stuffed animal or a rattle. If you choose to do this, you may also want to buy a little something for the existing kids from the new baby.

Try not to make changes that the older child will equate with the new baby's arrival. In other words, don't preface a change with, "Now that the baby's here . . ." An existing child may be inclined to think the change is because the new baby has come to live at her house; this might make her resent the baby. Most changes, such as going to preschool or moving from a crib to a bed, are age related and should be presented as such—not in relationship to the baby's arrival.

Emphasize each child's individuality. Although this new child is related to everyone equally, make the children know you see each of them as unique and that the new sibling will add happiness to their lives, not distract a beloved parent.

Be careful that the new baby does not dominate the lives of the existing children. A new baby is the parents' responsibility, not that of the existing children. Don't expect older children to clean up after the baby. Don't dump babysitting responsibilities on an adolescent. Until your existing children have accepted this child as a member of the family, try to maintain a babysitting swap with other parents. Watch how much you ask grandparents to watch the baby, too; older children might start wondering why their grandparents prefer the new baby to them.

Look for ways to spend one-on-one time with existing children. Even though a new baby will take up most of your time, existing biological kids and bonuskids still need private time with their parents and bonusparents. A great way to find "extra time" is to integrate existing children into your everyday routine. Let dad watch the baby and mom take the older child to the grocery store or vice versa. When it's time to change the oil in the car, ask one of the kids to come along for company. Grab a quick bite together while you are waiting. Use the time to talk.

Who Do You Like Best?

"I have two bonuschildren with whom I am very close. My husband and I were also blessed with a little girl three years ago. The ages of the children are seven, five, and three. I try to have alone time with all of

them and inevitably each one will ask, 'Who do you love best?' I am always at a loss what to say."

It's human nature for a child to wonder if she is as special to you as you are to her. When the question is presented, it's difficult to know what to say, especially if the question comes from a bonuschild. You may have conflicted feelings—yes, you care for them, but not in the same way you love your biological child. Perhaps you are one of the lucky ones who make no emotional distinction between biological and bonus. Either way, when you are asked the question, good ex-etiquette suggests that you have an answer prepared in advance.

When my youngest daughter asked me, "Who do you love best?" I was prepared to give her the same answer my father gave me; he told me he loved all of us equally. But I remembered that answer did not reassure me. I wanted to be special in my dad's eyes. Not necessarily loved more than my sister and brother, but I wanted him to know I was *me*. Every so often I would ask him the question again, hoping to get a different answer. I never did.

If you think about it, "I love you both the same," may actually promote rivalry between siblings. It puts children in a position to compete for their parents' affection—and if you add step allegiances to the mix, that particular response really complicates the issue. Both biological and bonus children have concerns about favoritism. Biological children want to reaffirm that you love them best. Bonuschildren want reassurance that they will not be overlooked. Both biological and bonus are looking for acceptance and reassurance. If one or the other asks which child you love best, and they get the "I love you all the same" answer, they are both bound to be skeptical.

When my youngest daughter asked me, "Who do you love best?" I tried to give her an answer that made her realize that I loved all the children in my care, but that I also saw her as an individual. "I love all my children," I told her. I then continued with,

"All of you are so different, I really can't compare you." And then I chose something that was special about her and talked about that. "Honey, how many three-year-olds do you think can sing the way you do? Sing me a song. I love it when you sing." She immediately started to sing, and the conversation switched to how she wanted to be a rock star when she was older.

Would I have given her the same answer if she were my bonus-daughter? Absolutely. When you are pointing out a child's good traits, the fact that she is your bonuschild is irrelevant. *All* children want to feel special.

When my daughter was a little older, she asked me the question again. That's when I had the opportunity to talk about the individual qualities that make her special. "Each of you is special, but you are all so different! *You* are so considerate. Yesterday when you were watching your big brother clean up the backyard? You noticed that he was very hot all by yourself and brought him a glass of ice water. I was so proud of you. You care about people, and that's a wonderful trait to have."

Did I answer the *exact* question I was asked? Not really; however, the answer she was given was the answer to the question she really wanted to ask. Like my question to my father years ago, my daughter wanted to know if I saw her as an individual. That's what all our kids are asking when they ask, "Who do you like best?" They are asking, "Do you see *me*? Do you see how special *I* am?" That's the question you answer. You tell them how special you think they are—all by themselves, not in relation to their siblings.

Will I Ever Love This Child?

"I am a bonusparent to a four-year-old boy. He lives at his mom's for the week and with us on weekends. I

have been in his life for three years, and I'm worried because I do not feel the love toward him I thought I would feel by now. When will I love him—or will I? I keep my distance from his biological mother because she is condescending and authoritative, and I get mad at my husband for not standing up to her. Help! I don't want to be angry all the time."

There is more than one troublesome issue here, but the writer is running them all together in her mind, allowing the anger she feels toward the mother to affect her feelings toward her bonus-son, thereby creating problems in her relationship with her partner. Angry and confused, the writer wonders when she will feel the love that she thought she would feel by now for this child. But until she has the ability to separate the issues and see each problem separately, it is doubtful she will find those loving feelings for the child. Right now, each time she looks at the child, she sees his mother, feels anger about her behavior, then gets angry with her partner for not taking a stand. The writer is the only one who can stop this negative thought/negative behavior chain. She must first address her feelings about the mother and accept that she can only control her own turf—she cannot control the mother's attitude—and move on from there. Once she stops the angry mental chain of events, her relationships with all three people—the mother, father, and child—will improve.

Will she ever love this child? Many bonusparents ask that question. I find it interesting that society accepts the fact that there is a courting period between two adults who plan to marry, yet fails to acknowledge that there must be a similar adjustment period dedicated to getting to know the children. You may be one of the lucky ones; you might adore your bonuskids right from the beginning. More often than not, though, the adjustment takes years, and as you get to know each other you develop a mutual respect that turns into a special affection for each other.

Dealing with a Change in Attitude

"I've been married to my husband for seven years. Because we have primary custody, his daughter and I have grown quite close. Lately, however, she's rude and standoffish, and I just don't know what to do. She hurts my feelings! Her mother recently got out of rehab and is trying to reenter her life, and I'm trying to be supportive. Last night she finally said the phrase I was dreading. 'You're not my mother! You can't tell me what to do!' Help!"

It's not uncommon for a bonusparent (or any parent, for that matter) to think her relationship with a bonuschild is wonderful right up to the point when adolescence and hormones set in. Then the child's moods shift radically, and the bonusparent takes the change very personally. She may think, "I didn't have to love you, you know. It was my choice, and now you're turning on me."

Another more important fact to consider is that children of divorce often live with an unwarranted adoration of the noncustodial parent. As they get older, they realize for themselves that mom or dad has a drug problem or is violent or neglectful, and this realization can put them into an emotional tailspin. At the same time the bonusparent is working hard to offer stability and camaraderie, the bonuschild may simply resent that this person who is being so nice isn't her "real" parent. And the nicer the bonusparent is, the angrier the child becomes. There is simply nothing the bonusparent can do about that.

The bonusparent in this case mentioned "hurt feelings." This is a trap that lots of bonusparents fall into because they are trying so hard to be perfect parents. When the child doesn't respond, the bonusparent becomes vindictive and resentful that all her hard work has been for nothing. She emotionally withdraws from the child, promising herself that "that little &*%$ isn't going to hurt me again." This attitude will not help the situation. The child was dealt something she did not ask for—her parents' divorce. If the bonusparent gives up, the situation will not get better on its own.

If a biological parent is not active in a child's life, it's even more important for you, the bonusparent, to continue to be a good role model. Always remember to separate your feelings from the bonuschild's negative reactions. Put up a mental shield that blocks out the negative comments, and don't let *your* feelings be any part of an interaction. If you are being a supportive, loving role model and the child is still lashing out, that's proof it's not related to something you are doing. It's the child's pain, and it is the bonusparent's responsibility to the child to stay positive, continue to initiate time together, and reach down inside for all the patience she can muster.

If you are faced with a child's abrupt change of attitude, it's a good idea to talk to her teachers or the school counselor to see if her attitude or behavior has changed at school. They may be able to give you some additional insights. If they verify that there has been a noticeable change, don't be afraid to seek counseling. A few sessions that allow a child to vent to an unbiased party may be all that is needed to get her back on track.

"So give me a good comeback for 'You're not my mother (or father)!'"

If you are using good ex-etiquette, you are trying not to be in the mind-set where you depend on comebacks to hold your ground. If you are hearing that statement from your bonuschild, a bond has not been built between the two of you. The child simply resents being told what to do by someone she regards as an outsider. The best response to "You're not my mother!" is acknowledgment of the fact, followed by your request for the good behavior. For example, you ask the bonuschild to flush the toilet after she uses it. The bonuschild says, "Don't tell me what to do. You're not my mother!" The appropriate acknowledgment is, "Yes, honey, I know that. Please flush the toilet, anyway" (in exactly the tone of voice the response implies—calm, matter-of-fact, and moving on).

The key is not to react to the statement emotionally. It's said out of frustration to hurt and upset the bonusparent. It's truly going for the jugular, so if you respond in the way that you would like, "Listen, you little turd, treat me with some respect!" the argument will just escalate, and you will have given the child a reason to be disrespectful. It's unlikely that you will be able to offer a zinger that will put the child in her place, so the best thing to do is stay calm.

One of the rules of ex-etiquette truly applies to this situation: "Don't hold grudges." If you hold on to the feelings of anger and hurt that you feel when you hear that statement, your relationship with your bonuschild is bound to suffer. From a practical standpoint, look for ways to bond when there is no conflict between the two of you. For example, when things are calm, ask the child for suggestions on what to have for dinner or what color to paint the house. Look for ways to make her feel that you value her opinion. As the bond between you grows you will begin to hear "You're not my mother!" far less often.

In the Name of Family Unity

"Recently my son expressed interest in Little League, and I took that request to my fiancé. His position is that he doesn't want my son involved in something that will leave his children out, and he doesn't think his children will feel included by simply attending my son's games. So because I've chosen to be part of this blended family my son can't play Little League?"

It is rare that a married couple with children would prevent one child from participating in sports because the others did not want to attend the games. So what makes this an issue is the fact that this is a combined family in search of its new family identity. They must make sure that in the pursuit of that new identity, they don't lose sight of each family member's individuality.

As parents, it is our job to reinforce the bonusfamily as a unit but also to recognize each child's distinctiveness. One of the things bonusfamilies have to consider is the uniqueness of each member of the new family. Each member should feel supported to excel in his or her own areas of interest.

Biological Parent in the Middle

"My husband is very tough on my daughter from a previous marriage. He has never had children, and it hurts me to see him hurt her feelings so often. I feel like I'm in the middle of the two people I love the most."

It's not uncommon for parents who have remarried to feel as if they must run defense for their child or their new partner to prevent hurt feelings or arguments. It usually starts with the parent feeling that the new spouse will be overly critical of her child, and the parent tries to serve as a buffer to protect the child from being hurt. By the same token, the same parent sees the child's interaction with the bonusparent as potentially disrespectful, and again intercedes to head off an argument. Although at the time many parents explain that they are trying to protect the two people they love most, their interference fails to give the bonusparent and child a way to work through their own problems. The parent's behavior diffuses the anger but prevents the bonusparent and bonuschild from developing their own relationship.

If there is ever a situation in which good behavior after remarriage is needed, it is this one. But surprisingly the parent, not the bonusparent, is the one who needs to be put on notice. Practicing good ex-etiquette means the bonusparent and bonuschild must be allowed time *and be trusted* to develop their own relationship with one another. There will surely be bumps in the road, but interference from the parent will only extend the period of adjustment bonusrelations need to form a caring bond.

Family Intimacy

"Should my bonuschild sleep with us?"

It is common for parents and bonusparents to have different opinions on this subject. To be blunt, professionals suggest divorced parents do not sleep with their children. This includes single divorced parents and parents who have remarried. Although both parent and child may find it comforting, when the parent becomes involved in a new relationship she automatically puts child and lover in competition with each other. When the child is told she can no longer sleep in the parent's bed, she may perceive that the parent loves the new partner more; feelings of insecurity and resentment may flare. By the same token, if the parent allows the child to continue to sleep in her bed, the new partner may believe the parent prefers to fulfill her child's wishes.

There's something else to consider—the feelings of the child's other biological parent. Most biological parents prefer that their child sleep separately from the other parent and her new partner. And if one parent allows the child to sleep with her and the other doesn't, this just makes the transition from house to house more difficult. To keep things calm between both homes, it's best not to sleep in the same bed with the child.

Take the following steps to ward off potential problems when the child makes the transition to sleeping alone.

Make your child's room a comforting, fun place to be. Decorate it the way she wants. Make it fun for her to stay in her bed by providing stuffed animals of her choice, cuddly quilts, and so on. Try using glow-in-the-dark stars on the ceiling—something she can see only when the room is dark to emphasize the necessity of turning out the lights.

Establish a ritual for putting your child to bed. Read a story or make up a handshake or kiss ritual. Another great idea for a goodnight ritual is playing a favorite cassette tape after you leave the room. My own daughter had a Snoopy cassette player. Every night I would put on a tape of a fairy tale told by a favorite cartoon character. After our goodnight kiss I told her to close her eyes, listen to the tape, and imagine she was right there in the fairy tale. It worked like a charm. She always fell asleep before the tape had ended.

Integrate the bonusparent into the goodnight ritual. This will reinforce the feeling of family and guard against problems should the biological parent be ill or out of town when it is time to put the child to bed. Start by allowing the bonusparent to observe the goodnights. The bonusparent's presence will give the subliminal message that this is a member of the family. Next, suggest that the bonusparent participate in the goodnight ritual along with you. Then, slowly ease the bonusparent into occasionally conducting the goodnight ritual alone.

If your child chooses to come into your room even after you have taken these precautions, gently take her back to her own room, and put her back into bed with the words, "This is your very own special place to sleep. Mommy (or Daddy) has her own special place to sleep." And then leave the room. If she continues to come back into your bed, simply do it again and again. Do not lose your temper. Ask your spouse to show patience until your child accepts sleeping in her own room. Remind your spouse that obvious frustration only makes the problem worse. Your child will see that there is a battle for your attention and will consequently fight for it. When that happens, you are right in the middle again. It's no fun.

Nudity

How you handle nudity in your own home is a very personal matter. Most parents tell us that they would prefer that bonusparents not appear nude in front of their children. Psychologists agree that it is best to be comfortably modest in front of bonuschildren. Good ex-etiquette is based on courtesy and politeness. Because of close quarters, of course, there may be a time when someone walks in on someone else while changing or showering, but this should be met with the appropriate "Excuse me." To keep embarrassment to a minimum, the subject should then be dropped.

I became Sharyl's children's bonusmom when her son was three years old. As the primary caregiver when he was with his father, I often bathed him, washed his hair, and performed all the other intimate duties a mother would perform when taking care of her own child. At one point he asked me to take a bath with him. He was four, soaking in the water, and simply said, "Hey Janna, why don't you take a bath, too?"

I did not have a response prepared. I never anticipated the question; therefore, without thinking, my first response was, "Honey, I can't take a bath with you." Well, that opened an entire can of worms. He wondered why. "We go swimming together. You've taken a bath with Anee. Why can't you take a bath with me?"

That was a good question and I had to think about it for a second. Anee is my daughter, and she had obviously mentioned that we bathed together when she was a baby. Since my goal was never to show open favoritism for any of the children, I had a problem. How could I communicate that I cared for my bonusson without showing an obvious preference for my biological child? Just as important, when family members are not biologically related, nudity is often not perceived as casual. I was particularly sensitive to how I might feel if my son came back from his dad's house with stories of bathing with his bonusmom.

After quickly running various scenarios over in my mind, I decided on a rather unorthodox approach. Here's an important distinction—it was the right decision for our family, but possibly not for yours. I said, "OK!" And I got into the bathtub . . . in exactly what I was wearing—my jeans and a T-shirt. I will never forget the look on his face. We laughed so loud that the other kids came running into the bathroom to see what the commotion was all about. They still talk about it years later.

Did I handle it the way other professionals say to handle such situations? Probably not. I can't imagine a child psychologist suggesting you get into the bathtub with all your clothes on—but the solution worked for our bonusfamily. The conversation ceased to be, "Will you take a bath with me?" It became, "Remember when you got into the bath with all your clothes on?" For us, the subject was over.

If you are faced with a similar situation, a more clinical response might be, "Honey, bath time is private time, and although I'm helping you now, there will be a time very soon when you can wash up all by yourself! I'll stay close by if you need me, but soon it can be your private time just as it is mine." Such words reassure a child. Essentially, you are telling him, "Don't worry, I'm here, and when you feel more confident, you can do things for yourself." Perfect.

Too Much Information

"My ten-year-old bonusdaughter started her period when she was at our home. She knew very little about what was happening to her body, and she was a little frightened. I did my best to tactfully explain the human reproductive system and what was happening to her. It was actually a lovely time, and we felt quite close. When her mother found out that I had discussed these

EX-ETIQUETTE FOR BONUSPARENTS 187

things with her, she became incensed; she felt that I had overstepped my bounds and that this was something she should have discussed with her daughter. Truthfully, I understand her feelings, but I was faced with the problem and handled it the best I could."

If you share custody of your child, she may not be with you when she is faced with a need for an explanation about such things as the human reproductive system. Therefore, it is important that parents and bonusparents take a proactive approach by anticipating the problem and coming to agreement on how they will handle such situations. I have heard everything from "Tell her what you want" to "Don't you dare say a thing. That's my job!" Somewhere in between is probably the kindest approach.

Most moms will tell you that they would like to be the one to discuss the human reproductive system with their daughters. However, the joint-custody lifestyle may not be conducive to mom or dad exclusively answering the intimate questions their children may ask. And new questions always come up. You think you have covered it, but when the child goes to the other parent's home, she may have new questions. For this reason, all parent figures must be allied on how best to handle such situations.

In this example, a young girl started her period while at her father's home, the bonusmom answered intimate questions, and the biological mother was angry. Truthfully, the bonusmom's actions were the proper ones; however, she should have phoned the mother with the news so that the mother could then also be supportive of her child. In this way the parents are working together for the benefit of the child. That's good ex-etiquette.

There may also be times when one parent has spoken to the child, but the child decides to ask the other parent or bonusparent the same question just to make sure the answer is correct. For example, Sharyl's daughter asked both Sharyl and me where babies come from. When I became pregnant the children were ten, nine, and six, and my pregnancy opened an entire line of discussion about the human reproductive system and how babies got in there. This is when it is imperative that parents—*all of them*—decide together what they feel is age-appropriate information, and then stand by the agreement.

How to Handle Attraction Among Stepsiblings

"My new spouse and I both have fifteen-year-old children. I have a boy, he has a girl, and it appears they may be attracted to each other. I'm afraid to leave them alone together. What should we do?"

One of the worst fears of parents who combine families is the thought of stepsiblings becoming sexually attracted to each other. Aside from a fear for the children's safety, there are quite a few other considerations.

Are their feelings mutually shared or is one child intimidated by the other?

How will the teens' relationship affect the dynamics of the new bonusfamily?

How will their relationship affect the younger, more impressionable children in the home?

Even though the kids aren't actually related, their relationship seems questionable as society wonders if the situation constitutes incest.

Probably the most difficult thing for the parents to address is their guilt that the decision to marry or live together caused the problem in the first place.

Let's address the most alarming thought first. Is this incest or not? What makes this sort of relationship questionable is that the parents are married and the children are living under the same roof. If these two teens had met under other circumstances, most parents would not be alarmed. Teens date. That's the normal order of things. The term *incest* never would have come up.

When teens live together in the same home, however, the situation changes drastically. Parents, who normally frown on teenagers of the opposite sex being alone in the home, have to consider that both the teens now *live* in this home. How can a parent limit their time alone in their own home? And would the question of incest even come into play if the parents were not officially married, but living together? Therefore, is it the parents' union that makes the teens' attraction a taboo? It is truly a perplexing problem.

Good ex-etiquette suggests that you once again take a proactive approach. If your children are teens when you marry, anticipate that you may be faced with their mutual sexual attraction, and put proper boundaries in place from day one. The kids must know what you expect of them.

These rules sound good in theory. But they may not translate into action. As parents, we would like to think our teens do exactly what we say, when in reality we know they may not. Our best hope as caring, involved parents is to offer information, guidance, and support. Judging, lecturing, and criticism will not solve the problem, and may shut down communication altogether. And judgmental stepparents are considered to be the very lowest life form. Be careful.

If you are faced with the problem of sexually attracted teens, as wrong as you may feel your children's actions are, now is the time to keep your head. Stay focused on what is really important—the teens need level-headed guidance to lead them through a very trying time. If you do not keep your head, the kids may keep up their relationship but hide it from you. If that happens, there is no way you can help.

Teens must understand that romantic relationships carry huge responsibilities and can have far-reaching consequences. A good way to call this to their attention is to have an open discussion and ask the teens to reflect on the following questions.

> How do you feel about the impression your actions will make on the younger children in the home?
>
> How will you feel if you break up and still have to live in the same house?
>
> What will happen to your friendship if the romance doesn't work out?
>
> How will you feel about the negative reactions of friends that perceive your relationship as forbidden?
>
> How will you feel knowing that it will make all the other members of the household very uncomfortable?

Notice that most of the questions start with, "How will you feel . . . ?" That is designed to help teens consider the consequences of their actions and then talk about their feelings rather than feel as if the parent is passing judgment. If teens feel a parent is passing judgment, they won't say a word. If their feelings are being considered, they will be more inclined to open up.

It is during this question-and-answer period that you can let your feelings be known. Use discretion when voicing your unhappiness with the situation. It may be a good idea to suggest that they put the relationship on hold; but they may not see the necessity to do so. At that point, it may be time to look for subtle ways to limit their time alone. Suggest an after-school job, cheerleading, volunteer work (most high schools require some community service work to graduate), homework club, or other extracurricular activities. You may have to get creative.

If your teens still refuse to end the relationship, you will have to set some strict limits. Be specific about the exact behavior you expect in your home. If you prefer no displays of affection in front of younger siblings, make that clear. This is not a time to be shy, but you must also understand that if you are too heavy-handed or if you demand that the involvement cease, the teens will probably continue the relationship in secret. A discussion about contraception may be in order. This will undoubtedly make things even more uncomfortable, but it's better to face the uncomfortable situation rather than the unfortunate consequences.

Professionals warn parents that they cannot control their teens' behavior, but they can become sought-after consultants while their children make their own decisions. If you listen and do your best to appear nonjudgmental, you will keep their trust. This situation is a real test for parents and children alike, but if you implement harsh disciplinary tactics, you will only drive them away. The most important issue in raising teenagers is to keep the lines of communication open. This will only happen if you remain calm and supportive during confusing and trying times.

It's important to note that this section refers to a situation in which the teens in question have a mutual attraction for each other. If you are faced with a situation in which one family member is sexually harassing another family member, get professional counseling for them immediately.

Dealing with Unaccepting Adult Bonuschildren

"I have just remarried after being divorced for twenty-five years. I never had children, but my new wife has three who are all well into their thirties. Even though their father is dead, they hate me. My spouse and I are very happy but these adult children are making our lives miserable. I don't know how to act when they are around, and now neither does my spouse!"

Ex-etiquette is based on courtesy, but it's difficult to be polite when you feel you are being misjudged based purely on circumstance. In this case, the man's crime was simply marrying someone with adult children who had a strong allegiance to a deceased parent.

Many people feel that they should be able to reason with the adult children of a spouse. When these children are difficult to reach, newly married older couples are at a loss. That's when frustration sets in on both sides and communication breaks down.

Being an adult does not diminish a son or daughter's feelings of sadness over a divorce or a parent's death. On the contrary, it can be more frustrating for an adult child because she is expected to act rationally when she feels the same base emotions a child might.

A person who has married someone with unaccepting adult children may take the adult children's behavior quite personally. He might look to his new spouse to curb her children's behavior. Although parents can have an impact on their adult children, they certainly cannot be expected to control their actions. This makes any sort of get-together very uncomfortable for everyone, and consequently many remarried seniors spend time away from their adult children to prevent confrontation.

In my conversations with adult children of divorce, I find they are often concerned with the appearance that things are moving too quickly. I often hear that a parent is being insensitive or even disloyal if he or she remarries within a time period the adult child perceives as being "too short." People need time to form bonds with one another. Therefore, to lessen the pain of remarriage or the death of a parent, adult children should be awarded the same courting period their parent's new partner would dedicate to getting to know younger children. They should use the same getting-to-know-you techniques prescribed when your partner has younger children. This can be accomplished by starting out slowly with lunch or brief get-togethers, and spending more time together as everyone gets comfortable.

Like many circumstances pertaining to good ex-etiquette, empathy for all concerned may be the key. When in doubt about how to behave, put yourself in the other's place and consider how you would like them to respond to you.

Divorce and the passing of a parent is a very painful experience, but it is ultimately the adult child's journey. Good ex-etiquette suggests both parties remain polite at all times and do their best to find comfort in the possibility of a newfound kinship in which both share a genuine affection for the same person.

Favoritism

"My husband and I have been married for five years. We have one son each from previous marriages, and now we have a third son together. His son is somewhat obnoxious, and I am having difficulty accepting him into my life. Since he is only with us every other weekend, I almost feel like we are watching my husband's ex-wife's son, and it makes me feel even more distant from him. I consider our family to be my son, the son we had together, and us. He considers our family to be three kids and us. It's causing us a great amount of stress."

Ex-etiquette tells us that the correct attitude in this case is as follows. He has a child, she has a child, they have a child; therefore, their immediate bonusfamily consists of three children and two adults, *plus* the extended-family members that this mother hasn't even begun to consider.

It is sometimes difficult to build a bond with stepchildren. They can look a particular way, have attitudes you dislike, and hold allegiances you do not care for. They are a constant reminder that your spouse was once intimate with someone else. But that's the challenge you accept when you divorce and remarry.

As a bonusparent you have the opportunity to make a difference in a child's life. You certainly do not want to be the stereotypical antagonist that you read about in fairy tales. Instead you would probably like to help mold a child through love and mutual respect. You can be someone that this child holds in high regard and goes to for advice and comfort. Or you can be someone who causes additional pain. If you harbor animosity for a bonuschild, it will eventually color every aspect of your married relationship, and that's when another divorce looms.

As I have said throughout this book, you control your thoughts and your behavior. *You* are the only one who can change your attitude about what makes a family. Instead of dwelling on the fact that a child is obnoxious, look for something positive he brings to the family. Start with just one thing—even if that one thing is that it makes your partner happy when the child is around. That's something. Hold on to that one thing. Soon your animosity will diminish because your ill thoughts about the child have diminished. Sounds easy, right? If this child drives you crazy, you will soon see that it is not an easy task at all. How long will this take? It could be days or it could be years. No matter how long it takes, it is your moral obligation. That's putting the children first.

7

IMPROVING EXTENDED-FAMILY RELATIONS

*"If you judge people, you have no time
to love them."*

—MOTHER TERESA

When couples marry for a second or subsequent time, they often forget to look past blending their immediate families to consider how they will integrate extended-family members—grandma, grandpa, aunts and uncles, and cousins who are not an immediate part of this blissful new union. Bonusfamilies must take special care to integrate extended-family members early in the process.

Communicating Clearly with Extended-Family Members

"My husband has two daughters and I have one son from previous marriages. My husband's parents are great, but sometimes they favor their biological grandkids over my son. When the two granddaughters turned eighteen, each was rewarded with a generous sum of money for college. My son, on the other hand, recently turned eighteen and was given a token monetary amount. Although he was happy they remembered him, I could see the pain this caused him. Should we say something to the grandparents about this?"

Naturally, this parent loves her own child. She's had years to get to know him. She's nurtured and raised him, and as a result, she loves him in spite of any foibles. New relatives that have not had that bonding time just don't feel the same way. If an adult extended-family member meets a child at six years old, by the time the child is eighteen, the adult and child may have had time to form a bond. If the adult meets the same child at sixteen, the relationship between adult and child is still quite new, and it is unlikely a bond has been formed. You can't change that. The best thing the parent in this case can do is to make sure the child understands it's not his fault if extended-family members treat him differently than biological family members. The adult may just need more time.

You can head off a lot of misunderstandings and speed up the bonding process if you have a formal conversation with extended-family members before you get married. As a new couple you should explain that when you marry, there will be more members of your family and that you hope that as your mother, father, sister, or brother, etc., they will support you and accept these new members as part of the extended family. *Invite* them to become members of your new family. For example, you might say, "We know you and the kids are not biologically related, but we value your place as a grandparent figure (or family member) in all of the children's lives." This may be all you need to do to break the ice.

Without having this type of conversation up front, extended bonusfamily members may have no idea that you want them to interact with your kids. They may be distant toward the new bonuschildren for two reasons. First, they don't want to hurt their biological relations' feelings (biological grandchildren, nieces, or nephews) by making a fuss over the new bonus additions. Second, they don't want to overstep their bounds. If you are a bonusrelative and no one has said anything to you about how they would like you to interact with the kids, don't be afraid to initiate the conversation. Ask them what they expect from you. Discuss how you will all go forward using your mutual love and respect as a guide.

Extended-Family Financial Obligations

"I have set aside some money to help my grandchild through college. My son recently remarried, and his new wife has three children. There's just not enough to help my stepgrandchildren through college. Am I obligated to provide for them too?"

It is important to clarify that when a family member marries someone with children, their financial obligation does not automatically become that of the extended-family members. Once again, good ex-etiquette suggests a frank conversation. Put your heads together. Talk about the possibilities. Pool your resources. The key is to discuss your available options and work together for the benefit of the children.

PUTTING GOOD EX-ETIQUETTE INTO

PRACTICE: INVOLVING EXTENDED-FAMILY MEMBERS

If you are having trouble integrating your partner's extended family with your new bonusfamily, perhaps it is because he or she is sending the wrong message. Extended-family members follow their relative's lead. Therefore, make sure you have your spouse's support. How does he feel about his parents becoming grandma and grandpa or auntie to your children? Without his knowing it, his statements may not suggest a feeling of unity.

For example, let's say a new husband is talking to his parents. Listen to his explanation when asked where his wife is: "Cindy took her kids to the mall." That statement very clearly says the kids in his care are not *his* kids, but his wife's.

This is not to imply that bonusparents should refer to their bonus-children as *my* children. But.read the following statements and make your own judgment about what each subconsciously says to others:

"Cindy took her kids to the mall."
"Cindy took the kids to the mall."
"Cindy took Billy and Mark to the mall."

When Extended-Family Members Do Not Accept Your Choices

"I'm happily remarried and my sister just doesn't like and won't accept my new family. We try to present everything in a positive light, but she's resisting."

As much as you would like your relatives to accept your choices, there may be times that you cannot sway them. One of the rules of good ex-etiquette tells us that we can only control our own turf. You cannot control others, and as much as it hurts that a loved one does not accept your new family, that is *her* choice. Good ex-etiquette suggests that you continue to be polite and courteous to her. All the rules of good ex-etiquette apply to extended family—no badmouthing, no holding grudges, etc. Always put the children first in all your decisions. Take comfort in the fact that you can only do your best.

Allegiance and Betrayal

"How many times am I supposed to welcome new children into my family? My son has been married three times. Each time they come and go, it's an adjustment."

If this mother-in-law is like the vast majority of in-laws I have worked with, her problem is not about welcoming new children into her family—it's about welcoming new children into her heart. She hasn't experienced the arguments or betrayal issues that served as the catalyst for her son's separations, so each time he divorces, she is left mourning the departure of a beloved family member. She questions if she should maintain the relationship and if she is being disloyal to her son if she wants to stay in contact with his ex.

"The day before yesterday, my ex picked up my son for a special fishing trip. After they'd left, my mother told me that my father had gone along with my son and my ex! I feel this is totally inappropriate. Once my husband and I divorced, that should have been the end of my father's relationship with my ex."

Divorce legally severs only the ties between the divorcing couple. It does not sever the extended family's affection for the divorced family member's ex-spouse. Another thing to remember is that, as in the case above, the ex is still related to the woman's father as the father of his grandson. A relationship may have been built over the years based on mutual respect and a love for the son/grandchild, and good ex-etiquette does not require that relationship to end merely because the marriage that produced the child ended. It is simply unfair for the mother to expect family members to reject her ex because her relationship with him has ended.

The divorced mother is not the only one who is not following the rules of good ex-etiquette, however. It goes without saying that divorced couples should always inform each other of their destinations and who accompanies them when taking the children on special outings. It is also the responsibility of extended-family members—in this case, the grandfather—to volunteer pertinent information. Sneaking around behind people's backs will only infuriate them and undermine any chance of an honest relationship in the future.

Granted, keeping the fishing trip a secret was probably done in an effort to keep the mother's discontent to a minimum. Deceiving her, however, sets a bad example for the young child. It also places the child in the middle and tests his allegiance to his parents. If he tells his mother about the fishing trip, he is betraying his father and grandfather. If he keeps the trip from his mother, he is betraying her. Putting the child in this position is very poor ex-etiquette.

In defense of all the players, this situation is confusing for all concerned, and good ex-etiquette may not come naturally. Most people regard their parents as *their* parents first, and their children's grandparents second. It would be completely understandable if the mother's first reaction was to be hurt by her father's apparent allegiance to her ex. However, in the midst of her hurt, she would do well to realize that her father's choice is not a betrayal of her, but merely a desire to maintain a relationship with his grandson and his grandson's father. This mother's ability to cope successfully rests on her ability to break the negative thought/negative behavior chain and make her judgments based on what is true:

> The mother's father loves his daughter, and his allegiance to her has not swayed.
> The grandfather loves his grandson.
> The grandfather wishes to maintain a relationship with his grandson's father.

When the mother allows all three relationships to be separate—not based on her relationship with her ex—she will feel less betrayed by her father, and her father will be able to maintain all the relationships he cherishes. This fishing trip might produce lasting memories for father, son, and grandfather that would have been missed if the family members had abided by the mother's original wishes. By the same token, when using good ex-etiquette you approach every interaction honestly. All three parent figures need to change their approach for the sake of the child they are raising.

Let's look at this same situation from another point of view.

"My husband recently took his son on a special fishing trip. When they returned, I found out that my husband's ex-wife's father also went along! I feel uncomfortable with my husband associating with his ex's parents. I feel like they are always comparing me to my husband's ex and what they really want is for my husband and their daughter to reconcile. This infuriates me. I want my husband to stop interacting with his ex's relatives!"

New spouses would do well to promote such relationships rather than undermine them. They should not expect their mates or bonuschildren to cut off ties to the children's extended-family members because of their personal insecurities. That needs to be understood *before* the second or subsequent marriage. In this case, this woman's husband's relationship with his ex-father-in-law—her bonusson's grandfather—should be perpetuated, divorce or not.

Good ex-etiquette for the new wife: She should be polite when in the former in-law's company and do her best to initiate positive interaction and maintain a positive mind-set. Any time she starts a sentence or thought with "I feel like . . ." she should make sure there is something positive following those words. Otherwise she is reaffirming a negative expectation. Buying into thoughts such as "I feel like they are always comparing me to my husband's ex, and what they really want is for my husband and their daughter to reconcile" undermines her own existence. She should work toward no preconceived notions for each meeting, no grudges, and no spiteful behavior.

If she is still met with resistance, it's the ex-in law's problem, not hers. What if she's right? What if her husband's ex-in-law *does* wish for that reconciliation? If it's true, then that is his desire, and as I have said over and over, you can't control anyone else's thoughts or feelings, or the way someone else runs their home. You can only control your own thoughts, feelings, and turf.

Good ex-etiquette for the new couple: It is the new husband's place to make his intentions clear to his former father-in-law while maintaining a healthy relationship with ex-relations for the sake of his child. If he sets the example, his ex-in-law will most likely follow suit. If the ex-in-law is openly disrespectful of his ex-son-in-law's new wife, it is up to the new husband to calmly confront the issue. If this does not rectify the situation, he should reduce the amount of personal interaction with the ex-father-in-law but continue to support a positive relationship between grandfather and grandchild.

Accepting a New Family Member After the

Death of a Loved One

"My grandmother died six months ago after a long illness. We loved her very much. My grandfather has recently started dating a woman he appears to like very much, but I am having a very difficult time accepting her. At twenty-two years old, I know I should be more accepting and I'm surprised by my reaction, but by the same token, I don't want another grandmother."

Although this may not seem like it at first, this is also an allegiance and betrayal issue. This young woman loved her grandmother and does not want to betray her memory by accepting someone else into her heart. It's important for her to remember that accepting someone new into the family betrays a deceased family member's memory only if she tries to replace her feelings about the relative who has passed with her feelings about the new relative. If she keeps the two relationships separate, respecting both people as individuals, she is then free to mourn one while befriending the other.

Everyone mourns at his own speed. Six months may seem like a very short time after the death of a loved one to recouple. However, something younger loved ones may not understand is that mourning can actually begin during a partner's illness. If it is a long illness, the well partner may subconsciously start the mourning process while his partner is still alive. What seems to this young woman to be a short mourning period could really have gone on for years before her grandmother's death. This may explain why the grandfather is able to move on more quickly than the granddaughter thinks is appropriate. After the death of a partner from a long illness, most are not looking to *replace* their partner; they are looking for companionship and a diversion from the pain of losing someone they loved. A new friend can be the best medicine.

For the adult bonuschild: Do not assume that the new bonus-relative wants to replace your deceased relative. Try to accept the new relative as a valued friend in support of your loved one.

For the new bonusrelative: Just as you would if the child was young, go slowly into the adult child's life. Look for common ground. Adult children can be more dedicated to a deceased loved one or an ex-relation, and therefore they may distrust your attempts to get to know them. Don't be too aggressive by acting as if you are taking their relative's place.

Becoming a Bonusgrandparent

"How can I maintain my close relationship with my grandchild and comfortably nurture a new relationship with a new bonusgrandchild?"

The following tips suggest good ex-etiquette when trying to get to know new bonusgrandchildren, but they can be used by any adult initiating the getting-to-know-you process with a new bonusrelative, such as a bonusniece or -nephew.

Eight Tips for New Bonusgrandparents

1. Remember that no two children are alike. Make a special effort to get to know your new grandchild. Find out about his likes and dislikes so you have more to say than "Hi, honey, how's school?" Most kids do not like to talk about school. They prefer to talk about their interests—skateboarding, snowboarding, cool movies they have just seen, the music they like to listen to, and so on. Ask them about those things and you will get an engaged answer. Ask them, "How's school?" and all

they are likely to say is, "Fine." And that's the end of the getting-to-know-you conversation.

2. Let them get to know you. Tell your new bonusgrandkids special stories about your past, just as you would a biological grandchild. Bonusgrandkids like to hear those "In my day I walked five miles in the snow to school" stories, too. And the more they know about you, the easier your interactions will become.

3. Go slowly into the new bonusgrandchildren's lives. Don't push yourself on them or force them to kiss or hug you. They will respond naturally to your kindness.

4. Don't say "I love you" if you don't mean it. Kids are very skeptical of declarations of affection from people they don't know well. By the same token, if you feel uncomfortable verbally expressing affection for your new grandchild, start with things like "Aren't you a smart girl!" "Great choice, Scotty!" or "How handsome you look today!" Positive reinforcement makes everyone feel more accepted.

5. Don't play favorites. When giving presents, try to give all grandchildren presents of equal value. Don't sneak extra money for that little something special to the children that are related to you biologically. You can be sure your grandchild, niece, or nephew will let their bonussibling know about the special gift, which will only reinforce the bonuschild's feeling of lack of acceptance. To reinforce that special relationship with your biological grandchild, niece, or nephew, you might set aside a special day or time on a regular basis for just the two of you. If you live far away, send e-mails, or connect via an occasional phone call.

If giving a grandchild *extra* cash is important to you, consider an individual bank account or college fund. You may never feel the same way about bonusrelatives as you do about blood relatives, and that is understandable. But when it comes to children, try to find a way to show your affection that does not make one feel *blatantly* less cared for than the other. This is especially true if the bonuschild's biological relatives are not in the picture. You may be the only chance at having a grandparent, aunt, or uncle, this child has.

6. Remember that children do not choose to get a divorce. It was their parents' idea. You should discuss any anger or resentment you may harbor because of the divorce with the divorced parents. Never direct it toward innocent children.

7. Don't compete with their biological relatives. Get to know them so that they don't feel like you are invading their territory. The biological grandparent may be close to your age and have a lot in common with you. This may be the opportunity to make a new friend who cares for the same people you do. The new bonusgrandchild will also follow the lead of their grandparent. If the grandparent is your enemy, don't expect to be openly accepted by the grandchild.

8. Try not to overcompensate. Being overly nice to the new bonusgrandchild can cause jealousy in your biological grandchild. Just be yourself, and if you aren't sure what to do, be honest. Talk to the parents, and talk to the kids. Talk to a counselor. Or write us via the Bonus Families Web site.

Allegiance to Divorced Friends

"My husband of ten years and I were just divorced. My best friend for twenty-five years has sided with him. I'm devastated about the divorce—and also about the loss of my friend, who is like family to me."

Unfortunately, allegiances are tested when marriages dissolve, and losing an old friend can be part of the fallout after a divorce. When I divorced I had two really good girlfriends that I had known for years. The first had been my best friend since high school. The second I had met in college. My friend from college had been a friend of my ex-husband's before we were married, and I automatically assumed that their relationship would continue after we divorced. By the same token, I assumed that my old friend from high school would automatically choose to continue our relationship. I was wrong on both counts. My friend from high school, now married to a man who had become my ex-husband's best friend, felt compelled to choose one of us over the other, and because the men were so close she felt she had to support her husband. My friend from college, on the other hand, the one I assumed would choose my ex-husband if a choice had to be made, stood her ground. "I love you both," she said. "And I want to remain friends with both of you." Thankfully, that is exactly what happened.

It is human nature to want to side with a friend, to take up his cause and defend him if you feel he has been wronged. Good ex-etiquette, however, suggests that friends do not take sides, but instead allow the couple to work through their differences on their own. By the same token those who are divorcing should not ask their friends to take sides. They should allow friends to make their own decisions about where their allegiance lies.

Part III

ADVANCED EX-ETIQUETTE

Managing the Formalities

8

INTRODUCTIONS, CORRESPONDENCE, AND OTHER CONVENTIONS

"Life is short, but there is always time for courtesy."
—RALPH WALDO EMERSON

Chance Meetings and Graceful Responses

Years ago the possibility of ex-spouses and new partners all show-ing up at Junior's Little League game was very small. Today it's commonplace. And if you are all there, at least one of you is going to be put into the position of introducing someone and explain-ing the relationship. Although this can be awkward, anticipating what you will say if you have to introduce—or be introduced by someone else—will eliminate some of the anxiety.

Good ex-etiquette dictates courtesy and good manners. When greeting new people, even ex-relations, it's best to be cordial. It will be rare that you have to interact with an ex-relation on a social basis when the kids are not present, so for that reason, keep your anger in check and say only what is necessary.

If you share custody of the children, you probably live near each other, and therefore a chance meeting is likely. This can be embarrassing if you are out with a new date and have yet to mention that you are divorced or separated. For that reason, it is best to let new dates know your marital status immediately, especially if you and the ex do not get along but are attempting to co-parent.

My husband, Larry, and his ex-wife, Sharyl, lived in a very small town when Larry and I began to date. There were only one or two nightspots in the entire town. Because Larry and Sharyl could barely speak to each other at that time, they made an agreement about designated days at either nightspot. I remember this because on one of Larry's and my first dates I suggested we go out for dinner, and I was told we couldn't go to the spot I chose "because it was Sharyl's night." An interesting way to handle the situation, but it did employ good ex-etiquette. Even though these two parents were at odds with each other they were looking for a way to eliminate heated confrontations.

When an Ex Asks How You Are

Good ex-etiquette means using tact and timing, and your response today to your ex's question will make or break your future communication. If you are looking for a fight or looking for a way to make an ex feel guilty for leaving you, then a response like, "How do you think I am since you have left us?" will do the trick. It is not, however, good ex-etiquette. Good ex-etiquette suggests you look for a way to have continued comfortable conversations for the sake of future co-parenting. Therefore, if you are having trouble with the breakup, an honest response of "As well as can be expected" rarely starts an argument, but lets the ex know you have a ways to go. If you are doing well, don't be afraid to say so. "Things are just fine. And how are things for you?" If you ask, "How are things for you?" be prepared to listen and respond civilly.

When Someone Compliments an Ex

"I was recently talking to an acquaintance who did not know I was divorced. She complimented my ex. I have to admit, it sent waves of anger through me. I wasn't sure how to respond."

Using good ex-etiquette means you always respond politely and with no apparent malice. This is done for two reasons. First, to squelch gossip. Second, to prevent embarrassing the obviously uninformed person offering the compliment.

The proper response would be to simply agree, "Yes, he is _____ (handsome, smart, a good dancer). But he is no longer my husband."

There will most likely be a pregnant pause. Fill it with something *polite*.

When Someone Inquires About an Ex

"I was recently at a party with friends that I had not seen in a year. One of them asked, "How is your wife?" In fact, my wife and I are now divorced and the marriage did not end on good terms. What is the proper response?"

Those who employ good ex-etiquette are polite at all times. The proper response would therefore be, "Very well, I hope, but we are no longer married." Then if you do not want to explain your personal business, change the subject. Ask them about *their* spouse . . . *their* children . . . how's that new house . . . and how about those Raiders?

Rude and Uncouth Comments

Unfortunately, friends or acquaintances may wonder how exes handle the fact that there have been intimate relations between past and present partners. Friends or acquaintances should not make, nor ask you to make, intimate comparisons of any sort— ever. It does happen on occasion, usually when people with a sarcastic or inquisitive nature have been drinking. I have faced this question a few times and have squelched it with a comment like, "How tacky." Do not feel compelled to discuss, compare, clarify, justify, or explain anything of an intimate nature that went on between past or present partners. It's hard enough to get past it for the sake of the children. You certainly do not have to verbalize your thought process to inquisitive gossipmongers.

Introductions and Announcements

Introducing Ex-Relations

To prevent confusion, it's best to introduce ex-relations clearly and concisely, leaving no room for speculation. For example, let's say you are a former mother-in-law introducing your ex-son-in-law. You would say, "Let me introduce Larry Madison. He was married to my daughter, Louise." If he has remarried, you might add, "But he is now married to Joyce McGregor."

Rather than use references that might promote additional embarrassing questions, always use a reference that can be easily understood. In other words, rather than saying, "This is Leanne Gonzales, my ex-mother-in-law," a preferable way to describe her may be, "This is Leanne Gonzales, my children's grandmother." The trick is to consider to whom you are introducing the ex-relation and then use the proper explanation.

For example, if you are introducing your ex at a social gathering, you may want to introduce him or her as your ex. However, if you are at a parent-teacher conference introducing your ex to your son's teacher, you might say, "This is Travis's father, Michael Smith." Introducing Michael Smith as your ex, in that instance, would be inappropriate and may make the teacher uncomfortable. She may wonder, "Will these two people cooperate? What will I do if they disagree in front of me?"

Some people feel uncomfortable offering personal information during an introduction—especially information that might raise eyebrows. To avoid embarrassment, it is acceptable to introduce an ex-relation to an acquaintance (someone with whom you do not anticipate further contact after this meeting) without an explanation of her relationship to you. To prevent a void in the conversation after the introduction, it is best to interject something that might spark a conversation between the new acquaintances after you leave, such as, "Let me introduce Michael Smith. You two have a lot in common. Mike is also an avid fisherman." If the acquaintance pushes for an explanation, "How did you and Michael meet?" You can then clarify by saying, "He is my son's father," or "He is my ex-husband," whichever you think is appropriate for the person to whom you are introducing Michael Smith.

It will not come as a surprise that Sharyl and I often have the opportunity to introduce each other. We both admit there are times we find it amusing to introduce each other as "my husband's ex-wife" or "my ex-husband's wife," however, under most circumstances I find the description "husband's ex-wife" problematic. Therefore, I often say, "May I introduce Sharyl Jupe." I then say nothing about our relationship but mention that we work together: "Sharyl is my coauthor on my latest book." Or Sharyl might say, "Jann and I write a column for divorced parents on the Bonus Families Web site."

As mentioned previously, the key is to consider to whom you are making the introduction. Most of the time, the best introduction for Sharyl is, "Let me introduce Sharyl Jupe, my bonuschildren's mother." And her best introduction for me is, "Let me introduce Jann Blackstone-Ford, my children's bonusmom."

Introducing Your New Romantic Interest to Your Ex

This was touched on in chapter 3, but it is important enough to be discussed in greater depth. First, if you live within a reasonable distance of each other, it is most respectful to all concerned to schedule a private adult meeting for your introductions without the children present. This may be awkward. Nonetheless, this approach will protect your children from a potentially uncomfortable situation. Nothing more need be discussed at the first meeting other than the introduction.

Even if you do live miles, states, or even countries apart, your child's other parent must be informed that there is someone new in your life. There are many different forms of communication available to you. Perhaps the easiest way to break the news begins with a letter and then a follow-up phone call to clarify any questions. The goal is to inform your ex politely that you are involved with someone and plan to make a life together.

Let's look at an example. Bill and Louise are planning to marry. Inez is Bill's ex-wife. Inez and Bill have one child, Joshua. I suggest Bill make the introduction in this way: "Louise, I'd like to introduce you to Inez, Joshua's mother."

The rules of formal etiquette suggest that a less important or prominent person is always introduced to a more important person, but this can be problematic. Who is the more important person in this situation—the mother of your children or your new partner? Both expect and deserve respect. There's a reason I suggest addressing the women in this particular order—semantics. If Bill introduced Inez to Louise he would have to say, "Inez, I would like to introduce you to my fiancée, Louise." Ex-wives and ex-husbands often cringe at the word *fiancée*, especially if the new couple has evolved very soon after the divorce or if there has been an affair. It may also be problematic to use the word *fiancée* if the man or woman making the introduction was never married to the father or mother of their child. The ex may think, "Oh, so he's marrying *her*, but he wouldn't marry *me*." In this case, using that simple word *fiancée* may set these counterpartners up for a turbulent relationship right from the beginning. No one will be upset at the introduction of Inez as Joshua's mother. She is and always will be.

Introducing Yourself

There are a few different cases in which you may find that you have to introduce yourself, usually because your ex has not done the honors. For example, let's imagine that you are dropping your son off at a birthday party his mother is throwing. Because the mother is busy with the preparations, you find yourself standing next to her new partner's parents. In this case, the most appropriate introduction would be a smile, an extended hand, and the words, "Hello, I'm Michael Smith, Lance's father."

When introducing yourself, it is important not to appear intimidating. As you extend your hand, be empathetic. Put yourself in their place: meeting an ex-relation can be uncomfortable for them. There's no need to stand around and chat about the latest football scores, but there is a need for courtesy. No snickering or sarcasm about your status as "the ex." Acting immature will just make future meetings uncomfortable for everyone, especially the children. If you feel compelled, just excuse yourself and leave politely after your introduction.

If You Are Introduced Incorrectly

At one time or another we have all been introduced incorrectly, but this can be especially embarrassing for both the host and you if you are introduced as the wrong husband or wife. For example, I am often introduced as Sharyl. She is frequently introduced as Jann. People have gone so far as asking us to clarify, "Which one are you?" This is very poor ex-etiquette. Each person is an individual and should be introduced as such.

When someone introduces you incorrectly, correct the person as soon as possible. Even though it can be irritating to be introduced by the name of an ex-husband or new wife, do not be rude. Good ex-etiquette suggests you politely point out the mistake.

If the host introduces you and then leaves, smile, make the correction to the group, and then, when it is comfortable to slip away, find the host and politely inform him or her of the mistake.

Announcing That You Are Getting Another Divorce

People can form allegiances in a very short amount of time. For this reason it is important to use discretion when you announce the dissolution of your second or subsequent marriage.

Begin by informing your children. Remember to inform their other parent (your previous spouse) personally so that she can offer her support should the children need an extra shoulder. Children can become quite attached to their bonusparents, and the support of an understanding parent who is not directly involved with the separation can greatly enhance a child's ability to cope with the disappointment associated with another divorce.

The next step is to tell your parents and extended family. Do not look for relatives to take sides, discuss preferences for one partner over another, or promote a discussion of fault or blame. Such discussions may come back to haunt you, especially if you choose to reconcile or maintain a cordial relationship for the sake of the children you have had together. And you never know when young ears may be listening.

Close friends should then be informed, but there is no need to call everyone you know. News like that travels fast. Occasionally, announcements of the separation are sent out; however, I believe that this is a tacky practice. Good ex-etiquette suggests that if you want people to know of your impending separation, you quietly inform them personally.

If you are a renter and you plan to move, write a letter to your landlord stating the date you will vacate the premises. Wait to inform credit card companies and other creditors until your ex and you have decided who is responsible for debts. You may want to discuss this aspect of the separation process with an attorney.

Names and Other Potentially Confusing Issues
When Parents Have Different Names than Their Children

It can be very confusing when a child has a different last name than her parent or stepparent. In these cases, the relationship should be clarified from the beginning. Let's say the bonusdad is doing the introductions. His name is Jim Brown, and he wants to introduce his bonusdaughter, Michelle Myers, to his friend Bill. Jim Brown could simply say, "Bill, I'd like you to meet my bonusdaughter, Michelle Myers." Or, if the child is old enough to understand proper introductions, she could introduce her bonusfather by simply saying, "This is my bonusdad, Jim Brown." In both examples the relationship between Michelle Myers and Jim Brown is easily clarified in the introduction, and the reason their last names are different is obvious.

Different last names can become a problem, though, when a divorced mother returns to her maiden name or remarries and takes the new husband's last name. Then the child and mother have different last names. The mother will be asked to clarify, and she may find that this causes resentment in the child ("Mommy has the same name as her new husband, but not me"). Some children take the different last name in stride; others find it troubling.

It can also cause problems when a mother remarries, takes the new husband's last name, and then has a child with her new husband. Now the mother has the same last name as one of her children but not the other. To ward off resentment and to prevent confusion, it's not uncommon for mothers in both of these situations to hyphenate their last name. Then she carries the last name of the older child, the younger child, and her new husband. For example, Marie Johnson married John Miller. She then became Marie Miller and had a child. Marie and John divorced, and she married Leo Dickerson. They also have a child. Therefore, Marie chose to use Miller-Dickerson as her last name.

Perhaps the most confusing name situation is when a mother resumes using her maiden name after she is divorced. This guarantees that her name will be different from that of her children. It is really only a problem when the children are young—say, when a mother is meeting teachers or the parents of playmates— but it can be explained in the introduction. It's the same type of introduction as when an older daughter marries and chooses to change her last name. For example, your last name is Miller, and your daughter's name after marriage is Owens. You would simply say, "Let me introduce my daughter, Janet Owens."

Sharyl went back to her maiden name after her divorce. Although I hyphenate my last name professionally, around my neighborhood I am simply Jann Ford. Sharyl's children's last name is Ford. Therefore, I share a last name with my bonuschildren but their mother does not.

I know these explanations sound obvious, but I have found people can be completely at a loss when they have to explain their relationship to ex-family members. A common consequence of their discomfort is that they volunteer far more information than necessary. Relax, consider who is being introduced and to whom, then use the appropriate description when performing the introduction.

When Ex- and New Partners Have the Same Last Name

Confusion often arises when former and new partners have the same name: "Pardon me, but which 'Mrs. Henderson' are you?" This is especially confusing if someone doesn't realize that a divorce and remarriage have occurred.

Some new wives want to be the *only* Mrs. Henderson and resent when the ex-wife retains her ex-husband's last name. It is a woman's right to change her name when she marries and change it back to her maiden name after a divorce. She also has the right to retain her ex-husband's last name if she chooses, and it should not be a bone of contention between ex-wives and new wives. New wives must realize that the first wife's decision to retain her ex's last name is not made just to irritate them. Most women who make the choice to keep their married name do it so that their name will match that of their children.

Although I hyphenate my last name professionally, there are times when I don't. Sometimes I am Jann A. Ford. Sharyl's name when she was married to my husband was Sharyl A. Ford. Jupe is her maiden name. To this day, however, we get each other's bills, bank statements, and junk mail. We can either get upset about it and let it bother us every time we hit the mailbox, or we can let it go. I choose to let it go. Thanks to Sharyl I have received many discount offers through the Victoria's Secret catalog.

When Stepsiblings Have the Same Name

"My husband and I each have young sons named Tom. The two Toms think it is fun right now, but we are concerned it may cause competition between them in the future. To complicate the issue, my child's father has passed away and my husband plans to adopt my son. Then both boys will have the same first and last name. Any suggestions about how to deal with this?"

Technically, this is no different than if these boys were biologically related and the father was Thomas Sr., one son was Thomas Jr., and the other Thomas III. In these cases family members often use nicknames to distinguish among them. The father might be called Thomas, while his son is called Tom or T.J. (for Tom Jr.), and the youngest is called Tommy. Some people also opt to call the third in a row Trey. We have a friend we call Buck to distinguish him from his father.

In this case of the two Toms, however, I suggest that the parents try not to let their own concerns complicate the issue. They should let the boys pick the way they would like to be distinguished from each other.

When People Confuse You with Your Spouse's Ex

I can't tell you how many times this has happened to Sharyl and me. Since we are together quite a lot we often hear, "Which one are you?" Before I changed my hair color, I often heard, "Oh, you're the brunette." I have to admit, I did resent being reduced to a hair color.

Using good ex-etiquette means you don't try to embarrass someone simply for being ignorant and insensitive or for making an innocent mistake. So decide if it is really necessary to make the clarification. Will you see this person again? Knowing any sort of clarification will most likely embarrass the person, consider whether it's worth the trouble.

Here's a perfect example. My family—my husband and all the kids, both bonus and biological—was having dinner at the local pizza parlor. Sharyl was not present, although she has joined us on many occasions. We live in a very small town. Everyone knows everyone. As my family was eating, a woman who knows all of us quite well stopped by the table to say hello. She called me Sharyl during the conversation. All the kids noticed, especially my eleven-year-old who always finds it quite amusing—but I didn't say a word. The woman knew that my name is Jann; she just slipped. So, rather than embarrass her, I let it go. It made for interesting dinner conversation after she left.

When You Are Mistaken for Your Bonuschild's Parent

Some people just assume when they see a child with an adult that the adult must be the child's mother or father. Many even comment on a family resemblance. In an age when biracial marriages, adoptions, and bonusfamilies are commonplace, people should not take for granted that a family resemblance is a uniting factor. A clarification on your part, such as "That's strange, this is my bonusdaughter," will certainly embarrass the person. I have tried it. That's when you get the awkward comment, "Well I guess people start to look alike when they spend a lot of time together." One person then interjected a comment about people looking like their dogs. Lovely.

As I mentioned, my hair is no longer dark like my oldest biological daughter's, but it's very similar in color to that of Sharyl and her daughter, Melanie. As soon as I changed my hair color, Melanie and I were mistaken for mother and daughter. Truthfully, we look nothing alike, but it happens all the time, most likely because of the familiarity of our interaction. At first we clarified the mistake. We stopped, however, when we noted the embarrassment it caused. These were people we met casually and would never see again. To correct them when they were just trying to make conversation seemed impolite.

On the other hand, to allow someone to make the mistake over and over is also impolite. For example, if you are the bonusparent, and while watching your bonusson's Little League game you are continually mistaken for the biological parent *when the biological parent is present*, it is only polite to clarify the mistake. If the biological parent is not active in the child's life, it may not be necessary to make the clarification. I have found that some children are embarrassed that their biological parent does not actively participate in his or her life. These kids would prefer to let people think their bonusparent is their biological parent. So it's best to check with the children and ask how they would like you to handle the situation, assuming that the child is old enough to make that sort of decision. Be very careful not to let your desires for an intact family cloud your decision as to whether you should clarify the relationship. There are plenty of biological parents who are active in their children's lives after divorce or separation, but who cannot get to sports activities because of work or time constraints. It will eventually be embarrassing for all concerned if you do not clarify the relationship in these situations.

What Should the Kids Call You?

Some families are so complex that it's difficult for the kids to describe the various relationships. In conventional families there are two parents. In single-parent homes, obviously, there is only one parent. But in bonusfamilies, your kids may feel overrun by parents—there may be two at mom's house and two at dad's house. If you have combined kids from two or more marriages, there are even more parents to contend with. It can be very difficult for kids to make verbal distinctions among their parents and their bonussibling's parents. When they speak, are they talking about their mom and dad, their mom and bonusdad, their dad and bonusmom, or their bonussiblings' biological parent? How do they keep it straight?

My children are not all related biologically, but after years of growing up together, they are quite close. To avoid saying "my dad and your mom" or "my mom and your dad," all the kids refer to my husband and me as "the parents." They distinguish Sharyl as a separate entity, either as "Sharyl" or "Mom," depending on who is speaking. This was not meant to slight Sharyl; she is also considered "a parent." For the kids it is just easier to distinguish among all of us using that chosen designation. How your children refer to their parents, bonusparents, or a combination thereof is something that will also evolve on its own.

Language Makes a Difference

It's easy to split families into factions without even knowing it. Your kids, my kids. My mom, Mommy's car, Daddy's house. It seems everything continues to be split up between the parents even after the divorce. Even though research tells us that both parents' continued interaction with the kids after divorce is best, the back-and-forth life does constantly remind everyone of the divorce. Without the proper precautions, that lifestyle will never let parent or child settle down into a regular life.

After their parents split up, it's important for kids to feel that they are settled and that they belong. Referring to everything as belonging to either one parent or the other continues to emphasize the split and never really gives kids a sense of their own identity. I am not saying deny the breakup. That's impossible, and certainly unhealthy, but it may be helpful to find ways to refer to cars or homes without personalizing them to be either mom's or dad's. Doing so will give the kids the sense that even though their parents are divorced, both environments, mom's and dad's, are *theirs* too.

For example, rather than always referring to mom's or dad's house, suggest the kids say, "My house with Mom or Dad." In other words, "I'm going back to Mom's house" becomes "I'm going back to my home with Mom." It's all in how you present it.

Here's another example of how we depersonalize things at our house. When we speak about our children, we refer to them as "the kids." Not "our kids" as so many bonusfamilies try, but "the kids." This word choice prevents having to distinguish Larry's child from my child. When we need to talk about an individual child, we simply call her by name. We make it a point never to refer to "your kids" or "my kids," especially when the kids are with us. Our children know who their parents are, but when we distinguish who belongs to whom in front of them, they get offended if one is singled out.

This is not always the case, however. Children who resent their bonusparents, or feel uncomfortable that their parent has remarried too soon after a split, do not like it when their parents and bonusparents refer to them as "our children." It's a loving thought, but the kids may get defensive if they are lumped into an "our" designation too soon. It also opens the door to the "You're not my mother (or father)" comment. The phrase "the kids" does not show favoritism, but includes them all.

What Should I Call My Ex-Stepparent?

"I am the adult child of twice-divorced parents: after my parents divorced each other, they both remarried others, then both divorced again. I had become rather close to both of my stepparents, but they are no longer my stepparents. Is there such a thing as 'ex-stepparents'? And if my parents remarry yet again, will I then have two stepfathers and two stepmothers?"

Just as after a divorce a spouse becomes an ex-spouse, so does a stepparent become an ex-stepparent to the children. Therefore, you cannot have two stepfathers or stepmothers, but you can have two ex-stepparents, or a current and ex-stepparent. This is yet another reason why the word *bonus* is a good choice. Unlike the term *step*, *bonus* is a term of endearment that does not depend on marital status. The title can remain the same even if the parent and bonusparent are divorced. Once a bonus, always a bonus.

Adult children may have complex and diverse relationships with their stepparents. Family membership after divorce is an honorary designation, and whether or not an ex-stepparent is still considered a family member really depends on the relationship that existed while the marriage was still strong. If a stepparent was close to her bonuschildren, and they regarded her as family while she and their father were married, they will most likely continue to regard her as family after divorce, and the relationship does not have to be severed. This often prompts questions of allegiance to and betrayal of the biological parent that should be discussed as openly as possible. As an adult, however, how you choose to maintain the ex-step relationship is ultimately up to you.

A Woman's Name After Divorce

The rules of old-school divorce dictated that a woman could not combine her first name with her ex-husband's last name. For example, if her name were Joy Lowell and she married then divorced Sam Sneed, her name was then Mrs. Lowell Sneed. There was no mention of Joy whatsoever. Using the old-school rule, everyone automatically knew the woman's marital status—she was divorced. It is now acceptable for a woman to use her first name in conjunction with her ex's last name. Therefore, rather than Mrs. Lowell Sneed, she would be Joy Sneed, married or divorced. And current ex-etiquette dictates that once a woman has been married, she may retain the courtesy title of Mrs. after divorce, if she likes.

Clearing Up Confusion at Your Children's School

For years schools have been facing the confusion brought on by divorce or separation. Kids often live in two houses and have more than one adult picking them up or dropping them off. A pet peeve of noncustodial parents is that they never know what is happening in their child's classroom. and if their ex is uncooperative, it can be like playing twenty questions to get some information.

The best approach to staying in contact with a child's school is to take the initiative to write a separate letter to both the teacher and the principal *each year* explaining the situation. Include the following in the letter:

> The proper first and last names of both parents and new partners
> Addresses and phone numbers (both home and work) of both partners
> E-mail addresses of both partners
> A request for two of everything—notices, conferences, and announcements for special events at the school

The letter could say something like "My name is Joyce Martinson. My son's name is Steve DeWitt. He is in Mrs. Livingston's third-grade class. Steven's father and I are divorced, but we share custody of Steve. Steve's dad has remarried. His wife's name is

Sylvia DeWitt. I just wanted to clarify the players to make sure that we receive information about Steve's schooling at both homes. Please make sure you have the following contact information on record. . . ."

Please take note: the most common custody arrangement today is joint custody. Joint custody allows both parents to sign papers for their children, no matter where the children reside. Although many bonusparents sign legal documents or school permission slips for their bonuschildren, by law, they are not supposed to. Some schools do accept the bonusparent's signature as a sign the parent has been notified and permission has been granted. It is best, however, to have an affidavit on file at the school that spells out what the biological parents feel are acceptable bonusparent responsibilities and grants the bonusparent permission to speak for or transport the children.

"Two years ago I was transferred to another state for work, and my ex continually neglects to send me copies of our daughter's schoolwork, progress reports, and report cards. What recourse do I have?"

I have heard many complaints from divorced or separated parents who are angry with their ex for not keeping them up to date on the child's progress in school. Although this is understandable, as a parent it is your responsibility to communicate firsthand with your child's teacher. In a perfect world, divorced parents cooperate with each other. More often they don't. In that case, don't bother to resent the other parent; get out there and get the information yourself. Just about every school today has a computer system, and most teachers are glad to communicate with parents via e-mail. Most elementary school teachers have a weekly newsletter they send home to keep parents up to date. If the child lives with the other parent on a full-time basis, and you do not receive regular information, arrange for your child's teacher to send that newsletter via e-mail. Don't be afraid to ask the teacher for his or her impression of how your child is doing and about what you can do to help her reach her potential.

If you can't be with your child on an everyday basis, there are great ways to work with her so that you know how she is doing in school.

If you live out of state and your child has to do a state report, suggest that she choose the state in which you live. Send travel brochures and pictures of you visiting the landmarks.

If you live in the same state as your child, but you live nearer a landmark of interest, send information and discuss your impression of the landmark to help her to understand why it is important.

Find out about her science projects and look up helpful Web sites to pass along to her.

As the child gets older and books are assigned, find out the titles and read the book along with her. Then, every other day or so, call or e-mail her to discuss your impressions.

When writing letters or e-mails to your child, make sure you use proper language and punctuation!

Correspondence

The Use of Courtesy Titles

When addressing mail to people who are divorced or remarried, formal rules are the easiest to follow. Use *Mr.* when corresponding with a married or divorced man, *Mrs.* for a married or divorced woman, and *Ms.* as a catchall when corresponding with a woman of indeterminate marital status or when the use of that title has been specifically requested.

When a Couple Separates

When a married couple separates, correspondence should no longer be addressed to "Mr. and Mrs." Friends should use good sense and never invite both to a party or get-together without first informing both of them. At that point, it's up to the separated couple as to how they will handle the invitation.

Inappropriate Correspondence

Although it is admirable for exes to stay on cordial terms with each other, this should not be taken to the extreme. It is in very bad taste to use cards, letters, e-mails, or phone calls to commemorate a past anniversary or another special event the couple once shared. A breakup is the end of that relationship as it once existed. Co-parenting after divorce can extend a relationship indefinitely—but not on the same terms as before.

9

BABIES, WEDDINGS, SHOWERS, AND ANNOUNCEMENTS

"We are all serving a life sentence, and good behavior is our only hope for a pardon."

—Douglas Horton, theologian

Many parents who choose to marry have either been married before, have children from previous relationships, or choose to have more children with their new spouse. For these families, old-school etiquette simply doesn't apply. They need new guidelines when interacting with an ex or ex-relatives. This chapter discusses the new acceptable rules of behavior for integrating past and present in these big life events.

Ex-Etiquette When There Is a New Arrival

Good ex-etiquette suggests that your ex be notified well in advance of the arrival of your new baby. Some people may find this odd.

Why would you need to let your ex know that you are having a child with your new partner? If the child you and your ex share is an active member of both of your families, then it is only fitting that the other family be notified of an important event in your child's life. Adding a new child is a milestone, and the existing children need support from both parents' families to help them make the adjustment. Notifying the other parent will enable the parent to be supportive and help prepare the existing child for the new addition.

"What is my role now that my ex is having a child?"

If your ex is having a child, your role is that of the mother or father of the existing children. Your job is to offer helpful, reassuring advice to your children that reminds them that they will not be forgotten because of the birth of a new baby. Saying "Don't worry, honey—you still have *me*" will not comfort your children. It will only serve to undermine their sense of security. Although you are important, the parent whose affection they fear losing at this moment is the one having the new child. They know where you stand. No matter who's having the baby, it's your job as a parent figure to support and reassure the existing children. The best thing you can do for your children when their other parent is adding a child is to reassure them that the other parent's love will not waver. That's good ex-etiquette. Do not use this time as a subtle way to reinforce the child's anxiety, believing it will benefit your relationship with the child in some way. It won't. That sort of behavior only backfires.

"Is it appropriate to buy a gift for my ex's new baby?"

Presents from an ex for the new baby are always welcome, but they should be unemotional in nature and given as a gesture of peace and goodwill. Never include anything that is reminiscent of your past life with your ex: no baby blankets crocheted by your great-aunt for the child you had together and then passed on to this new baby as an heirloom. Your ex's new partner may perceive a gesture of that sort to be inappropriate. It is appropriate, however, to return a baby blanket crocheted by *his* great aunt in order to pass on to the new baby.

If you give a present to your child's new half-brother or -sister, it may be nice to offer a small gift to your child at the same time. This can go a long way toward warding off sibling rivalry. A note reiterating your love and saying how confident you are that he or she will be a terrific big brother or sister may help to dampen the jealousy a new arrival can bring on.

"Who gives the baby shower?"

Previous etiquette rules suggest that the mother and sister of the mother-to-be should not host the baby shower, although sisters-in-law, close friends, aunts, or cousins may. Mothers and sisters should be invited, and may even help with the expenses behind the scene, but it is not good manners for a blood relative to host a shower when a present is expected. Contemporary ex-etiquette follows suit with this rule; however, it could cause problems when there are allegiance issues between the first wife, second wife, and extended family. Let's look at an example.

Michelle was married to Rick for thirteen years and became very close with Rick's sister, Susan. When Michelle and Rick divorced, Michelle and Susan continued their close relationship. When Rick remarried, his new wife, Lara, and Susan also forged a friendship. Susan kept the relationships separate and never talked about one to the other. Then Lara became pregnant. It was her first baby, and she was ecstatic. Although Rick already had two children with Michelle, he, too, was very excited about the new baby. This was a new beginning for them. Being that Susan was Lara's sister-in-law, she was the most likely candidate to host a baby shower. Michelle was furious. "You have been my best friend for more than thirteen years!" she cried. "You are my children's auntie! How could you betray me like this?"

Something that Michelle did not take into consideration was that Susan would also be auntie to Lara's baby. An ex cannot expect an ex-relative to choose between past and present. It is simply unfair for the first wife to expect her former in-law's allegiance to the exclusion of the new relative. Allegiance to former extended-family members must be handled delicately with the understanding that the children are the ties that bind. The former sister-in-law, in this case, Susan, is aunt to her brother's children, no matter who is the mother. These relationships do not change, and if the former sister-in-law were a true friend, she would understand this and not ask extended-family members to choose.

"Should ex-wives be invited to baby showers?"

I am not discounting the possibility, but it is rare for a relationship between the first wife and second wife to progress to the point that both feel comfortable attending a baby shower for the second (or subsequent) wife. The ex-wife's presence may make the other attendees uncomfortable and prompt comparisons that are not in good taste. In general, it is best that ex-wives do not attend the baby showers of the next wife.

There is a time when the first and second wife may feel comfortable attending the same baby shower—when the baby shower is for their daughter or bonusdaughter. If they have worked through their issues and can be in the same room together, it is perfectly acceptable for both to attend. It is very selfish to tell an expectant mother, "If *she* is going to be there I won't come." Offering ultimatums of that sort is in extremely poor taste and goes against every rule of ex-etiquette. Follow the daughter's lead. If she is comfortable with both being in attendance, then both may happily accept the invitation. Of course, first wives and second wives are both free to attend the baby shower of a mutual friend.

"Should baby showers be held for single mothers?"

It is not uncommon today for babies to be born outside of marriage. Whether it is your moral choice or not, baby showers are celebrations designed to help the parents prepare for the new arrival. If anyone needs help preparing for a new arrival, it's a single mother. Therefore, the same rules of ex-etiquette mentioned for all baby showers apply to showers for single mothers.

"I am going to be a single mother. How should I handle the announcement?"

If the mother has never married, she should sign the birth announcements using her first and last name, with either Miss or Ms. if she chooses to use a title. If the mother is recently divorced from the father of the child, the birth of a child is nonetheless a happy event, and therefore an announcement of a birth is still in good taste. In this case the announcements should not be signed Mr. and Mrs. Bill Morrison, but with the name the mother will use after the breakup—Jenny Morrison (if she's decided to retain her husband's last name). If the father of the child passed away before the birth, the mother should sign the birth announcement using either Mrs. Bill Morrison or Jenny Morrison, but not Mr. and Mrs. Bill Morrison.

Bonusfamily Bridal Showers, Wedding Showers, and Weddings

Bonusfamily weddings are typically more complicated than first marriage ceremonies because they involve so many people with highly charged emotional attachments to one another. First, there is the new couple with kids from a prior union. Add to that three or more sets of relatives, extended family, and friends, including at least one and maybe more ex-partners, and you have quite a tangled endeavor. Bonusfamily weddings can also be problematic because there are no established rules to help couples or clergy resolve the questions brought about by these complex unions. Hopefully this section will serve as that much needed guideline.

When This Is Your First Marriage

Just because there are children and an ex, that does not necessarily mean that either partner has previously been married. If this is your situation, you may be looking forward to a wedding shower and a large formal wedding. There are some things to consider, however. Getting married with children is not the same as getting married without children. Children's allegiances vary a great deal, and you must take that into consideration when you bond with another partner. When there are children, first marriages are often smaller, more discreet, and centered around family rather than merely the union of the two adults.

When Only the Groom Has Been Married Before

If the bride has not been married before, but the groom has, the wedding can be approached as a conventional first marriage, but there will be some exceptions to consider. If your fiancé has been married, but had no children, you might think there are no "ex" issues to consider. This is not so. For example, if your partner's ex has died, your fiancé may still be close to his ex-in-laws and ex-extended-family members and want to invite them to the wedding. You must be gracious and accept his obligations to past relatives.

If your fiancé has children from a previous marriage or relationship, the children will become part of your family and should be included in the wedding ceremony. Examples of how to include children in your wedding ceremony will be discussed later in this chapter.

When Only the Bride Has Been Married Before

If the bride has been married before but has no children, the wedding can be as elaborate as the couple would like. Actually, *any* wedding can be as elaborate as the couple would like; it just depends on how much scrutiny they want from the outside world. For example, let's say the bride is a widow, has stayed in contact with her ex-in-laws and extended family, and now wishes them to share in her happiness of finding another. If this is the case, it would be in poor taste to have another wedding of the same caliber as the first wedding. If the bride's previous wedding was annulled, then, technically speaking, the bride has never been married and her wedding may be approached as a first wedding.

The Encore Wedding (Second Weddings)

For simplicity's sake, I refer to second or subsequent weddings as "encore weddings" and women marrying for the second or subsequent time or women with children from previous relationships, "encore brides." I know that women who have never married are not technically encore brides, but most who have had children had rather lengthy previous relationships; therefore, they may also be referred to as "encore."

While parents or relatives usually finance first weddings for younger brides and grooms, a couple marrying for the second time—or a couple that has lived together for a great amount of time—usually pays for their own wedding. The ceremony and reception should be designed around their interests as individuals and their mutual interests as a couple. Second wedding celebrations tend to be more casual than first weddings. Interestingly, I have found that in couples marrying for the second time, the grooms tend to be more involved in the wedding planning, and many of the decisions are made as a couple rather than by the bride and her mother, as in first weddings. It can be a great help when the groom gets involved—or it can be exasperating. Before they begin to plan the wedding, couples must come to an agreement about which of them has the final word. Otherwise they might not make it to the altar!

Showers for Encore Brides Legend suggests that the first bridal shower was given for a Dutch bride who chose to marry a humble miller with little money. The bride's father disliked her fiancé because he was poor, so he refused to give her a dowry. The couple married in spite of the father's discontent, and the groom's friends pitched in to "shower" the bride with gifts of household necessities for the couple's new home. Thanks to the shower, the couple had the necessary items to begin their life together.

Bridal showers are perfectly appropriate for encore brides. In fact, a shower is an excellent way for a bride to include her fiancé's children in the planning and celebration. Here are some suggestions about how children can help in the preparation for both a shower and the wedding.

> Children can help make favors for both the shower and the wedding.
> Children can help with the planning, setup, and cleanup of the shower.
> Children can help greet and seat guests at the bridal shower. The ushers usually seat guests at the wedding. If a child is an usher, he may also seat guests at the wedding.
> Children can take notes when the presents are opened at the shower.

"Who throws the bridal shower for an encore bride?"

The matron or maid of honor or other good friends are most often the ones to host a bridal shower. Parents, brothers, sisters—either biological or bonus—or other extended family may help financially, but usually they are not the ones to send out the invitations. This is because bridal showers—even encore bridal showers—are meant to show support from the community, and it would appear rather self-serving if a blood relative hosted a party for the sole purpose of recruiting presents for an immediate family member.

"Who is invited to the encore bridal shower?"

It's usually mostly women that attend bridal showers. The bride prepares the guest list and passes it along to the person hosting the shower. No one should be invited to a shower who is not invited to the wedding. Important people to remember are the bride's or her fiancé's older children, the mother and bonusmother of both the bride and the groom, and any ex-relatives the bride feels it is important to include. This is especially true if either the fiancé's previous relationship or the bride's previous relationship ended because of the death of a past partner.

No matter how close the connection may be between the new bride and her fiancé's ex-wife (perhaps the couple has lived together for years before marrying, and the women have been coparenting and come to know one another well), it is inappropriate for the ex-wife to attend the bridal shower. This is a celebration of the new bride's upcoming union. The presence of a past partner at the bridal shower may prompt inappropriate comparisons that may embarrass the new bride or the children from previous relationships, should they be in attendance. Let me clarify this statement. The couple knows who qualifies as "a past partner" and who is truly a friend. Many people stay friendly with someone they have dated in the past and, together with their new partner, maintain that friendly relationship. If this is the case, and the bride is comfortable with that person being in attendance, it is up to the bride to decide.

If you are an ex-partner in this situation, you should be aware that if you are asked how you know the bride, an appropriate answer would be, "I have known Jerry, Lucy's fiancé, since college. When he met Lucy we became friends." Not, "Oh, Jerry and I dated all through college and now I'm friends with Lucy." Frankly, talking about dating all through college implies that you have slept with Lucy's fiancé, and that sort of information at Lucy's bridal shower can only bring her embarrassment. It is inappropriate to volunteer information that may bring on gossip and speculation. If you are attending Lucy's bridal shower, you owe your allegiance to Lucy.

In the past, etiquette dictated that if a friend attended the festivities associated with a first wedding, she need not attend the festivities associated with the second, but this is no longer the case. Many people stay friends through thick and thin, together surviving the turmoil of divorce and then celebrating when the divorced friend finds someone new with whom to share her future. A friend who attended the first bridal shower may again offer a present for an encore bridal shower, though it need only be a small token that represents her best wishes for the future. One of the most cherished gifts I received was from a very old friend for my second marriage: a book of love poems by Emily Dickinson, a bottle of wine, and two lovely wine glasses.

"What is the difference between a bridal shower and a wedding shower?"

The original purpose of the bridal shower was for the community to help young couples just starting their life together. It was rare that couples lived together before marriage, and the bridal shower helped the bride acquire the little extras needed to start married life. People who have children or have been married before rarely need those little extras to begin their life together, and the shower serves another purpose—a celebration of the upcoming marital union. For this reason, wedding showers as opposed to bridal showers are quite popular for second marriages or for couples who are marrying and have children from previous relationships (or couples who are marrying and have children together). Both the bride and the groom attend a wedding shower. Wedding showers often have a theme, such as:

Couples shower (other couples are invited)
Lingerie shower

Recipes shower

Activity shower (for example, if the new bonusfamily enjoys snow skiing, the gifts would be related to that activity)

Entertainment shower (guests offer presents in the form of gift certificates to a favorite restaurant, movie, or concert)

Spa getaway shower

Period shower (attendees dress up according to theme and the entertainment is centered around the theme; for example, a Great Gatsby wedding shower)

Gardening shower (gardening tools or landscaping accessories)

Barbecue shower

Surprise showers are not in good taste. After all, the bride suggests the guest list. If she does not know there will be a shower, someone may be forgotten—especially if this is a second marriage with new relatives. Anyone who wishes to throw a shower for a friend or a couple about to be married should ask permission. She should also ask for the couple's help in developing a schedule, a theme (if any), and guidelines concerning gifts.

Encore Registry Many couples, even those entering a second or subsequent marriage, register for gifts at department stores. This should be noted in the invitation. Guests are not required to buy a gift from the bridal registry; the registry merely offers suggestions. Guests should always feel free to bring special gifts that express their personal wish to the couple for happiness in the future.

Encore Bachelor and Bachelorette Parties Bachelor and bachelorette parties are adult affairs that serve as a symbolic right of passage from single to married life. The best man or maid of honor usually hosts the bachelor or bachelorette party. There is no etiquette associated with today's bachelor or bachelorette parties, and just about anything goes—from spa weekends to strippers. The conversation and antics associated with bachelor and bachelorette parties are inappropriate for children. If the bride or groom has kids, babysitting arrangements should be made.

Bachelor parties are rarely held for grooms marrying for the second or subsequent time, but it's not unheard-of. I have attended bachelorette parties for women who are planning a second or subsequent marriage. Truth be told, they were rather brazen affairs, far more racy than any first-time bachelorette party I ever attended.

Encore Protocol—How Long Should You Wait Before Remarrying? The time you spend grieving the death of a spouse is very personal, but etiquette suggests widows and widowers wait at least a year before remarrying. There are a few reasons for this. First, it shows respect for those who have died. Second, the more time between marriages, the less likely it is that the second or subsequent marriage will be a rebound relationship. If there are children, there is another reason couples should wait at least one year. It shows respect for the kids. Actually, children will most likely prefer that their parent wait even longer than a year after the death of a beloved parent. The parent may be ready to move on, but the kids, no matter their age, will probably need more time. Although it is important to move on, parents should be sensitive to their children's mourning period when they set their wedding date.

Ex-etiquette suggests that a divorced individual may remarry the day after their divorce is final. Although few follow the rule, a divorced person should not announce his or her desire to remarry until both parties are legally divorced. A woman may accept, but should not wear her new engagement ring in public, until both she and her fiancé are legally divorced.

When a widow becomes engaged after the death of a spouse, she should stop wearing her engagement ring from her first marriage, but she may continue to wear her wedding ring until she officially remarries. It's not uncommon for widowed mothers to save rings from their first marriage for their children to use when they marry. Or, the mother may choose to have another piece of jewelry made from the stones.

When a woman divorces, she does not continue to wear her ring on her wedding finger, and she, too, may choose to pass her wedding ring on to the children of that marriage. She may wear the ring on her right hand or have the stones reset in another piece of jewelry. She may wear the new piece or pass it on to a child.

Encore Wedding Notification When you decide to get remarried you should tell your children first. Your ex should be notified soon after. Next, notify the bride's parents. If they are divorced, tell the custodial parent first, and then move on to the noncustodial parent. If both parents shared custody equally, the decision about whom to call first is up to you. The next people to receive a call are the groom's parents. If they are divorced, again, start with the custodial parent.

Preparing the Children for Your Encore Marriage If you have followed the rules of ex-etiquette up to this point, getting married is a natural progression to your relationship, and your children should not be surprised. It is important that you and your spouse-to-be discuss with the existing children your hopes and dreams for the future. Even more important, however, is that the children are able to be frank about their concerns. They should feel comfortable expressing their excitement or apprehension about the upcoming event.

As a rule, it's best to let the biological parent tell her children about her decision to marry. If a couple chooses to be together when they tell the kids, it is also important to find private time to address any concerns the children may have that they do not want to raise in front of the fiancé. The parent can then calm their fears and understand if the children have any reservations.

Some children struggle with feelings of disloyalty to the other parent if they openly show their excitement about the upcoming wedding. All parent figures—not just mom or dad, but extended-family members, as well—must be prepared to respond to the children's concerns and offer soothing support when they express their insecurities about a parent remarrying.

I must say, as a woman excited about her remarriage, it was difficult to hear my eight-year-old bonusdaughter express her concern for her mother, Sharyl. She was worried that her mommy would feel left out because of all the excitement surrounding the approaching wedding. It's a very natural reaction. We had to take great care for fear of severely alienating the kids as well as Sharyl.

Support from the other biological parent cannot be overemphasized. It is to Sharyl's credit that she reassured her daughter that she was just fine and even helped Melanie press the dress she was wearing in the ceremony the morning of the wedding. Sharyl's response to her child's anxiety helped our wedding run smoother.

Make sure that your excitement does not blind you to the fact that your children or bonuschildren are having a difficult time of it. Look for clues as to how they are feeling and don't be afraid to initiate family counseling if you do not feel equipped to tackle the emotional turmoil sparked by your desire to marry.

What to Do with the First Wedding Ring and Other Heirlooms Family heirlooms should be returned to the family of origin when a couple divorces, unless a pledge is made to pass the heirloom on to a child produced from the union. For example, my wedding ring from my first marriage was a family heirloom cherished by my ex-husband's family. It was made of gold that had been panned in the California Gold Rush. The dates of four marriages were set in the ring—the date my ex-husband's great-grandparents wed, the date his grandparents wed, the date his parents wed, and the date we wed. To ensure safekeeping, when my first husband and I divorced, I returned the ring to his family. Sharyl had the diamond from her first wedding ring made into a ring for her daughter.

Preparing the Children for the Encore Wedding Day A child's response to the news that you are getting married may be dampened by the fact that kids don't know what to expect. Upon hearing that her mother and bonusdad were getting married, one four-year-old girl with whom I have worked in the past said, "No! I don't want to go up in a balloon!" It seems that the only wedding she had ever seen was one on television. A minister married the couple, both of whom were hot-air balloon enthusiasts, as they floated over Napa Valley. The little girl was terrified by the heat blasts that lifted the balloon, and she had no desire to participate in such an event. So when her mother told her she was getting married and wanted to plan the wedding, the first thing the little girl imagined was being up high, near fire, with no way to get down.

Most kids have never been to a wedding. Their frame of reference is what they have seen on TV or what their friends have told them. When talking to them about upcoming nuptials, don't assume that they know what to expect or that they understand their responsibilities. Make sure you clarify what a wedding means to your family. Is it a formal affair in a church? Is it a party at grandma's house? Is it just the family skiing in Colorado? After you have given them enough information that they understand what you envision, that's when you can ask them how they would like to participate. If you ask them to participate without clarification, you may not see the enthusiasm you hoped for.

Addressing Adult Children's Concerns About a Parent's Encore Marriage
Many children—and adult children are no exception—find a parent's remarriage a confusing time. Even if a divorce or a parent's passing happened years ago, the news of remarriage stirs all sorts of feelings. The older the child, the greater his sense of loyalty to the other parent—or perhaps more accurately, the more verbal he may become about his loyalty to the other parent. All kids may have the same issues of allegiance and betrayal; older children are just more inclined to voice them.

My experience tells me that older children's primary concern is that not enough time has passed before the remarriage. This is particularly common in cases where a parent has died and the surviving parent wishes to remarry. At that point it is vital that the proper preparation is done—open conversations, counseling, and lots of interaction between the new bonusparent and the adult child. The bonusparent should reinforce that he in no way wants to compete with the memory of the parent who has passed, but rather to share in the family's future. He should be willing to discuss the parent who has died and not let possible insecurities about "competing with a ghost" get the best of him.

Choosing Attendants for Encore Weddings Some parents who are remarrying feel compelled to ask their child to be best man or maid of honor. While this is a lovely gesture, there are some practical matters to consider. If you are having a large wedding, the maid of honor and best man are the logical choices to help with the organization. If you have chosen your young child to be your primary attendant, you will be on your own in terms of getting everything in order. If this is your choice, you may want to explain to one of the ushers and/or bridesmaids that you have chosen your child for that spot as a sign of your love for him, but you could really use an *adult's* help.

My husband and I married at home in front of about seventy-five people. My husband's son was barely four, but he loved the idea of being his father's best man. My daughter and my bonus-daughter were my attendants. Our children stood next to us as we married, and we all exchanged rings to symbolize the joining of our two families in marriage.

We did not approach the decision to handle our wedding in this manner without a lot of soul-searching and family meetings. If our children had not been ready for our marriage, to ask them to be our personal representatives would have put too much pressure on them. Our children were quite ready for the wedding to take place, but this is not always the case. Before you ask your child to be your best man or maid of honor, make sure he views your invitation—to stand beside you as you marry another—as the compliment you feel it is. It is also important to consult the child's other parent when a child plays such an active part in the wedding ceremony. He or she may view this participation as placing the child in the middle, so special care must be taken.

The Guest List for Encore Weddings Just as in a first marriage, the guest list should include the bride and groom's family, plus mutual friends. If one of the people marrying has been widowed and has remained close to his or her in-laws after the death of his spouse, then of course those former in-laws should be invited. This may be difficult for new partners to understand until they consider that the in-laws of the deceased spouse are their new bonuschildren's grandparents. It is the responsibility of new bonusparents to continue to support an existing relationship between grandparent and grandchild, or aunt or uncle and niece.

Ex-in-laws are rarely invited to a second marriage if the first marriage ended in divorce. The exception is when everyone involved has remained friendly enough that the children would think it strange that their relatives were not included on the guest list. The gauge is the comfort level of all concerned. It can easily be explained to children that "I also love grandma and grandpa very much, but they are not coming to the wedding." I suggest you say it exactly that way—use the phrase "not coming." The phrase "not invited" will perhaps hurt the children's feelings. A personal phone call to the ex-in-laws explaining your continued affection—and the awkwardness of the situation—will likely be accepted and understood. Suggest a private dinner where you can all meet, talk, and relax.

Wedding Invitations for Encore Weddings Wedding invitations for second or subsequent weddings can be anything from traditional to quite creative. The wording, again, is up to you, especially if both partners were previously married. Following are some examples of encore wedding invitations for just about every situation.

When the bride and groom issue their own invitations:

The honor of your presence

is requested

at the marriage of

Mary Elisabeth Alexander

to

Michael Kenneth Buttons

on

Saturday, the fourth of June

Two thousand and four

at four o'clock in the afternoon

Christian Country Church

Grass Valley, California

or

Ms. Mary Elisabeth Alexander

and

Mr. Michael Kenneth Buttons

request the honor of your presence

at their marriage

on

Saturday, the fourth of June

Two thousand and four

at four o' clock

Christian Country Church

Grass Valley, California

When guests are invited to a reception that immediately follows the ceremony, then this would be noted at the bottom of the invitation:

Reception immediately following at

Discovery Bay Country Club

Discovery Bay, California

It is not uncommon for second weddings to be small and private, but have a large reception. The reception can follow the wedding or be held at another time. If this is your choice you may want to invite the guests to the wedding personally, and then send out an invitation to the reception that looks similar to this one:

Mary Elisabeth and Michael Buttons

request the pleasure of your company

at the reception of their marriage

Saturday, the fourth of June

Two thousand and four

four o'clock

Discovery Bay Country Club

Discovery Bay, California

When a couple has been living together:

Mary Elisabeth Alexander

and

Michael Kenneth Buttons

invite you to share in the joy of their marriage

Saturday, the fourth of June

Two thousand and four

at four o'clock

Christian Country Church

Grass Valley, California

When a couple would like to include the names of their children:

Mary Elisabeth Alexander and Michael Kenneth Buttons

together with their children,

Samantha Alexander and Susan Buttons

request the honor of your presence

at their marriage

on the fourth of June

Two thousand and four

at four o'clock

Christian Country Church

Grass Valley, California

If the bride is a widow or divorced:

The honor of your presence

is requested at the marriage of

Mrs. Mary Elisabeth Alexander

to

Mr. Michael Kenneth Buttons

Saturday, the fourth of June

Two thousand and four

at four o'clock

Christian Country Church

Grass Valley, California

If the divorced or widowed bride feels the title "Mrs." is too formal or inappropriate, she may choose to not use it.

When the grown children of an older couple host the wedding:

Mrs. Mary Lions

Mr. and Mrs. Larry Ford

Mr. and Mrs. Mark Buttons

Mr. Scott Buttons

request the honor of your presence

at the marriage of their parents

Mary Elisabeth Alexander

to

Michael Kenneth Buttons

When the bride and groom's children are hosting the wedding, then their names may appear on the invitation, listing the oldest child first. In the example above, the oldest daughter of Mary Elisabeth Alexander is divorced and uses her married last name. The next one listed is Mary Elisabeth's younger daughter who is married to Larry Ford. She could have also been listed as

Bridget and Larry Ford. The next couple listed, Mr. and Mrs. Mark Buttons, is Michael Buttons's oldest son and his wife. Mr. and Mrs. Mark Buttons could also have been listed as Mark and Louise Buttons. Or, if Mark has a partner and they are not married but consider themselves life partners, they may be listed as Mr. Mark Buttons and Ms. Louise Lewis. Mr. Scott Buttons is Michael Buttons's youngest son. Courtesy titles can be left off if the people hosting the wedding want a less formal tone for the invitations.

No Kids Allowed It is impolite to mandate "No children" on the invitation. The easiest way to approach this is to list only the names of the adults on the envelope accompanying the invitation. This is where things get tricky. If you list your children on the invitation, some guests with children may assume that children are invited to the wedding. If you get a phone call asking if children are invited, that would be your opportunity to clarify that only adults will be attending the ceremony and to state whether children are invited to the reception.

Once you make your decision, there should be no exceptions. It is sure to alienate guests when they realize that some children were invited while their children were not.

When Children Are Invited Children should sit with their parents at the wedding, but at the reception a separate table is often set for older children, ages eight through approximately twelve. The quickest way to alienate teenagers and therefore make their parents (your guests) miserable is to expect them to sit with the little kids. A separate table should be set for teens.

Encore Wedding Attire for the Wedding Party Long gone are the days of a rigid dress code, and second-time brides can feel free to wear almost anything they want at their wedding. From a traditional wedding gown to a suit or simple dress, anything is fine. Ex-etiquette tells us that white is now considered symbolic of joy rather than virginity, so if the bride has dreamed of that long flowing wedding dress but could never afford it, now is the time to consider it—or not. It's up to her. Some people believe frilly traditional white wedding gowns look silly on brides who are over forty. If you are a member of this club, there are lots of tasteful dress designs from which to choose.

If the bride does choose to wear a traditional wedding dress, she should consider a simple off-the-face veil—nothing too long or covering her face. That style is still reserved for first-time brides who have never had children.

Wedding attire is really dictated by the formality of the wedding. If you have chosen to marry in a church or synagogue, then a formal wedding gown or even a dressy suit is appropriate. The groom should wear the appropriate tux when the bride chooses a gown, or a nice dark suit if the bride chooses a dressy suit. Colors should be coordinated and the style of the bridesmaid's dresses should follow the same lines as the bride's choice of dress. If the bride chooses even less formal attire, like a sarong on the beach, then the groom and wedding party follow suit.

Wedding Attire for Single Mothers and Pregnant Brides There are all sorts of moral and religious implications associated with this question, so I will answer it purely from an ex-etiquette standpoint.

Having children outside of marriage is not as frowned upon as it once was. And pregnant brides may not be commonplace, but they are certainly not the moral dilemma they were once considered to be. With this in mind, a single mother or pregnant bride may feel free to wear white, which is no longer symbolic of virginity but of joy. A traditional wedding gown is fine, but elaborate veils are inappropriate.

Ultimately, good taste is what really dictates the choice of dress for a pregnant bride. If she is three months pregnant and barely showing, then a conventional gown may be fine. If she is eight months pregnant and waddling down the aisle, a more conservative outfit would be more appropriate. The final goal is to look dignified, cut gossip to a minimum, and not bring embarrassment to any member of your family. That is the essence of good ex-etiquette.

Involving the Children in the Encore Wedding When you have children, it's not just you and your partner making a commitment to marry, you are making the commitment to combine your two families. Research tells us that children who actively participate in the wedding seem to adjust more easily to family blending.

Of course all parents want their children to be as enthusiastic about their wedding as they are, but the degree to which your children participate in the ceremony should be up to them. Talk to your kids and ask them if and how they would like to participate. Some kids love the idea of reciting something poignant at the ceremony, while others shudder at the thought of standing up in front of a lot of people and would be content with just a reference about them in the vows.

There are many age-appropriate ways kids can participate. Young children can be flower girls or ring bearers. Older children can be ushers or bridesmaids. My own bonusson was four at the time of my marriage to his father, and he was delighted by the fact that he was asked to be best man. We let him pick the color and the style of his tux. It was the smallest tux I had ever seen, but a tux all the same, and helping to pick it out made the occasion fun for him. Weddings are serious occasions, but kids are kids. Include them in the preparations and make them fun and interesting, and the kids will look forward to the wedding. Portray the preparations as a stressful time, and your kids will see the wedding as stressful and be more inclined to dread the upcoming event.

Here are some other ways to incorporate your children into your wedding ceremony:

Have them sit in the front row, and reference them during the ceremony.

Allow them to light a candle at some point during the ceremony.

Offer them a flower from your bouquet at some time during the ceremony.

Allow them to read a favorite verse or simply talk about their
expectations at the appropriate time in the ceremony.

Have them sing a song.

Have them pass out programs, throw rice or birdseed, or blow
bubbles (whichever the wedding party chooses to use).

Have them oversee the guestbook.

Our children joined us when the vows were exchanged and
they were presented with small gold rings as a symbol
of family unity.

When a date has been set, it is important to notify your child's
other parent and discuss his feelings about the children participating in your wedding. Whether the other parent approves of the children's participation or not, children should always be allowed to
attend their parents' weddings. The only exception is if the children
choose not to attend. If this is the case, it's an obvious red flag that
should be addressed immediately in family counseling.

The Processional for Encore Weddings For encore weddings the processional, or the trip down the aisle, can be as traditional or as
nontraditional as you like. At the most touching encore wedding
I have ever attended, the entire bonusfamily walked down the
aisle of the church together. Each adult had one child from a previous relationship and they each held their own child's hand as
they walked. The minister waited for them at the end of the aisle,
before walking up the three stairs to stand at the pulpit, the
mother and father of both the bride and groom who sat in the
front row on their designated sides of the church, both rose,
walked over and kissed their adult child on the cheek, then they
kissed their adult child's new partner on the cheek and sat down
as the ceremony began. The children then sat in the front row
with their grandparents until they were asked to rise, walk up the
three stairs to their parents and the minister, and light a candle
with their parents as a symbol of unity. The symbolic message of
cooperation and acceptance was lovely and that was the feeling

communicated throughout the ceremony and into their life together.

The choice for the family to walk down the aisle together does not follow old-school etiquette rules, but the choice was lovely and communicated exactly what this family wanted to say to their guests. According to good ex-etiquette, as long as your processional communicates love and cooperation, it is the right choice.

Demonstrating Family Unity at Encore Weddings There are quite a few different ways to symbolize family unity during a bonusfamily wedding ceremony. Perhaps the most dramatic is when both parents and their children stand together during the ceremony and pledge their commitment to combine families. Wedding rings are exchanged between the parents while smaller rings are offered to the children as a gesture of family unity.

I am currently aware of two resources for symbols of family unity suitable for wedding ceremonies. Roger Coleman, a Christian minister from Kansas, developed the Family Medallion as a symbol for incorporating children into a wedding ceremony. The Family Medallion symbol includes three equally merged circles. Two circles represent the marriage union while the third symbolizes the importance of children within the family. You can learn more about the Family Medallion by visiting www.familymedallion.com.

After years of being asked, Bonus Families also offers jewelry designed specifically for weddings that combine families. You can view the designs at www.bonusfamilies.com.

If the Kids Are Very Young As a special wedding present to yourself and your new spouse, ask a trusted friend or relative to watch the little ones so you can attend to your guests without worrying about the children.

Encore Wedding Vows One of the most difficult decisions I had to make when I chose to remarry was which passage to use for our vows. We wanted something poignant and meaningful, and it was difficult to find anything that really communicated how we felt. We wanted something lovely and simple that would integrate the children into the ceremony. Following are some ideas for vows for a variety of second-wedding situations.

If you are having a religious ceremony, begin by checking with the minister, priest, or rabbi to see if there are any standardized words of faith you might use. You may have to adapt the words of a first-time wedding ceremony to something more appropriate to your situation. There is one line I always remind encore couples to modify: "Who gives this woman in marriage?" This is an appropriate question at a first wedding when the father "gives away" the bride. It is rare that a father plays the same role at an encore wedding, so this question is not appropriate. A more appropriate version might be, "Who will support this new family with their love and prayers?" Everyone attending the wedding can answer that one with a hearty "I do!"

There are many books and Web sites that offer help with choosing the words exchanged during encore marriage vows. The vows I've listed here are some that I felt might be helpful. At the very least they may start you on the road toward writing your own vows. Feel free to select different portions of these suggested vows and fine-tune them to your own needs.

Traditional wedding vow:

"I, _____, take you, _____, to be my lawful wife/husband, to have and to hold from this day forward. For better, for worse, for richer, for poorer, in sickness and in health . . . for all eternity."

or

"I, _____, take you in the presence of God and these witnesses, to be my wife/husband. I promise to love you, to honor you in good times and in bad, to respect our dif-

*ferences and cherish our similarities, to confide my feel-
ings and listen to yours, and to console you when you are
in despair. I will give thanks for you each and every day,
and cherish you with all my heart until our time on earth
together has ended.*"

or

"*I, _____, standing beside you in front of these witnesses, say to you with all my love that in finding you,
God has given me a second chance at happiness—a
chance I never thought possible to find again in my lifetime. He has given me you not to lead nor to follow, but
to stand at my side as my partner through life. I come
today to offer my love and to join my heart with yours.
Because of you I laugh and smile and dream again, and I
again look forward to the future.*"

If you do not feel comfortable with the reference to God in
the above vow, you may want to make the following changes:

"*I, _____, standing beside you in front of these witnesses, say to you with all my love that in finding you,
Life has given me a second chance at happiness—a chance
I never thought possible to find again in my lifetime. You
are here not to lead nor to follow, but to stand at my side
as my partner through life. I come today to offer my love
and to join my heart with yours. Because of you I laugh
and smile and dream again, and I again look forward to
the future.*"

Reference to your children in your vows:

*_____, I choose you as the person with whom I will
spend my life. I take you, with all your faults and your
strengths, as I offer myself to you with my faults and my*

strengths. I will trust in you, and I will keep your confidences. I will help you when you need help, and will turn to you when I am in need. I will care for all of our children and offer them a strong and loving home. Before these witnesses I pledge to love and care for you and our family as long as I live."

or

"_____, I promise to be a good and faithful husband/wife to you, and also a patient, loving parent figure to (children's names). I promise to care for them and provide for them as my own. I promise to be their strength and their emotional support, and always hold them dear. I promise to respect this new family and do everything in my power to make it be a safe haven for each of us."

The children can repeat a variation of the above, either separately or together, or the person performing the ceremony can ask the children the following questions. The children should repeat "We do" after each question.

Officiate: *And now, (children's names), do you promise to care for _____ as your bonusparent?*

Children: *We do.*

Officiate: *To treat him/her with respect as a member of your new bonusfamily and know that he/she cares for you as one of his/her own?*

Children: *We do.*

Officiate: *Do you promise to be an active member of this new family with the understanding that your mother (or father) and _____ understand the importance of both of your*

families, your new bonusfamily and your other family with your father (or mother), and do not wish you to choose one over the other, but to love and be loved by both?
Children: *We do.*

or

"I, _____, choose you, _____, and our children, _____, to be my family. I promise to honor and respect all of you, and to make our home a sanctuary where trust, love, and laughter abound. I make these promises with all my heart and soul, and vow to honor them all the days of my life."
The children repeat the same pledge.

"The Blessing of the Apaches" (author unknown)

*"Now you will feel no rain,
for each of you will be shelter for the other.
Now you will feel no cold,
for each of you will be warmth to the other.
Now there will be no loneliness,
for each of you will be companion to the other.
Now you are two bodies,
but there is only one life before you.
Go now to your dwelling place,
To enter into the days of your togetherness.
And may your days be good and long upon the earth."*

"Wedding Blessing" (author unknown)

"Treat yourselves and each other with respect, and remind yourselves often of what brought you together. Give the highest priority to the tenderness, gentleness, and kindness that your connection deserves. When frustration, difficulty, and fear assail your relationship—as they threaten all relationships at one time or another—remember to focus on what is right between you, not only the part which seems

wrong. In this way, you can ride out the storms when clouds hide the face of the sun in your lives—remembering that even if you lose sight of it for a moment, the sun is still there. And if each of you takes responsibility for the quality of your life together, it will be marked by abundance and delight."

Passage from *Corinthians 13:4–7*

"Love is patient; love is kind and envies no one. Love is never boastful, nor conceited, nor rude; never selfish, not quick to take offense. Love keeps no score of wrongs; does not gloat over other men's sins, but delights in the truth. There is nothing love cannot face; there is no limit to its faith, its hope, and its endurance."

"The Art of a Good Marriage" by Wilfred Arlan Peterson

"Happiness in marriage is not something that just happens. A good marriage must be created.
In marriage the little things are the big things.
It is never being too old to hold hands.
It is remembering to say "I love you" at least once a day.
It is never going to sleep angry.
It is at no time taking the other for granted; the courtship should not end with the honeymoon, it should continue through all the years.
It is having a mutual sense of values and common objectives.
It is standing together facing the world.
It is forming a circle of love that gathers in the whole family.
It is doing things for each other, not in the attitude of duty or sacrifice, but in the spirit of joy.
It is speaking words of appreciation and demonstrating gratitude in thoughtful ways.
It is not looking for perfection in each other.
It is cultivating flexibility, patience, understanding, and a sense of humor.

It is having the capacity to forgive and forget.
It is giving each other an atmosphere in which each can grow.
It is a common search for the good and the beautiful.
*It is establishing a relationship in which the independence is
   equal, dependence is mutual, and the obligation is recip-
   rocal.*
*It is not only marrying the right partner, it is being the right
   partner.*

Encore Wedding Gifts Many couples marrying for the second or
subsequent time already have all the necessities of everyday life.
That said, it is possible that they have registered with a department store for a china pattern that they could never afford the
first time around or for other things they might need, so always
check their registry first for easy gift selection. If they have not
registered, gifts that decorate their home, theater or concert tickets, a gift certificate for a nice dinner, or a night at a lovely bed-
and-breakfast are good ideas for encore wedding gifts. I always
like to get the couple something extravagant that I know they
would like but would never buy for themselves— perhaps a really
good bottle of wine. Or I take a special photograph of the couple, have it enlarged, and enclose it in a beautiful frame. I stay
away from giving gifts of art, such as paintings or sculpture. Taste
in art is very individual and unless you know the couple well, it
can be very hit-or-miss.

Here are some more ideas for encore wedding gifts.

If they are collectors, a trinket to add to their collection.
If the couple has children, an offer for dinner and sitter
   service.
A plant (live orchids are far hardier than most realize).
A basket of prepared foods and cheeses or even CDs that
   you know they like.
Bath accessories "for the couple."

No Gifts, Please Old-school etiquette dictates that it is inappropriate to state "No gifts, please" on the wedding invitation. I do not agree with that philosophy for encore weddings. Many people marrying for the second or subsequent time are quite settled and are embarrassed to receive a present for a marriage celebration they are hosting for themselves. I handled this situation by having the following printed in very small letters at the bottom of the response cards accompanying our wedding invitations: "The honor of your presence is the greatest gift we can receive." My invitations were not formal, but they were printed and placed in matching envelopes with response cards. If you feel as strongly as I did about not receiving gifts, and your invitations are more formal, you may want to consider printing a sentiment similar to mine on a separate note card and including it in the invitation envelopes. Another way to state it is, "Your love and friendship are our cherished gifts. We respectfully request no other." In our case, some friends still felt compelled to bring presents, but most understood that their company and good wishes were what we really wanted on our special day.

Encore Wedding Receptions An encore-wedding reception can be as individual as the wedding ceremony. It's not uncommon for second-wedding receptions to be held at a friend's home, even the home of the bride and groom. If the reception is a large one with many guests, then it, like most first-wedding receptions, is usually held at a meeting hall, country club, or even the reception room of the couple's favorite restaurant. There is no formal rule that dictates where a reception should be held. The key is for guests to be comfortable while celebrating the marriage of loved ones.

There is a consideration for encore receptions that one may not have to consider for first-time wedding receptions—not all the people invited to the reception necessarily feel friendly toward each other. Ex-in-laws or ex-extended-family members may be present, and couples should take special care when considering the seating arrangements. It's a good idea to introduce everyone and to keep interaction as comfortable as possible.

Wedding Pictures for Encore Weddings The following graphics give you some ideas for properly positioning bonusfamily members for wedding photographs.

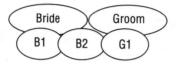

B1 and B2 are the bride's children, and G1 is the groom's child.

If the bride and groom have a child together, the arrangement would then be:

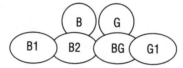

BG is the child the bride and groom have together.

As family members are added to the picture, they should stand on the side of their blood relative. The bride's parents would stand on her side, whereas the groom's parents would stand on his. If the bride and groom's parents were divorced, the blood parent would stand closet to their child.

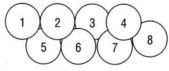

1. Bride's bonusmother
2. Bride's father
3. Bride
4. Groom
5. Bride's child #1

6. Bride's child #2
7. Bride and groom's child
8. Groom's child #1

Should We Just Elope? Eloping may be more convenient than planning a full-blown encore wedding—and it can even be romantic—but all too often when divorced parents choose to elope, their kids feel left out. It can feel to them as if their mom or dad is choosing another over them.

A Wedding Alternative There's an encore wedding option that has worked out well for quite a few bonusfamilies who choose not to marry. The wedding picnic is a lovely idea that easily prepares new family members for what lies ahead and starts a family tradition or ritual that will help to solidify the new family ties. Usually held a few days before the ceremony, the wedding picnic is a private get-together for just the new family. It can take place at a quiet park, or perhaps the beach. The family can eat their favorite foods in a casual setting and discuss their aspirations for their new life together. It's a good time to answer any questions the kids might have and clarify how their life will change. They all have fun together and devote the day to becoming a new family.

Some of the best family pictures I have seen were taken at wedding picnics. They are casual—it's just the bonusfamily—and it's a day to remember. That day becomes the day the family officially united, which makes it the *family's* anniversary date. The kids will feel as if they are part of something, not an afterthought to a big celebration at which someone is taking their mommy or daddy away.

Wedding picnics work just as well for families who do not choose to officially marry, but want a day to celebrate their family union.

Along the same lines, Christine Borgeld, a bonusmom and board member of the Stepfamily Association of America, has been working hard since 1997 to bring us Stepfamily Day. It officially falls on September 16. In celebration of this special day, National Stepfamily Day picnics take place across the nation, usually on the Sunday preceding National Stepfamily Day. For more information please visit the Happy Stepfamily Day Web site (www. happystepfamilyday.org). You can also find out more about Stepfamily Day by visiting the Stepfamily Association of America's Web site at www.saafamilies.org.

When Adult Children of Divorced Parents Marry

The wedding of a bride or groom whose parents are divorced is handled just as any wedding would be, with a few special considerations, discussed in this section. If the parents' relationship is strained, the situation could be uncomfortable for everyone. Things get more complicated if *both* the bride and the groom's parents are divorced. This is when practicing good ex-etiquette is a must.

If the thought of dealing with your ex regarding your child's upcoming nuptials makes the hair rise on the back of your neck, remember, this isn't your wedding; it's your child's. Both the bride and the groom are going to need you to stay calm and help make decisions during a very stressful time. You will not be able to offer them that help if you are obsessing over dealing with your ex or his or her new partner. Even if your child is an adult, keep the first rule of good ex-etiquette in the forefront when making all decisions—put your child first.

Bridal Showers for Adult Children of Divorced Parents
The biggest question concerning bridal showers for brides with divorced parents is whether to invite the bride and/or groom's mother and bonusmother to the same shower. That could add up to a total of two mothers and two bonusmothers with lots of issues between them. Still, the answer is yes. The bride should make the gesture and let the mothers and bonusmothers decide whether or not to attend.

If the bride is planning to have more than one bridal shower, perhaps one for her side of the family and one for the groom's side of the family, then it would be appropriate to invite her mother and bonusmother to one shower, and her fiancé's mother and bonusmother to the other shower. Of course, this does not eradicate the possibility of tension, because mother and bonusmother will still be invited to the same bridal shower. Sooner or later the subject will have to be addressed.

As a special note to mothers and bonusmothers with issues between them—it's time to put those issues aside. Whatever happened before is in the past and needs to be left there. What is current is the fact that a child who is loved by many needs as much love and support from family members as possible. If anyone ought to understand how difficult it is to make a go of a marriage today, it's a divorced parent. She should offer that knowledge in the form of love and support and use it as a building block for future relationships with extended-family members. (These people will all share grandchildren in the future.) To dampen a bride's enthusiasm for the future with an attitude of "I won't go if *she* is there" is selfish—and very poor ex-etiquette. Of course, this also applies to fathers and bonusfathers.

The Finances Traditionally, the father of the bride pays for the wedding and reception. Today, however, the parents of the bride and groom often share expenses. If the parents of the bride or groom are divorced, then the expenses designated for the bride's or groom's parents are often shared equally between them. Of course this is not a rule. Once divorced, how the parents divide the expenses for their child's wedding is up to them.

Because of the high cost of weddings and receptions, it is not uncommon for the bride's parents to pay for the wedding while the groom's parents host the reception. If the bride's parents are divorced, another approach is for the bride's mother to host the wedding while her father hosts the reception. It is also fairly common for grandparents or other relatives to help with the expenses.

The Guest List

"My fiancé and I have been together for over a year. He has been separated for four years, and we plan to get married as soon as his divorce comes through. His eldest son is getting married and recently told his dad that I am not invited to the wedding. I was very hurt. I felt I was being treated like a mistress."

Although people nowadays rarely get bogged down by such propriety, it is regarded as very poor etiquette to attend a family gathering, such as the wedding of an immediate family member, with a man who is not yet divorced when the ex-wife is present. If the man in question is determined to have his new partner accompany him, every effort should be made to finalize his divorce before the ceremony.

In this case, it's difficult to know why the fiancée hasn't been invited. It may be that the ex-wife is uncomfortable with the state of affairs or that the son is the one who is offended. And one might wonder why, after four years, the parents' divorce is not final. Extending the time between separation and divorce often gives exes and children a false hope of reconciliation, and then when a parent starts to date, the mourning intensifies. That may be exactly what has happened in this case. Even though the parents in question have been separated for four years, the father has been dating this woman for only one year, and that is not much time for wounds to heal.

Good ex-etiquette suggests that the father first speak to his ex to verify her position. Then, move on to the son and prospective daughter-in-law. If they are both uncomfortable *because the father and mother are not divorced*, the new partner should not attend. However, this would not be the case if the parents' divorce has been finalized. For parents who never marry, protocol is not so strict, but politeness and consideration should always be motivating factors.

Family members' acceptance of a new partner is largely determined by how the new partner is presented. Therefore, a person who wants his new partner to be accepted by extended-family members must make his regard and respect for his new partner obvious. Hopefully, extended-family members will then follow his lead. The father can propose a toast that makes his intent obvious: "Now, let's lift our glasses to the bride-to-be. Donna [the father's new partner] and I are so happy to have you as a member of our family. I have also spoken to John's [the son] mother, and I know that she is pleased, too."

That should make it apparent to everyone where things stand. But remember, this is a toast to be given in private, *not* at the ceremony.

Wedding Invitations for Adult Children with Divorced Parents The following examples are designed to help you understand how to list the family members on wedding invitations when the parents of the bride or groom are divorced and/or remarried. A traditional invitation is presented first as a reference point.

Traditional invitation to a first wedding issued by the bride's parents:

Mr. and Mrs. Michael Smith

request the honor of your presence

at the marriage of their daughter

Jeanne Marie

to

Kenneth Michael Blackstock

Saturday, the twentieth of June

Two thousand and four

at four o'clock

Christian Country Church

Grass Valley, California

When the parents are divorced (note: if the parents of the bride are divorced, their names are not written on the same line):

Mrs. Louise Baldwin Smith

and

Mr. Michael Smith

request the honor of your presence

at the marriage of their daughter

Jeanne Marie

to

Kenneth Michael Blackstock

Saturday, the twentieth of June

two thousand and four

at four o'clock

Christian Country Church

Grass Valley, California

In the above example, the mother's maiden name is Baldwin. If she has resumed using her maiden name rather than her married name, she has the choice of being listed as:

Louise Baldwin

Mrs. Louise Baldwin

Ms. Louise Baldwin

When the mother is divorced and has not remarried, but issues the invitations:

Mrs. Louise Baldwin Smith

requests the honor of your presence

at the marriage of her daughter

Jeanne Marie

to

Kenneth Michael Blackstock

Saturday, the twentieth of June

Two thousand and four

at four o'clock

Christian Country Church

Grass Valley, California

Alternatives for the mother's name are:

Mrs. Louise Smith

Ms. Louise Smith

Louise Baldwin Smith

When the mother has remarried and issues the invitations with the father:

Mrs. Braden Stephenson

and

Mr. Michael Smith

request the honor of your presence

at the marriage of their daughter

Jeanne Marie Smith

to

Kenneth Michael Blackstock

Saturday, the twentieth of June

two thousand and four

at four o'clock

Christian Country Church

Grass Valley, California

"Mrs. Braden Stephenson" may also be listed as "Mrs. Louise Stephenson."

When the mother has remarried and issues the ceremony invitation without the bonusfather:

Mrs. Braden Stephenson

requests the honor of your presence

at the marriage of her daughter

Jeanne Marie Smith

to

Kenneth Michael Blackstock

Saturday, the twentieth of June

two thousand and four

at four o'clock

Christian Country Church

Grass Valley, California

Note that the daughter's last name is listed in this invitation because the mother and daughter's last name are no longer the same now that the mother has remarried and taken her new husband's name.

When the mother is remarried and issues the invitations with the bonusfather:

Mr. and Mrs. Braden Stephenson

request the honor of your presence

at the marriage of her daughter

Jeanne Marie Smith

to

Kenneth Michael Blackstock

Saturday, the twentieth of June

two thousand and four

at four o'clock

Christian Country Church

Grass Valley, California

Again, note the last name of the daughter is listed because it is different than the mother's last name. When describing Jeanne Marie Smith, there are three alternatives:

her daughter (as in the above example)

Mrs. Stephenson's daughter

their daughter

"Their daughter" is used when the biological father is deceased, out of the picture, or on very friendly terms with the mother and bonusfather and has agreed that his daughter can be listed as "their daughter." When there is a question of offending the biological parent, this phrase should not be used.

When the mother has remarried, the father has not remarried, but the invitation is issued jointly:

Mr. and Mrs. Braden Stephenson

Mr. Michael Smith

request the honor of your presence

at the marriage of their daughter

Jeanne Marie Smith

to

Kenneth Michael Blackstock

Saturday, the twentieth of June

Two thousand and four

at four o'clock

Christian Country Church

Grass Valley, California

When the father is not remarried and issues the invitation alone:

Mr. Michael Smith

requests the honor of your presence

at the marriage of his daughter

Jeanne Marie

to

Kenneth Michael Blackstock

Saturday, the twentieth of June

Two thousand and four

at four o'clock

Christian Country Church

Grass Valley, California

When the remarried father issues the invitation with the bonusmother:

Mr. and Mrs. Michael Smith

request the honor of your presence

at the marriage of his daughter

Jeanne Marie

to

Kenneth Michael Blackstock

Saturday, the twentieth of June

Two thousand and four

at four o'clock

Christian Country Church

Grass Valley, California

When describing Jeanne Marie Smith, there are three alternatives:

his daughter (as in the above example)

Mr. Smith's daughter

their daughter (again, if there is a possibility that the
other parent will take offense, the phrase "their daughter"
should not be used)

When the father has remarried, the mother is not married,
but the invitation is issued jointly:

Mrs. Louise Baldwin Smith

Mr. and Mrs. Michael Smith

request the honor of your presence

at the marriage of their daughter

Jeanne Marie

to

Mr. Kenneth Michael Blackstock

Saturday, the twentieth of June

Two thousand and four

at four o'clock

Christian Country Church

Grass Valley, California

When the mother and father have both remarried and issue
invitations together without new spouses:

Mrs. Braden Stephenson

Mr. Michael Smith

request the honor of your presence

at the marriage of their daughter

Jeanne Marie Smith

to

Kenneth Michael Blackstock

Saturday, the twentieth of June

Two thousand and four

at four o'clock

Christian Country Church

Grass Valley, California

"Mrs. Braden Stephenson" can also be:

Mrs. Louise Smith Stephenson

Louise Stephenson

Ms. Louise Stephenson

When the mother and father, both remarried, issue the invitations with their new spouses:

Mr. and Mrs. Braden Stephenson

Mr. and Mrs. Michael Smith

request the honor of your presence

at the marriage of their daughter

Jeanne Marie Smith

to

Kenneth Michael Blackstock

Saturday, the twentieth of June

Two thousand and four

at four o'clock

Christian Country Church

Grass Valley, California

If the parents of the groom have helped to host the wedding and wish to be added to the invitation:

Mr. and Mrs. Braden Stephenson

Mr. and Mrs. Michael Smith

Mr. and Mrs. James Blackstock

request the honor of your presence

at the marriage of

Jeanne Marie Smith

to

Kenneth Michael Blackstock

Saturday, the twentieth of June

Two thousand and four

at four o'clock

Christian Country Church

Grass Valley, California

When both the bride and groom's parents have divorced and remarried, and everyone, including the couple to be married, is pitching in, rather than list everyone's names individually, the invitation may begin with the marrying couple's names (the bride's name always comes first) and follow with "together with their parents" before the request line. For example:

Jeanne Marie Smith

and

Kenneth Michael Blackstock

together with their parents

request the honor of your presence

at their marriage

I recently received a wedding invitation that used this no-non-sense approach:

The parents and stepparents of

Jeanne Marie Smith

and

Kenneth Michael Blackstock

request the honor of your presence

at the wedding of their children

Who Gives the Bride Away?

"Although my parents divorced when I was very young, and I lived primarily with my mother growing up, I have always had a lovely relationship with my dad. My mother remarried when I was nine, and over the years I have also grown very close to my bonusfather. I plan to marry next year and would like both my father and bonusfather to walk me down the aisle, but I'm getting some resistance. My father says he will not come to my wedding if my bonusfather also walks me down the aisle. What do I do?"

This young woman's father is asking her to choose between himself and her bonusfather on one of the most important days of her life. He has forgotten the primary rule of ex-etiquette, "Put your children first."

Statistics tell us that most divorced parents remarry or live in another long-term committed relationship. Therefore, when a couple divorces, they should know that their ex-spouse will most likely remarry, and there will eventually be another parent figure in their children's lives. If they put their child first, their hope should be that their ex will find a partner who will truly care for their child and treat her with love and respect.

Obviously, the divorced mother in this example chose her new partner well. She chose a man who accepted her child and through the years forged a loving bond with her. Rather than be resentful and require her to choose, her biological father should rejoice that his daughter has been loved, not resented; protected, not abused. The gesture this young woman proposes, having her father and her bonusfather walk her down the aisle, is based on her deep and loving feelings for both men. To issue an ultimatum forcing a child to choose between biological parent and bonusparent is breaking every rule of good ex-etiquette. The decision about who walks the bride down the aisle is the bride's to make; it should be openly accepted by all parent figures.

I have seen this subject handled tastefully in three different ways. First, the father and the bonusfather stand on either side of the bride as they walk down the aisle. The bride's father is at her left side; her bonusfather is at her right side. If the bride would like a gesture that distinguishes the father from the bonusfather, aside from the side on which they are walking, the bride may take her father's right arm as they walk.

Another approach is the bonusfather walks the bride down the aisle to the row in which her father sits. The father rises and then walks his daughter the rest of the way.

A third possibility is for the father, standing at the bride's left, to walk her down the aisle to the row in which the bonusfather sits. The bonusfather rises and walks his bonusdaughter the rest of the way. This choice was made by a bride who was somewhat estranged from her father, but wanted to include him in the wedding ceremony. She explained to us that her bonusfather had raised her, and she felt he was her father. That's why she opted for him to be the one to present her to the groom. Remember, the final decision lies with the bride.

There are, of course, brides who ask grandfathers or uncles to take on this honor. Perhaps the most untraditional choice I have heard of was a bride whose single mother, after struggling for years to raise her daughter alone, walked her daughter down the aisle. It was a day of triumph for them both—the daughter had just graduated from college the day before.

In Jewish wedding presentations, the bride's and groom's parents *both* walk them down the aisle. If the parents are divorced, it is still appropriate for the bride's or groom's parents to stand on either side of their child as they walk down the aisle. If the new spouse of the divorced parent finds this offensive, the mother and her spouse may walk the bride or groom halfway down the aisle, and then the father and his spouse can walk the bride or groom the remaining half.

Who Gives This Bride in Marriage? Just as tricky as the choice of who walks the bride down the aisle, is the decision of who responds when the officiate asks, "Who gives this bride in marriage?" Tradition stipulates that the question is asked by the one officiating over the marriage, and then the father replies "I do" or "Her mother and I do." If the father is not present and the bride wishes it, her bonusfather answers the question. He may want to answer "We do," as a symbol of the joint effort it took to raise the bride to adulthood. If the mother walked her daughter down the aisle, then the mother of the bride would answer, "I do." I recently attended a wedding ceremony where the bride's adoptive father lived with a male partner. His response to "Who gives this woman to be married?" was "My partner and I do."

The Groom and His Mother and Bonusmother One of the most touching ceremonies I have attended was that of a dear friend's son who lived most of his life with his father and bonusmother. As the wedding music began, he first walked his mother down the aisle and brought her to her seat. He then went to his bonusmother, walked her down the aisle, and brought her to her seat. It was a lovely sentiment showing respect to both his mother and his bonusmother.

Seating If Both the Bride's and the Groom's Parents Are Divorced

"My stepdaughter is getting married next week, and I need some advice on how to cope with my husband's ex. My husband and I have been married for fifteen years. His ex hates that I have anything to do with her child and has always been very unpleasant to me.
I have forged a close relationship with my stepdaughter, in spite of her mother's behavior, but I am afraid my husband's ex will cause trouble at the wedding and reception. Where do you suggest I sit, and how long should my husband and I stay at the reception? It's a formal wedding, and I do not want to contribute to a scene in any way."

Because there is a history of run-ins with her husband's ex, it's easy to understand why this woman predicts the worst for the upcoming wedding. However, she must remember who it is really hurting when she spends time and energy anticipating a negative outcome: *herself*. Agonizing about what *may* happen simply keeps her upset and has no effect on her husband's ex—except maybe to give her the satisfaction of knowing that she is keeping everything stirred up.

If the husband's ex-wife has indeed caused trouble for years, I suggest that the husband tell her that he wishes no ill will, but that he simply will not tolerate the behavior any longer. He should remind her that it is their daughter's wedding, and now is the time to put their own issues aside and make the day as special for their daughter as possible. There is no occasion at which it is more important for divorced parents to demonstrate their love for their children by displaying good ex-etiquette than at their child's wedding.

As for the seating arrangement at the wedding, the current wife sits next to her husband. They should sit on the bride's side, behind his ex-wife's extended family. If there is great animosity, it is understandable (and acceptable) if his current wife wishes to sit toward the back of the church, but the father of the bride should still remain in his designated pew.

Ex-etiquette dictates the following seating arrangement when the bride's parents are divorced or separated. The bride's mother and partner sit in the front pew on the left side of the aisle. If the bride has bonussiblings, they are seated in the second pew. The bride's grandparents and other extended family sit behind them. The bride's father sits with his wife and their family in the next pew. If her father and not her mother raised the bride, the seating arrangement is reversed—the father of the bride and his wife sit in the front pew.

The groom's family seating matches the bride's, but on the right side of the church.

In terms of the reception, in this case, if the father of the bride and his current wife are going to host it, they should stay until the end. There may be some last-minute things they need to tie up with the caterers or music, and it would be very impolite to leave that responsibility to someone else. If they aren't hosting the reception, then I would suggest that they bring a lovely wedding present to the couple and stay as long as they feel comfortable.

The Receiving Line for Adult Children with Divorced Parents Receiving lines are a formal way for your hosts to greet their guests and thank them for sharing the day. The first rule of ex-etiquette and receiving lines is not to be a stickler about protocol. The goal is to keep everyone comfortable and avoid public confrontations. If the parents of the bride and groom are at odds, a formal receiving line may not be your best option.

If bonusparents helped to sponsor the wedding and reception, they are also hosts and should thank their guests for coming. Ideally, the divorced parents hosting the wedding and reception understand that this is a day for cooperation. If, after weighing the issue carefully, they find that a receiving line is their only option, ex-etiquette suggests that divorced parents *do not* stand next to each other in the line. Biological moms and bonusmoms or biological dads and bonusdads also should not stand next to each other. Their child, their child's new spouse, or a member of the wedding party should separate them.

There are a couple of reasons I suggest this. First, just in case someone forgets the basic rules of ex-etiquette and provokes an argument, it is always wise to separate people who have issues between them. Second, although divorced parents and their new mates may have worked through their problems to the point where they can be cordial in public, guests who do not know the family well will inevitably be confused by the divorce players' casual interaction. This could provoke requests for clarification that may cause the bride or groom embarrassment.

10

HOLIDAYS AND SPECIAL OCCASIONS

"Often, the less there is to justify a traditional custom, the harder it is to get rid of it."

—MARK TWAIN

The concept of family seems to be synonymous with holidays and celebrations—no matter what your religion, no matter the holiday. And if you are reevaluating your family identity because of divorce and remarriage, it's easy to be confused about what is and isn't acceptable behavior.

The decision to spend any holiday together is a personal one. For many, the animosity between ex-partners is so strong that spending the holidays together seems impossible. The tiebreaker is always how it will appear to the children. If divorced parents cannot be civil with each other, for the sake of the children, they should not attempt to spend holidays together.

For those who do choose to spend holidays together, what is the proper holiday ex-etiquette? Should you bring your new girlfriend to Johnny's birthday party? Is Halloween a good time to introduce your kids to your new partner and his kids? This chapter will take a look at how applying the rules of good ex-etiquette at holiday times can help parents better cope with the problems they face when co-parenting their kids after divorce.

Children's Birthdays

Children's birthday parties can get very complicated when the parents of the birthday child are divorced or no longer live together. Biological parents often face feelings of insecurity and jealousy, and this prompts rude behavior such as demanding that your ex's new spouse not attend your child's birthday party.

There is always some emotional adjusting to do, but you must eventually accept that your former partner has a new partner whose place it is to be at your ex's side on special occasions.

There are three main considerations when divorced or separated parents plan their child's birthday party.

1. Who will host the party?
2. Who will attend?
3. Where will the party take place?

When considering who will host the party, divorced parents must first decide if there will be one party or two. Estranged parents usually opt for the two-party solution, but that may not be the best idea. Does a child really need two of everything, including parties? If a child's parents were not divorced, a child that got two of everything would be regarded as spoiled. But, it appears, a child of divorce who has two of everything is not spoiled—a very strange double standard.

Perhaps the best solution for divorced parents is to switch off—one hosts the party one year, the other hosts it the next year. This brings the guest list into question. Who is invited? Ideally, both sides of the family—complete with extended family—should be invited. If anyone feels uncomfortable attending, it should be that person's option to decline the invitation. Some family members may feel inclined to inquire who is invited to the party. For example, this may happen when an ex-in-law holds a grudge against a former son- or daughter-in-law because of the divorce. The knowledge that he or she is attending the party may then prompt comments along the lines of, "If he's coming, I'm not!" It is very poor ex-etiquette to agree to go to a party based on who is attending rather than based on a wish to help the guest of honor celebrate the special occasion. Openly snubbing an ex-relative is also very poor ex-etiquette.

When planning a child's birthday party, parents and bonusparents should ask themselves the following questions:

Who is this party for? Your child, not you. If you are the host of a party, you make your decisions based on what the guest of honor would like, not what you would like.

Will the absence of the uninvited person appear as an obvious snub? If so, a child's birthday party is not the correct place to make such a statement.

Where will the party be held? If divorced parents and new spouses are to attend together and if interacting with each other is a new experience, it should be on neutral territory—a skating rink or bowling alley, for example—rather than the home of the parent hosting the party.

If parents and bonusparents simply cannot put their feelings aside and remain civil in the presence of an ex-relative or counterpartner, then for the sake of the child, they should not attend parties together. Experts agree that it is better for the child if divorced parents keep things separate after divorce than to attempt to spend time together and fight in front of the child.

> *"Today is my nine-year-old son Johnny's birthday, and he seemed somewhat grumpy. Suddenly, he ran to the bathroom and locked the door. When he finally did let me in, he fell into my arms sobbing. Through his tears he explained that his mother had forgotten his birthday. What should have been my response?"*

Birthdays are always important to children, no matter what their age. It's the one day they are singled out to be the star, and if mom or dad forgets their day it can be devastating for the kids but also for the parent who has to watch the child be hurt. That's where the rules of ex-etiquette can really help parents and bonus-parents keep their wits about them.

The next time the parent in this example speaks to the offending parent, his first inclination may be to lash out, "How could you do this to Johnny?" but right now what he really needs is a way to help Johnny cope.

First, he must remove the emotion from the interaction, not only with his ex, but when talking to his child. Of course compassion and empathy are necessary as his child needs comfort. But he must take care not to let his empathy for his child's hurt feelings allow him to break other rules of ex-etiquette that prevent arguments with his ex in the future. His responsibility is to his child. He should help Johnny cope with this disappointment, not make the ex pay for her misdeeds. Right now, the child is afraid his other parent doesn't love him. That's the important issue.

An appropriate response to this situation might be, "Just because we are your parents and all grown up doesn't mean we don't have things to learn. You are a wonderful, talented kid with amazing creativity, great ideas, and lots of love to give. Aren't you lucky that you already know how important it is to share your love with the people that you love? Remember all the people in your life who do show you love on a daily basis." Then start naming them together—grandma and grandpa, friends, teachers, and most of all, *you*. Now your child is thinking about the people who love him rather than the one who he fears may not. Although I don't believe there is much that can fill the gap left by a parent's insensitivity, this is a step in the right direction.

Holidays

To help any holiday run smoothly, families associated with divorce or separation first need a solid plan. Without one, scheduling becomes overwhelming, and divorced parents find it impossible to coordinate visitation, presents, and gift giving. Being organized will ensure that the kids feel safe and secure and willing to accept the change between past and present. Holidays become stressful for children when they perceive that their parents (both bonus and biological) are vindictive, floundering, and disorganized.

Have Reasonable Expectations

It's not uncommon that after the first few years as a stepfamily, the stresses associated with coordinating the holidays become the catalyst to just stop celebrating. Although they put on a smiling face when the kids are around, some divorced parents have told us it's all they can do just to decorate the Christmas tree. It is true, yours is not a nuclear family, and the holidays may not be what you remember as a child, but that doesn't mean they can't be a wonderful time of year. Don't set yourself up for disappointment by expecting things to be perfect or even the way it used to be—that only leads to frustration and disappointment. Look for ways to make it new by integrating past and present.

Helping Your Child Transition from House to House During the Holidays

There are some changes divorced parents can make that will help ease their children's transition from house to house during the holidays. Notice I didn't say "suggestions for parents to cope with the holidays." If you are practicing good ex-etiquette, your goal is to create an environment where your children can flourish; therefore *you* have to make the necessary changes. Your ability to cope is a result of the positive changes you make.

Begin by making the transition from house to house as stress-free as you can by coordinating efforts with your child's other parent well in advance. Knowing exactly what time your child will leave (or when you will pick them up) and planning for it—bags packed at the door rather than scrambling around at the last minute—will help. Avoid saying things like, "I'm going to miss you so much." Even if you are, saying so just makes the transition more difficult for the child. Give him a hug and tell him you love him and then send him on his way.

Agree on a time you will check in and stick to it. Do not call him every five minutes to check up or to remind him that he is the most important thing in your life. This is quite disruptive for the other home and actually causes the child more anxiety than comfort. If your child is truly the most important thing in your life, allow him to settle in at his other parent's home so they can enjoy their time together. A constant reminder that you miss him is not putting your child first—it's putting your child in the middle.

To save on expenses, it also helps to coordinate presents with your child's other parent. Decide who is going to give Billy the bike and Mary the roller blades. Follow the rules of good ex-etiquette and look for the compromise. Then let everything go. Don't stew over the agreement you just made. Move on and celebrate the day.

Gift Giving at the Holidays

"Should we buy a present for my partner's ex?"

When people divorce and remarry, gift giving at holidays gets really complex. Rather than decreasing, the number of presents you may be required to give can actually grow, and you may find yourself buying presents for people you never would have dreamed you'd be buying them for.

"If someone had told me I would someday be buying a present for my ex-wife's husband," one divorced father confided, "I would have laughed in their face. But there I was last year buying him a box of golf balls for Christmas."

Interacting with an ex's new partner in such a casual manner would have been unthinkable even a generation ago, but today it is far more common. Good ex-etiquette suggests that if counterpartners become friends over the years, then it is appropriate to exchange gifts. Gifts can also be symbolic in nature. A gift given to or by an ex can serve as a peace offering, a gesture of goodwill, or even an example for the children.

Take special care when choosing a gift for an ex-relation or counterpartner. Never choose a gift that may be misconstrued as a show of criticism or disapproval or a reminder of their past relationship. It would be inappropriate, for example, to give your ex a CD that included the special song the two of you enjoyed. Presents that are noncommittal in nature are best for this occasion. Flowers, candy, dried fruit, or a candle are all good choices. They provide the gesture without any possibility of offense.

Buying Holiday Presents "from the Kids"

"My husband has two children, ages thirteen and fifteen. His ex has really been a pain and has tried to cause many problems for my husband despite the fact that he has made an effort get along. My husband

always takes his kids out to buy a Christmas gift for the ex. Is this appropriate? She never reciprocates!"

Of course we all get angry with exes at times, and it's easy to forget that the reason we are buying presents for them on special occasions is because the presents are supposed to be from the children, not us. It is important for exes to remember that assisting their children in buying a present for the other parent is setting a good example. The parent's actions demonstrate that he respects his ex simply because she is his child's other parent. That's good ex-etiquette. The fact that the recipient does not reciprocate should never play a role in the decision of whether to buy a present.

"Are you saying that even though my ex has moved across the country, is behind on child support, and never sees his kids, the appropriate thing to do is to take my kids shopping for him? Last year I asked my kids if they wanted to get anything for their dad, and they actually said no! Should I leave it to them to decide?"

Each situation is different. That's why it's difficult to make blanket statements concerning problems such as these. Let's analyze what may be going on here. The father sounds like someone the mother would prefer not have in contact with her children. Her anger, and her children's anger, helps to keep the father at bay. Even the smallest gesture—a card, for example—may appear as a symbol of truce to the father, which might bring him back into their lives, if only temporarily. So her anger and the children's anger are serving a purpose—the flaky dad stays away.

There is something more important going on here. Let's use our empathetic abilities to analyze this mother's approach to gift giving. As a young child, if you knew your mother was extremely angry with your wayward father, and she asked you if you wanted to send a present to your father for Christmas, how would you respond? It's likely that you would say no even if the answer were yes because you would know your mother is angry and you would want your mother's approval. Putting a child in this position encourages the child to reject his or her wayward parent, and that's too much pressure on the child. From working with hundreds of kids over the years, I have found that many children still have a great deal of affection for their parents, no matter what the parents have done.

A better way to present the option to the children would be to state the truth, then follow their lead. "You know I am angry with your dad, but I don't want to stand in your way if you would like to send him a present for Christmas." Then listen, don't lead. If they state they don't want to interact with their other parent, don't push. Consider that counseling may be in order to help them sort through their anger and resentment.

In cases such as this one, good ex-etiquette suggests that sending a card as a gesture may still be appropriate. If a divorced parent absolutely refuses to do anything, the bonusparent may have to step up to the plate. Remember, the important thing is what you are teaching your kids by offering the gesture, not what you are teaching the wayward parent.

"When is it not appropriate to take the kids out to buy presents for their other parent?"

It may not be appropriate to support interaction (e.g. gift giving) between parent and child when the child is estranged from the parent for the following reasons:

The parent is addicted to drugs or alcohol to the extent that his behavior is unpredictable and the child's safety at risk.

The parent has exhibited past violent behavior toward the other parent or the child.

The parent has committed a crime against the child.
The parent is mentally ill and seeing the parent in such a
state would be upsetting for the child.

In other words, interaction should not be initiated with a parent whose behavior makes the child uncomfortable or has been determined to be detrimental to the child. When in doubt, a parent should always check with a professional who is familiar with the family's case.

"Should we make the kids use their own money to buy presents for the noncustodial parent?"

When children use their own money to buy presents, it teaches them responsibility and reinforces that it is better to give than to receive. Parents should make sure they have the correct motivation though. They shouldn't make the kids buy the gift just because they don't want to use any of *their own* money to buy the other parent a present. Parents, biological and bonus, have to be bigger than that.

"Today my husband called from work and asked me to buy a present for his ex from the kids. Is that my responsibility?"

In old-school divorce, the thought of buying a present for your spouse's ex was unheard-of! Exes stayed on their own side of the fence. Today, good ex-etiquette tells us it's not automatically a person's responsibility to buy presents for their spouse's ex, but there may be times when it is necessary.

Supporting the relationship between your bonuschildren and their parent (your counterpartner) will strengthen your relationship with everyone concerned. It promotes trust, which is the basis of any good relationship, and proves to your bonuschildren that they can depend on you. A story I heard years ago from a new bonusmom that demonstrates this:

"One morning recently, when my bonusdaughter heard her mother's car pull into the driveway, her face went white. She had suddenly remembered it was her mother's birthday, and she hadn't gotten her anything. She was very upset. As I tried to calm her down I remembered that I had recently bought a gift certificate for a massage for a friend. We quickly put it in a gift bag, and she presented it to her mother at the door. As her mother opened the gift, the smile on my bonusdaughter's face made it all worthwhile. She knew I was on her side. My helping her to reinforce the bond she had with her mother reinforced the bond we were building."

This is a perfect example of the positive results of good ex-etiquette. In addition to reinforcing her relationship with her bonusdaughter, this woman reinforced her relationship with the biological mother. The mother knew that the bonusmom was the one to help her daughter pick out the present, and that went a long way in healing the bitterness between the two women.

Keeping Everything Fair

Something bonusfamily parents rarely address around the holidays is that the youngest child—the one they have created together—needs reassurance too. He may not understand why kids who he has been told are his siblings get extra presents from other parents.

To confront the extra-presents dilemma, have a conversation with the other children's parent to make sure the presents they gave their child really have to go back to your house. It's understandable if a child wants to take them back and forth; however, if there are other children in the home, bonus- or half-siblings, it may cause problems.

Once a divorced parent gets involved with someone with children, *all* the children's best interests must be at the forefront.

When I explained this to a divorced parent who shared custody of his children with his ex, his comment was, "I understand the need to cooperate, but I'm certainly not going to take her children with her new husband into consideration when I make decisions for my own." This attitude is understandable, but there will be times that your decisions for your children will affect an ex's partner's children—and vice versa. Notice that the primary rule of good ex-etiquette, "Put the children first," does not include a reference as to whose children they are. That's because it really doesn't matter.

In my family's case, working out of my home office allowed me to spend lots of time with the kids while Sharyl juggled work to find extra moments with them. Sometimes all Sharyl could do was run to the mall for pizza with her kids and then rush them back to our home for the evening. Meanwhile my daughter would sit patiently waiting for her bonussiblings to return. In they would walk with a special lollipop or a little stuffed animal, and my daughter would begin to cry. She was being raised to think that Larry and Sharyl's kids were her brother and sister. If that was so, why did her brother and sister get a present when she didn't?

Sharyl had no idea that buying her children a little gift would prompt such sadness in another child. This went on for a month, and it did give us the opportunity to discuss "bragging" and "flaunting" with the children, but those conversations did little to appease my eight-year-old.

Although I dreaded the conversation, I called Sharyl and appealed to her sense of fairness. I asked her to please consider whether the presents had to return to our house with the children. If they did, then of course I understood, but if they didn't, keeping the presents at her house would give the children something special when they were at Sharyl's and eliminate hurt feelings at my house. In the true sense of good ex-etiquette, the next time the children returned to our house with a special lollipop, they also had one for my daughter. I was not expecting that approach, but it was a welcome solution.

Gift Giving and Extended Family

Some grandparents or other relatives balk at the idea of giving presents to children to whom they are not biologically related. Even my own mother, in the midst of all my bonus talk, used to sneak my daughter, her oldest biological grandchild, an extra fifty dollars when no one was looking. As adults we inherently understand the blood-relation preference, but young children wonder what they did to make grandma not like them. Older children may understand better but still feel rejected when an adult obviously prefers another member of their family.

If becoming a bonusfamily makes your family huge, and gift giving grows troublesome, try picking numbers or names of family members; buying present for only the kids; or agreeing on a price ceiling for each present.

The goal is for everyone to feel included. Even though some extended-family members may at first be unwilling to participate as part of a bonusfamily, over time they will probably begin to understand and accept their responsibility to help the children cope.

Holiday Traditions and Rituals

Traditions and rituals associated with nuclear families evolve over generations. After a divorce or separation, conflict results when traditions from the past interfere with celebrating in the present.

What is the difference between family tradition and family ritual? Tradition is what families *do*—for example, decorate the Christmas tree. Ritual is *how* they do it; for example, the dad strings the lights while the mom sings a song. The lighting of the menorah during the eight days of Chanukah is a family tradition in Jewish households. If the family does it in a special manner— say the dad wears his red socks while lighting the candle each night—that's the family ritual.

Part of what is special about family rituals is who participates in the ritual ceremony. If the players change—say, the mom and dad divorce—and one is no longer there to participate, the tradition is broken. In situations like this, you may hear the words "It just feels like something is missing." And those who once looked forward to a particular time of year stop wanting to celebrate. The truth is, something *is* missing. Divorce changes everything. That's why divorced parents must try as best they can to maintain past family rituals around the holidays. But if that becomes too painful for the children, the family should not be afraid to modify the ritual.

When a divorced parent meets someone with children, it may again be time to modify a past family ritual or tradition. Look for ways to integrate the preferences of new family members without completely abandoning past traditions. A well-adjusted combined family attempts to combine family rituals to create new family rituals that work for them. They cherish the similarities and respect the differences. And, if need be, they start from scratch and establish new rituals of their own.

On the other hand, holidays, especially holidays involving specific family traditions (such as trick-or-treating with the neighbors or stringing popcorn for the Christmas tree) are not good times to *introduce* new girlfriends or boyfriends for the first time. And if your prospective new partner has children, that makes it twice as bad. You may think they are getting along just fine—and they may be—but more often than not it registers with the kids that there's new competition encroaching on their family tradition. Better to set aside an afternoon for the first meeting and keep it light. Ease into it, for the kids' sakes—*all* the kids' sakes. Holidays can eventually be a great time to combine family fun; they're just not a good time to make the first introduction.

"What if I don't want to spend a holiday with my ex? Specifically, do I have to go trick-or-treating with my ex and the kids?"

The ultimate goal in co-parenting after divorce is to be able to exist comfortably in the same room with your ex-spouse for the sake of the kids. Therefore, the goal is for both parents to go trick-or-treating with the kids—yes, at the same time. This mom doesn't have to hold hands with her ex while the kids skip from house to house, but a cordial conversation will put the kids more at ease—and help them to create positive memories.

Ask most children of divorce about holidays, and they will tell you they do not have happy memories. Holidays, from birthdays to Christmas, are reminders that their dad and mom stopped living together. And if the parents add to that stress by squabbling over whose time it is with the kids, why so-and-so was late, why he brought *her*, etc., it just puts more pressure on the kids. If parents can change that trend, for their kids' sakes, they should do it.

If this mother absolutely does not want to see her ex, then the kids should spend one Halloween with their mom and the next with their dad. That is the fairest way to approach the holidays. For Halloween trick-or-treating, the noncustodial parent should go to the neighborhood of the custodial parent so that the kids can trick-or-treat with their friends in a familiar neighborhood.

Taking Holiday Photographs

The placement of family members in bonusfamily holiday photos, such as Christmas cards, should easily communicate parentage. Therefore, place the children on the side of their biological parent, and place children shared by the parents between their parents.

For example:

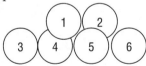

1. Father
2. Mother
3. Father's child
4. Father's child
5. Shared child of mother and father
6. Mother's child

In the above diagram, the family is made up of two parents who had children from previous marriages and share one child they created together. It does not matter if the mother or father choose the right or left. If the mother chooses the right, then her children from her first marriage stand on the right side of the picture.

If you want a photo that includes all the parent figures (parents and bonusparents) and children together, the family members should assemble to best communicate the biological parentage of the children. I will use Sharyl's and my family names and associations as a guide:

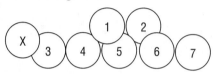

1. Larry, the father
2. Jann, the bonusmother
3. Sharyl, the mother
4. Steven (Larry and Sharyl's son)
5. Melanie (Larry and Sharyl's daughter)
6. Harleigh (Larry and Jann's daughter)
7. Anee (Jann's daughter from a previous marriage)
X Sharyl's partner would stand at her left.

Obviously, lining everyone up in a straight line does not make for the best pictures. It's better to get creative, use different levels, perhaps have some people sitting and some standing. Divorced parents should not stand next to each other. Ex-spouses and current spouses should not stand on either side of the spouse who was married to both. The children of divorced parents stand between them. This rule makes it very clear who is currently married to whom and which people are the parents of the children pictured.

Mother's Day and Father's Day

Mother's Day or Father's Day may be the most emotional days on the calendar for divorced parents. Ironically, Mother's Day, the first of the two holidays to come into being, began as a day of peace. In 1872, overcome by the suffering of war, Julia Ward Howe wrote a proclamation suggesting that mothers come together to stop the bloodshed. This eventually turned into what we now know as Mother's Day. Father's Day soon followed.

When Mrs. Howe wrote her original proclamation, she had no idea her day of peace would someday actually initiate conflict. But parents who are already at odds with their counterpartners know that on this special day the conflict between parent and bonusparent can become even more apparent. Many parents are as possessive of the day as they are of their children, and each time Mother's Day or Father's Day rolls around it opens a wound. These parents fear that their children will prefer another and resent having to share their children's affections. Sharing the day does not come naturally.

Sometimes anger and jealousy cloud our reason, and our kids have to watch our struggle to rise above. That's not necessarily bad. If you realize it's time to change your behavior, what better lesson than to change it right in front of your kids?

The rules of ex-etiquette dictate that the kids should be with their mother on Mother's Day and their father on Father's Day. Efforts should be coordinated among adults so that the child can spend that day with the appropriate parent. Of course, if the parent does not wish to spend the day with the child, no issue should be made. I mention this rule specifically for parents who demand that visitation schedules are adhered to strictly, without weighing the true impact of their decision. An example would be when the divorce decree states that a parent should spend every other weekend with a child without considering that the designated weekend may be Mother's Day or Father's Day and the child will be with the other parent. In these cases, good ex-etiquette asks parents to consider making the appropriate changes in the best interests of the child—and as a courtesy to the other parent.

Religious Training and Education

When couples marry outside their religion, they often agree on how their children will be raised before they are born. If this agreement is sincere, then divorce should not change the decision.

Ex-etiquette urges exes to be honest and straightforward. If the parents, when together, agree to raise a child Jewish, for example, then after a divorce, ex-etiquette suggests the child be raised in the original agreed-upon faith. If one of the parents remarries someone from another faith, whether the parent converts to the new faith or not, it is still that parent's responsibility to uphold the original agreement. If both parents agree to move away from the original religion, then the agreement may be changed.

Coming-of-Age Celebrations

Depending on the culture or religion, coming-of-age ceremonies note some sort of achievement or milestone for a child. Like weddings, coming-of-age ceremonies are occasions where families meet and celebrate together, and if the parents or other extended family are divorced and estranged, the social and financial considerations can be quite complicated.

Good ex-etiquette suggests that divorced or separated parents always remember that coming-of-age events are celebrations of their children's achievements. Parents should set aside their personal vendettas.

Christenings and Baptisms

"My husband was divorced and had two children when I married him. We have worked hard to include the mother of his children in all decisions, and we really do have quite a cordial relationship. However, I am expecting my first child in July, and his ex-wife expects to attend the christening! As much as I want to keep the relationship comfortable, I don't want to invite my husband's ex to my baby's christening. What do we do?"

It's a thin line we walk when we become friendly with the ex. Parents must set boundaries from the beginning or else they will find themselves constantly juggling what's appropriate and what's not. In this case, ex-etiquette does not apply to the new wife's concern over what to say as much as it applies to the ex-wife's overstepping her bounds.

It's extremely rude to invite yourself to any occasion. When ex-spouses and new spouses become close, they may come to think of each other as extended family—but their relationship is very tricky. They are not family in the true sense of the word. Their relationship has become intertwined because of the shared children in their care. But there is more here to consider. Once a person remarries, the new spouse becomes his partner. They are the primary relationship, and they build their new family as such. Of course ex-etiquette teaches us to integrate past with present, but present must also be allowed to exist on its own. Baptisms and christenings are exclusive to the new family; they are not focused on the shared children. Therefore, the befriended ex becomes a potential invited guest—just like everyone else.

For most people, it would be inappropriate if an ex-spouse of one of the parents attended a new child's christening, and it would certainly be understandable if the new spouse did not want her in attendance. However, I have run into counterpartners who have so overcome their animosity for each other that they have asked their spouse's ex to be the godparent to their newborn. If something happens to Larry and me, my sister is first in line to assume parenting responsibilities, but Sharyl is second. Based on that, I certainly do not want to discourage positive relationships between counterpartners, but I must reiterate the appropriateness of waiting for an invitation before discussing attendance at such an event.

Bar Mitzvahs and Bat Mitzvahs

A Jewish child comes of age upon reaching thirteen. Elaborate bar mitzvah and bat mitzvah ceremonies and receptions are commonplace today; they often cost in the tens of thousands of dollars. If the parents of the child are divorced, the planning and financing of the bar mitzvah can be just as complicated as planning a wedding and reception. This is where good ex-etiquette comes in.

Parents are responsible for the invitations, decorations, food, and reception hall. For invitation ideas for divorced parents in all situations, see chapter 9. Although these are examples of wedding invitations, much of the same wording applies.

There is no formal seating guide at these ceremonies. The celebrant is called up to the Torah to recite a blessing over the weekly reading. The parents usually sit closer to the front of the temple to watch their child, but there is no formal etiquette guide for where the parents sit other than common sense if they are estranged. Divorced parents that have remarried sit with their new spouse. If this upsets the ex-spouse, good ex-etiquette says the unmarried, divorced parent keeps her discontent to herself, and the remarried couple may sit a distance away to prevent confrontation that may embarrass the child and other family members.

If the parents divorce before the child comes of age, they should make decisions about the cost of the upcoming bar mitzvah or bat mitzvah at the time of the divorce and include that information in the divorce decree. If they don't do this, then they must agree about the finances at the time of the ceremony. The most common solution is to split the cost equally.

Bar mitzvahs and bat mitzvahs are the most important occasions for Jewish children aside from their wedding. Both parents, regardless if they are married to each other, should attend. Ex-etiquette dictates that divorced parents should put their differences aside for the day and help to create a pleasant memory for their child.

Graduations

Every year, around the month of June, I am bombarded by requests for proper ex-etiquette concerning graduation. Divorced parents with exes tend to find all sorts of reasons why they should not attend their child's graduation if their ex is planning to show up with someone that does not suit them. To some, the mere threat that their ex will be in attendance is enough to keep them from attending the ceremony. That is extremely poor ex-etiquette. The parents are not graduating. Their child is.

A parent's main consideration concerning graduations, as with every other coming-of-age ceremony children experience, is to support the child's achievements. Caring parents should exhibit cordial behavior toward one another in public. If a man is at odds with his ex-wife, he does not have to sit in the same vicinity, but both parents should attend, and the child should know where both of them are sitting. If one parent has remarried or has a partner, that person should also be there. Graduations and other "family" celebrations are not times to introduce casual dates to the family. If the parent does not have a partner at the time, he or she should go alone or with an extended family member who also cares about the child.

School Plays, Little League Games, and Other Events

Divorced parents should approach school plays, Little League games, and other sporting events in the same manner as graduations. They are there to support the child. Their goal is to be cordial in public for the sake of the child, but if their relationship is estranged, the best course of action is for them to sit in different areas so that they will not cause a scene. Both are there to support the child, not establish territory or make a statement about their love lives. They should refrain from any behavior that would cause the child embarrassment. They should certainly avoid confronting an ex or an ex's new partner while their child, his friends, or other parents look on. If there is something that must be discussed, they should make an appointment to discuss it privately at another time. They should never leave a child's extracurricular activity without first acknowledging the child.

"My ex and I had a rocky marriage, and it ended with her walking out on me with another man. This man shows up at all my children's Little League games. Is it asking too much for him to stay away on my days with the kids? I don't want to see him at my kids' games."

My answer to this type of question depends upon how long the parents have been apart. If the separation is new—less than a year—then it is very insensitive to both the ex-husband and the children for the ex-wife to show up at the children's activities with a new love interest. Whether or not the new man was the cause of the separation, it's much too soon to introduce a new partner into the scenario. Better to let the children get used to the idea that their parents are no longer together, make sure the divorce is final, then slowly introduce the new love interest with as much sensitivity as possible.

This doesn't really help the ex who doesn't *ever* want to be confronted by his ex-wife's current boyfriend. He feels that the new boyfriend's presence at his kids' Little League games is going too far. But if it has been a while since the separation, the divorce is final, and the ex-wife has remarried, there's not much this dad can do to stop his ex's new partner from going to the children's extracurricular activities. The new partner is not going away. He is trying to be supportive, and it is in the children's best interest that he is involved in their extracurricular activities.

This father should do his best to keep his emotions in check in front of the kids. He should try not to badmouth his ex-wife or her new partner. Harboring anger or resentment will not change the situation. It will only cause him anxiety, and that will inevitably affect the kids and make them feel even more insecure than the divorce did. The best revenge for this dad is to rise above the conflict. The easiest way to do this is to remember to put the children first.

Funerals

Although divorce can cause very bitter emotions, some relationships are never completely severed. If relations between exes are cordial, then it is appropriate for a divorced man or woman to attend the funeral of an ex's relation with whom he or she may have had a close relationship, especially if that relationship was maintained after the divorce. A brief visit to the funeral home is also appropriate. When attending a memorial service or funeral, however, the ex should not try to join the bereaved family unless he or she has been formally invited to do so. It is more appropriate to sit in the back of the church to pay respects.

Another potential problem surrounding funerals is when the person who passed had divorced and remarried, and there is bitterness between past and present spouse. In this case it may be more advisable for the ex-spouse to send flowers and a note expressing sympathy rather than attend the funeral. The main goal is to be supportive of the family no matter what went on in the past. If the ex-spouse's presence would be more disruptive than comforting, it is best for him or her to stay away.

If one member of a divorced couple with children dies, then the remaining parent should sit with the children at the funeral.

One of the most lovely tributes I received after my mother's death was a note from my ex-husband. Although we were cordial because of co-parenting our daughter, conversation did not flow easily at times. In his note he expressed his deep sorrow and his affection for my mother and offered his assistance in any way. It was a lovely sentiment and greatly appreciated by not only me, but the rest of my family as well. When my extended family met with the minister before my mother's memorial service, my ex-husband timidly entered the room and was warmly embraced by all family members. All were there to support each other.

Don't discount the fact that the death of a loved one can break down previous barriers and put many issues into their proper perspective. Although I had remarried, and my daughter had formed a loving bond with her bonusfather, there was nothing like having her daddy next to her in her time of grief after her grandmother's passing. My ex-husband's kind words and loving presence at my mother's funeral allowed everyone to interact more easily in the future.

When the propriety of an ex-spouse's attendance at a funeral is in question, the children can be the best barometer. Although Sharyl remained close to my husband's parents after she and my husband divorced, she was quick to allow our family private time in the days before my mother-in-law's passing. When it looked as if the time was getting near, she sent a message through her daughter asking if she could pay her respects to her former mother-in-law. Asking in this manner made it very easy for us to invite her or graciously decline her request without embarrassment.

"My ex-sister-in-law just lost her son. She and I were good friends during the twenty years her brother and I were married, but I've only spoken to her once since I filed for divorce three years ago. Both my ex and I have remarried. I would like for my new husband and me to attend the funeral to show our respects, and I would like to be there for my ex. Is this something I should consider?"

Going to the funeral would be a good way for this woman to let an old friend know she hasn't forgotten her, and it's only natural that she would want to be accompanied by her partner. But, given that she has not spoken to her ex-sister-in-law in years because of the divorce, showing up with a new husband might appear to be a slap in the face and completely inappropriate in a time of mourning. Under the circumstances, a heartfelt letter may be all that's needed to let her ex-sister-in-law know that she is sorry for her loss. This woman might tell her ex-sister-in-law how often she thinks of her and how much she wishes that there was some way they could put the past behind them. Tragedies like this are sometimes the catalyst for resolving past conflicts. If the ex-sister-in-laws sees it that way, she will give the woman a call to thank her for her kind thoughts.

Notice that there is no mention of the ex-husband in my response. That is because both partners have remarried. Although it is important to remain cordial for your children, it is not this woman's place to "support" her ex at this time. It is his new partner's responsibility, and privilege, for that matter. If it feels as if some communication is necessary, again, a note is appropriate.

All that said, if you feel you must make an appearance, sit in the back quietly, pay your respects, and then leave without calling attention to yourself.

Anniversaries

It is inappropriate to call attention to a former anniversary at any time. Sending e-mails or cards, or leaving a message on the answering machine asking, "Do you know what day it is today?" are in poor taste. Don't do it. You are divorced, and if your ex has remarried you must respect the union.

Extended-family members and children of the previously married couple also should not call attention to a past anniversary, unless their relative is a widow or widower and they are paying their respects to the past marital union.

BIBLIOGRAPHY

American Heritage® Dictionary of the English Language. 4th ed. Boston, Mass: Houghton Mifflin, 2000.

Barash, Susan Shaprio. *Mothers-in-Law and Daughters-in-Law*. Far Hills, N.J.: New Horizon Press, 2001.

Bazerman, Max, and Margaret A. Neale. *Negotiating Rationally*. New York: The Free Press, 1991.

Berstein, Anne. *Yours, Mine, and Ours*. New York: W. W. Norton & Company, 1989.

Blackstone-Ford, Jann. *The Custody Solutions Sourcebook*. Chicago: Lowell House, 1999.

_____. *Midlife Motherhood*. New York: St. Martin's Press, 2002.

Catholic Community: Support Roman Catholic Life and Faith. "Holy Communion." http://www.catholic.org.uk/library/basics/fhc.shtml

Curtis, Jill. "Second Weddings with Children." *Getting Remarried*. http://www.gettingremarried.com/child_wedding.html

Engel, Margorie. *Weddings: A Family Affair*. 2d ed. New York: Wilshire Publishers, 1998.

Faber, Adele, and Elaine Mazlish. *How to Talk So Kids Will Listen and Listen So Kids Will Talk*. New York: Quill Publishers, 1982.

Gray, John. *Men Are from Mars, Women Are from Venus*. New York: HarperCollins Publishers, 1992.

Horn, Sam. *Tongue Fu!* New York: St Martin's Press, 1996.

Madonik, Barbara. *I Hear What You Say, But What Are You Telling Me?* San Francisco: Jossey-Bass, 2001.

Nettleton, Pamela Hill. *Getting Married When It's Not Your First Time*. New York: Quill Publishers, 2001.

O'Connor, Anne. *The Truth About Stepfamilies*. New York: Marlow & Company, 2004.

Oxhorn-Ringwood, Lynne, Louise Oxhorn, and Marjorie Krausz. *Stepwives: Ten Steps to Help Ex-Wives and Stepmothers End the Struggle and Put the Kids First*. New York: Simon and Schuster, 2002.

Page, Susan. *How One of You Can Bring Two of You Together*. New York: Broadway Books, 1997.

Petersen, Gayle. "Helping 4 Year Old Understand Why Family Is Not Together Anymore." Ask Dr. Gayle. 1996-2003. http://www.askdrgayle.com/qa69.htm

Post, Peggy. *Etiquette: The 16th Edition*. New York: HarperCollins Publishers, 1997.

Ricci, Isolina. *Mom's House, Dad's House*. New York: Simon and Schuster, 1980, 1997.

Rich, Tracey R. "Bar Mitzvah, Bat Mitzvah and Confirmation." Judaism 101. 1996–2001. http://www.jewfaq.org/barmitz.htm

Ross, Julie, and Judy Corcoran. *Joint Custody with a Jerk*. New York: Saint Martin's Press, 1996.

Ury, William. *Getting Past No*. New York: Bantam Books, 1991.

Warshak, Richard. *Divorce Poison*. New York: Regan Books, 2001.

Resource Guide

Helpful Organizations

Al-Anon/Alateen Family Group Headquarters
Corporate Landing Parkway
Virginia Beach, VA 23454
757-563-1600
888-426-2666
www.al-anon.alateen.org

This organization has information and support groups for family members in an alcoholic's life and for children of alcoholics.

Alcoholics Anonymous World Service
475 Riverside Drive, 11th Floor
New York, NY 10015
212-870-3400
www.alcoholics-anonymous.org
This international organization has information on alcoholism and local support groups for its twelve-step recovery program.

American Academy of Child and Adolescent Psychiatry
3615 Wisconsin Avenue, N.W.
Washington, DC 20016
202-966-7300
www.aacap.org
This organization offers important information as a public service that assists parents and families in their most important roles. AACAP does not provide individual consultations or referrals to specific child/adolescent psychiatrists.

American Psychological Association
750 First Street, N.E.
Washington, DC 20002
800-324-2721
www.apa.org
The American Psychological Association promotes research and represents the professional interests of psychologists in the United States.

Association for Conflict Resolution
1015 18th Street, N.W., Suite 1150
Washington, DC 20036
202-464-9700

202-464-9720 (fax)
acr@ACRnet.org
http://acrnet.org/
This is a professional organization dedicated to enhancing the practice and public understanding of conflict resolution.

Children's Rights Counsel
200 I Street, N.E.
Washington, DC 20002
202-547-6227
800-787-KIDS
www.gocrc.com
CRC works to strengthen families through education and advocacy. The organization's motto is "The Best Parent Is Both Parents."

Marriage Care
Clitheroe House 1 Blythe Mews
Blythe Road
London, England W14 0NW
020-7371-1341
info@marriagecare.org.uk
www.marriagecare.org.uk
Marriage Care offers relationship counseling for couples and individuals. The organization offers a premarriage program, support during marriage, and counseling on new beginnings after marriages fail. Sixty-four centers across the United Kingdom.

National Mental Health Association
2001 N. Beauregard Street, 12th Floor
Alexandria, VA 22311
703-684-7722
800-969-NMHA
703-684-5968 (fax)
www.nmha.org

This is a nationally recognized resource for information on mental illnesses and treatments. It offers referrals for local treatment services.

Stepfamily Association of America
650 J Street, Suite 205
Lincoln, NE 68508
800-735-0329
www.saafamilies.org
This is a national nonprofit membership organization dedicated to successful stepfamily living.

Books

Courtship/Planning to Remarry

Barash, Susan Shapiro. *Second Wives: The Pitfalls and Rewards of Marrying Widowers and Divorced Men*. Far Hills, N.J.: New Horizon, 2000.

Coyne-Hennessey, Bobbi. *Once More with Love: A Guide to Marrying Again*. Notre Dame, Idaho: Ave Marie Press, 1993.

Gerlach, Peter K. *Stepfamily Courtship: How to Make Three Right Remarriage Choices*. Philadelphia, Pa.: Xlibris Corp., 2002.

Keener, Craig S. . . . *And Marries Another: Divorce & Remarriage in the Teaching of the New Testament*. Peabody, Mass.: Hendrickson Publishers, 1991.

Second Weddings

Engel, Margorie. *Weddings: A Family Affair*. North Hollywood, Calif.: Wilshire Publishers, 1998.

Nettleton, Pamela Hill. *Getting Married When It's Not Your First Time*. New York: Quill Publishers, 2001.

Stepfamily Life

Bernstein, Anne. *Yours, Mine, and Ours: How Families Change When Remarried Parents Have a Child Together*. New York: W. W. Norton & Company, 1989.

Carlisle, Erica and Vanessa. *I Was My Mother's Bridesmaid: Young Adults Talk About Thriving in a Blended Family.* Berkeley, Calif: Wildcat Canyon Press, 1999.

Dale, James, and Alex Beth Schapiro. *Step Wise: A Guide to Family Mergers.* Kansas City, Mo.: Andrews McMeel Publishing, 2001.

Frydenger, Tom. *Stepfamily Problems: How to Solve Them.* Grand Rapids, Mich.: Baker Book House, 1997.

Gerlach, Peter K. *Build a High-Nurturance Stepfamily: A Guidebook for Co-Parents.* Philadelphia, Pa.: Xlibris Corp., 2002.

_____. *Who's Really Running Your Life? Free Your Self from Custody, and Guard Your Kids.* Philadelphia, Pa.: Xlibris Corp., 2002.

Glassman, Bruce. *Everything You Need to Know About Stepfamilies.* New York: Rosen Publishing, 1994.

Kelly, Patricia. *Developing Healthy Stepfamilies: 20 Families Tell Their Stories.* Bridgehampton, N.Y.: Haworth Press, 1995.

Newman, Margaret. *Stepfamily Realities: How to Overcome Difficulties and Have a Happy Family.* Oakland, Calif.: New Harbinger Publications, 1994.

O'Connor, Anne. *The Truth About Stepfamilies: Real American Stepfamilies Speak Out.* New York: Marlow and Company, 2003.

Reed, Bobbie. *Merging Families: A Step-by-Step Guide for Blended Families.* St. Louis, Mo.: Concordia Publishing Company, 1992.

Robinson, Roxana. *This Is My Daughter: A Novel.* St. Louis, Mo.: Scribner Paperback, 1999.

Shomberg, Elaine Fantel, et al. *Blending Families: A Guide for Parents, Stepparents, and Everyone Building a Successful New Family.* Berkeley, Calif.: Berkeley Trade Publications, 1999.

Visher, Emily, and John Visher. *Stepfamilies: Myths and Realities.* Sacramento, Calif.: Citadel Press, 1993.

Wright, Janet M. *Lesbian Stepfamilies: An Ethnography of Love.* Bridgehampton, N.Y.: Haworth Press, 1998.

Stepmothers and Stepfathers

Barnes, Bob, et al. *Winning the Heart of Your Stepchild.* Grand Rapids, Mich.: Zondervan Publishing, 1997.

Goodman, Karon Phillips. *The Stepmom's Guide to Simplifying Your Life.* Culver City, Calif.: EquiLibrium Press, 2002.

Margolis, David. *The Stepman.* Sag Harbor, N.Y.: The Permanent Press, 1996.

Oxhorn-Ringwood, Lynne, Louise Oxhorn, and Marjorie Krausz. *Stepwives: Ten Steps to Help Ex-Wives and Stepmothers End the Struggle and Put the Kids First.* New York: Simon and Schuster, 2002.

Smith, Donna. *Stepmothering.* New York: St. Martin's Press, 1990.

Williams, Stephen J. *The Stepparent Challenge: A Primer for Making It Work.* Hurst, Tex.: MasterMedia, 1993.

Wilson, K. C. *Where's Daddy? The Mythologies Behind Custody-Access-Support.* Richmond, Va.: Harbinger Press, 2000.

Co-parenting

Bernstein, Anne C. *Flight of the Stork.* Indianapolis, Ind.: Perspective Press, 1994.

Bloomfield, Harold H. *Making Peace in Your Stepfamily: Surviving and Thriving as Parents and Stepparents.* New York: Hyperion, 1993.

Clapp, Genevieve. *Divorce and New Beginnings: An Authoritative Guide to Recovery and Growth, Solo Parenting, and Stepfamilies.* New York: John Wiley & Sons, 1992.

Faber, Adele, and Elaine Mazlish. *How to Talk So Kids Will Listen and Listen So Kids Will Talk.* New York: Quill Publishers, 2002.

Gerlach, Peter K. *Build a Co-Parenting Team After Divorce and Remarriage.* Philadelphia, Pa.: Xlibris Corp., 2002.

_____. *Build a High-Nurturance Stepfamily: A Guidebook for Co-Parents*. Philadelphia, Pa.: Xlibris Corp., 2002.

Ross, Julie, and Judy Corcoran. *Joint Custody with a Jerk: Raising a Child with an Uncooperative Ex*. New York: St. Martin's Press, 1996.

Sandoz, Bobbie. *Parachutes for Parents: Seven Keys to Raising Wise and Loving Children*. Lincolnwood, Ill.: NTC/Contemporary Publishing, 1997.

Schaefer, Charles, and Theresa D. Geronimo. *How to Talk to Your Kids About Really Important Things: Specific Questions and Answers and Useful Things to Say*. San Francisco, Calif.: Jossey-Bass, 1994.

Wisdom, Susan, and Jennifer Green. *Stepcoupling: Creating and Sustaining a Strong Marriage in Today's Blended Family*. New York: Three Rivers Press, 2002.

Wittmann, Jeffrey P. *Custody Chaos, Personal Peace: Sharing Custody with an Ex Who Drives You Crazy*. New York: Penguin, 2001.

For Children

Boudish, Lynea. *Living with My Stepfather Is Like Living with a Moose*. New York: Farrar Straus & Giroux, 1997. (Ages 4–8)

Braithwaite, Althea. *My Two Families*. London: A&C Black, 1998. (Ages 9–12)

Christopher, Matt. *Spike It*. New York: Little, Brown, 1999. (Ages 9–12)

Cook, Jean Thor. *Room for a Stepdaddy*. Morton Grove, Ill.: Albert Whitman & Co., 1995. (Ages 4–8)

Fine, Anne. *Step by Wicked Step: A Novel*. New York: Little, Brown, 1996. (Ages 9–12)

Ford, Melanie, Annie, and Steven, as told to Jann Blackstone-Ford. *My Parents Are Divorced Too*. Washington, D.C.: Magination Press, 1998. (Ages 8–13)

Holt, Kimberly Willis. *Mister and Me*. New York: Putnam, 1998. (Ages 9–12)

Kransky, Laurie, and Marc Brown. *Dinosaur Divorce*. New York: Little Brown & Company, 1998. (Ages 4–8)

Lewis, Beverly. *California Christmas*. Grand Rapids, Mich.: Zondervan, 1994. (Ages 9–12)

Martin, Ann M. *Dawn's Wicked Stepsister*. Milwaukee, Wis.: Gareth Stevens, 1995. (Ages 9–12)

McCann, Marcy. *Chelsea's Tree*. Woodstock, Va.: Inspiration Publications, 2001.

McGinnis, Lila. *If Daddy Only Knew Me*. New York: Albert Whitman & Co., 1995. (Ages 4–8)

Weitzman, Elizabeth. *Let's Talk About Living in a Stepfamily*. New York: Powerkids Press, 1997. (Ages 4–8)

For Teens and Young Adult Stepchildren

Block, Dr. Joel D., and Dr. Susan S. Bartell. *Stepliving for Teens*. New York: Price Stern Sloan, 2001.

Denny, Kevin M. *A Teenager's Guide: How to Manipulate Your Way To Happiness*. West Orange, N.J.: Warthog Publishing, 1997.

Reisfeld, Randi. *Extreme Sisterhood*. New York: Archway, 1999.

Snelling, Lauraine. *Close Quarters*. Minneapolis, Minn.: Bethany House, 1998.

Stine, R. I. *The Stepbrother*. New York: Golden Books Publishing Company, 1998.

Williams, Ginny. *A Matter of Trust*. Eugene, Ore.: Harvest House Publishers, 1994.

Legal Matters

Blackstone-Ford, Jann. *The Custody Solutions Sourcebook*. Los Angeles: Lowell House, 1999.

Leving, Jeffrey M. *Father's Rights*. New York: Basic Books, 1998.

Tong, Dean. *Ashes to Ashes, Families to Dust: False Accusations of Child Abuse*. Tampa, Fla.: FamRights Press, 1996.

Zagone, Frank, and Mary Randolph. *How to Adopt Your Stepchildren in California*. Berkeley, Calif.: Nolo Press, 1994.

Family Growth—General

Bartell, Susan. *Mommy or Daddy: Whose Side Am I On?* Avon, Mass.: Adams Media, 2002.

Riera, Michael. *Staying Connected to Your Teenager: How to Keep Them Talking to You and How to Hear What They're Really Saying.* New York: Perseus Publishing, 2003.

———, *Uncommon Sense for Parents With Teenagers.* New York: Perseus Publishing, 1995.

Viorst, Judith. *Grown-Up Marriage.* New York: Free Press, 2002.

Divorce

Ahrons, Constance. *The Good Divorce.* New York: Basic Books, 1994.

Blau, Melinda. *Families Apart: 10 Keys to Co-Parenting.* New York: Perigee, 1995.

Engel, Margorie, and Diana Gould. *The Divorce Decisions Workbook: A Planning and Action Guide.* Columbus, Ohio: McGraw-Hill, 1992.

Everett, Craig, editor. *The Consequences of Divorce: Economic and Custodial Impact on Children and Adult.* Bridgehampton, N.Y.: Haworth Press, 1996.

Hickey, Elizabeth. *Healing Hearts: Helping Children and Adults Recover from Divorce.* Mt. Clemens, Mich.: Gold Leaf Press, 1994.

Jarratt, Claudia Jewett. *Helping Children Cope with Separation and Loss.* Boston, Mass.: Harvard Common Press, 1994.

Lansky, Vicki. *Vicki Lansky's Divorce Book for Parents.* Minnetonka, Minn.: Book Peddlers, 1996.

Vaughan, Diane. *Uncoupling: Turning Points in Intimate Relationships.* New York: Oxford University Press, 1990.

Web Sites

General

American Family Therapy Academy
http://afta.org/

This is a nonprofit organization of leading family therapy teachers, clinicians, program developers, researchers, and social scientists dedicated to advancing systemic thinking and practices for families in their ecological context.

Bonus Families
www.bonusfamilies.com
A nonprofit organization dedicated to peaceful coexistence between separated or divorced parents and their new families. The "Ex-Etiquette" department of the site is written by a mother and stepmother of the same children and offers insight into getting along with an ex or an ex's new partner.

Building a Successful Stepfamily
www.swfamily.org/stepfamily
This Web site is designed for Christian stepfamily couples, those considering remarriage, and single parents. Discover keys to healthy stepfamilies, and gain strength and wisdom in meeting the challenges of stepfamily life.

Children's Rights Council
www.gocrc.com
This is a national nonprofit organization based in Washington, D.C., that works to ensure children have meaningful and continuing contact with both their parents and extended family regardless of the parents' marital status.

Family Medallion
www.familymedallion.com
This is an organization dedicated to celebrating and strengthening family ties.

Forever Families
www.foreverfamilies.net
Here family members will find practical, scholarly, and faith-based information for strengthening and enriching families of all denominations.

Parenting with Dignity
www.ParentingWithDignity.com
This is a resource where parents learn essential parenting skills and develop the tools necessary to create an encouraging and loving home for their children.

Parentline Plus
www.parentlineplus.org.uk
This organization offers support and information for parents on issues related to parenting and relationship breakdowns.

Relate
www.relate.org.uk
This organization provides counseling and psychosexual therapy, as well as courses on marriage and counseling for teenagers whose parents are separating. Relate has more than 100 branches in England, Scotland, Wales, and Northern Ireland.

Selfgrowth.com
www.selfgrowth.com
This Web site provides a central resource for information on self-improvement, self-help, and personal growth.

Smart Marriages
www.SmartMarriages.com
This is a resource-rich national clearinghouse for educational and support programs for couples.

StepCarefully for Stepparents
www.stepcarefully.com
This organization was created by stepparents, for stepparents. It offers on-line support, as well as a series of resources for step-parenting needs, and a newsletter designed to help stepfamilies not only to survive, but to succeed.

Stepfamily Day
www.happystepfamilyday.org
   This Web site is dedicated to the movement toward a day dedicated to the American stepfamilies.
Stepfamily inFormation
www.stepfamilyinfo.org/
   This nonprofit research-based educational site is for prospective and current stepfamily members and their supporters. It suggests twelve ongoing projects that co-parents can work at together to overcome five re/divorce hazards, and build a high-nurturance stepfamily. Browse more than 450 Web pages geared toward helping you understand and resolve typical stepfamily problems.

The Stepfamily Network
www.stepfamily.net
   This is a nonprofit organization dedicated to helping stepfamily members achieve harmony and mutual respect within their family lives.

Stepfamily Solutions
www.stepfamilysolutions.net
   This organization offers individual, couple, family, and group counseling for stepfamilies. Workshops and classes provide training to mental health professionals and organizations.

The Stepfamilyzone
www.stepfamily.asn.au
The Stepfamily Association of South Australia Inc. and
   Stepfamily Australia
   This organization actively promotes the *positive* aspects of stepfamily life. Stepfamilies *can* work and be successful! The Stepfamilyzone believes that providing information is the first step to successful stepfamily life.

StepTogether
http://steptogether.org
    StepTogether provides educational material and support resources for all persons who are, or have been part of a step-family, or who are otherwise related to a stepfamily environment.

A Successful Family
www.asuccessfulfamily.com
    This organization offers tools to help families get to know each other better and communicate more effectively.

Your Stepfamily Online
www.yourstepfamily.com
    This is a bimonthly Web magazine created just for moms, dads, and kids who want to learn from and enjoy the relationships they're creating as they evolve as a stepfamily.

Stepmother/Second Wives Links
CoMamas Association
www.comamas.com
    CoMamas' goal is to teach stepwives and their families how to develop cooperative and respectful relationships so they can end their war and get along for the sake of the children.

Life in a Blender
www.lifeinablender.org
    This is an organization of dedicated biological moms and stepmoms of blended families.

The Second Wives Club
www.secondwivesclub.com
    This is a comprehensive, interactive site for second wives and stepmoms.

WIFE (Women's Institute for Financial Education)
www.wife.org

The nonprofit Women's Institute for Financial Education provides financial education and networking opportunities to women of all ages. It features a dynamic on-line magazine updated several times each month.

Stepfather/Biological Father Links

American Coalition for Fathers and Children
www.acfc.org
This organization dedicates itself to the creation of a family law system and public awareness that promotes equal rights for *all* parties affected by divorce and the breakup of a family.

Families Need Fathers
www.fnf.org.uk
134 Curtain Road
London, England EC2A 3AR
020-7613-5060
0870 760 7496 (24-hour helpline)
This organization is dedicated to helping maintain relationships between children and both parents following divorce and separation.

The National Father's Resource Center
www.fathers4kids.org
This Web site features information about, and referrals to, attorneys and other professionals who understand fathers' issues and effectively represent the interests of fathers and children in family court in all jurisdictions.

Fatherville
www.fatherville.com
This is a resource for fathers, by fathers, and about fathers. Its goal is to equip men to become better fathers through the sharing and application of articles written by fathers at many different stages of fatherhood (and bonusfatherhood).

National Center for Fathering
www.fathers.com
This organization inspires and equips men to be better fathers. It conducts research on fathers and fathering and develops practical resources to prepare dads for nearly every situation fatherhood might bring.

National Fatherhood Initiative
www.fatherhood.org
This nonprofit, nonpartisan, nonsectarian national civic organization was founded in 1994 to stimulate a society-wide movement to confront the growing problem of absent fathers. It is dedicated to improving the well-being of children by increasing the number of responsible and committed fathers.

Single and Custodial Fathers Network
www.scfn.org/index.html
This is a nonprofit organization dedicated to helping fathers meet the challenge of custodial parenthood.

United Fathers of America
www.ufa.org
The goal of United Fathers of America is to provide an interactive medium for people experiencing the effects of dissolution, parenting arrangements, and other family law issues. Its secondary purpose is to provide information and resources in the aid of Internet Legal Research.

Divorce-Support Links
Beyond-Divorce.com
www.beyond-divorce.com
This Web site specializes in topics related to divorce, single parenting, remarriage, and stepfamilies.

Dad's Divorce Rights
www.dadsrights.com
    Via this organization, experienced attorneys help fathers with litigation and negotiation strategies while staying focused on what is best for the children.

Divorce Central
www.divorcecentral.com
    This organization offers help, support, and information, and gives divorced couples the opportunity to communicate with others who are in various stages of decision-making.

Divorce Info
www.divorceinfo.com
    This Web site is designed to help you get through divorce and move on with your life.

Divorce Net
www.divorcenet.com
    This Web site offers a state-by-state resource center and interactive bulletin boards (forums) to help people deal with various divorced family and stepfamily issues.

Divorce Online
www.divorceonline.com
    This is an electronic resource for people involved in, or facing the prospect of, divorce.

Divorce Source.Com
www.divorcesource.com
    This site offers state-specific information on divorce and stepfamily issues.

Divorce Support
www.divorcesupport.com
   This site offers support with divorce and child custody.

DivorceInteractive.com
www.divorceinteractive.com
   This is a comprehensive divorce resource with survival tools, information, and helpful resources for anyone involved in or considering a divorce.

MillennumDivorce.com
www.millenniumdivorce.com
   A site devoted to providing information and help, MilleniumDivorce.com was developed and written by divorce lawyers and family law attorneys to answer just about any question related to divorce.

Second or Subsequent Weddings Links
Bride Again Magazine
www.brideagain.com
   Bride Again is the only magazine specifically designed for the encore bride. Quarterlies cover issues, both psychological and material, that meet the unique needs of the thousands of women who are planning a second or subsequent marriage.

GettingRemarried.com
www.gettingremarried.com
   This site has loads of wedding ideas for anyone planning a second or subsequent marriage.

The Knot
www.theknot.com
   A comprehensive resource for couples seeking information and services to help plan their weddings and their future lives together.

INDEX